Nirali's New Series

# CONCISE STUDY SERIES

# MICROCONTROLLER AND APPLICATIONS

For
**T.E. SEMESTER – I**

**THIRD YEAR DEGREE COURSES IN ELECTRONICS/ ELECTRONICS AND TELECOMMUNICATION ENGINEERING**

As Per New Revised Syllabus of UoP, 2014

**Dr. ST Patil**
M.Tech. CSE, Ph D. Computer
Professor, Computer Engineering,
Vishwakarma Institute of Technology (VIT),
Pune-411037.

N3173

**MICROCONTROLLER AND APPLICATIONS (TE E&TC SEM. – I)**  ISBN : 978-93-5164-137-7

**First Edition** : August 2014

© : Author

The text of this publication, or any part thereof, should not be reproduced or transmitted in any form or stored in any computer storage system or device for distribution including photocopy, recording, taping or information retrieval system or reproduced on any disc, tape, perforated media or other information storage device etc., without the written permission of Authors with whom the rights are reserved. Breach of this condition is liable for legal action. Every effort has been made to avoid errors or omissions in this publication. In spite of this, errors may have crept in. Any mistake, error or discrepancy so noted and shall be brought to our notice shall be taken care of in the next edition. It is notified that neither the publisher nor the authors or seller shall be responsible for any damage or loss of action to any one, of any kind, in any manner, therefrom.

---

**Published By :**

**NIRALI PRAKASHAN**
Abhyudaya Pragati, 1312, Shivaji Nagar,
Off J.M. Road, PUNE - 411005
Tel - (020) 25512336/37/39, Fax - (020) 25511379
Email : niralipune@pragationline.com

**Printed By :**

**REPRO INDIA LTD**
50/2 T.T.C. MIDC
Industrial Area, Mahape, Navi Mumbai
Tel - (022) 2778 2011

---

## DISTRIBUTION CENTRES
### PUNE

*Nirali Prakashan*
119, Budhwar Peth, Jogeshwari Mandir Lane
Pune 411002, Maharashtra
Tel : (020) 2445 2044, 66022708, Fax : (020) 2445 1538
Email : bookorder@pragationline.com

*Nirali Prakashan*
S. No. 28/25, Dhyari,
Near Pari Company, Pune 411041
Tel : (022) 24690204 Fax : (020) 24690316
Email : dhyari@pragationline.com
bookorder@pragationline.com

### MUMBAI
*Nirali Prakashan*
385, S.V.P. Road, Rasdhara Co-op. Hsg. Society Ltd.,
Girgaum, Mumbai 400004, Maharashtra
Tel : (022) 2385 6339 / 2386 9976, Fax : (022) 2386 9976
Email : niralimumbai@pragationline.com

## DISTRIBUTION BRANCHES

**NAGPUR**
*Pratibha Book Distributors*
Above Maratha Mandir, Shop No. 3, First Floor,
Rani Jhanshi Square, Sitabuldi, Nagpur 440012,
Maharashtra, Tel : (0712) 254 7129

**BENGALURU**
*Pragati Book House*
House No. 1, Sanjeevappa Lane, Avenue Road Cross,
Opp. Rice Church, Bengaluru - 560002.
Tel : (080) 64513344, 64513355,
Mob : 9880582331, 9845021552
Email : bharatsavla@yahoo.com

**JALGAON**
*Nirali Prakashan*
34, V. V. Golani Market, Navi Peth, Jalgaon 425001,
Maharashtra, Tel : (0257) 222 0395
Mob : 94234 91860

**KOLHAPUR**
*Nirali Prakashan*
New Mahadvar Road,
Kedar Plaza, 1st Floor Opp. IDBI Bank
Kolhapur 416 012, Maharashtra. Mob : 9855046155

### CHENNAI
*Pragati Books*
9/1, Montieth Road, Behind Taas Mahal, Egmore,
Chennai 600008 Tamil Nadu, Tel : (044) 6518 3535,
Mob : 94440 01782 / 98450 21552 / 98805 82331, Email : bharatsavla@yahoo.com

---

## RETAIL OUTLETS
### PUNE

*Pragati Book Centre*
157, Budhwar Peth, Opp. Ratan Talkies,
Pune 411002, Maharashtra
Tel : (020) 2445 8887 / 6602 2707, Fax : (020) 2445 8887

*Pragati Book Centre*
Amber Chamber, 28/A, Budhwar Peth,
Appa Balwant Chowk, Pune : 411002, Maharashtra,
Tel : (020) 20240335 / 66281669
Email : pbcpune@pragationline.com

*Pragati Book Centre*
676/B, Budhwar Peth, Opp. Jogeshwari Mandir,
Pune 411002, Maharashtra
Tel : (020) 6601 7784 / 6602 0855

*PBC Book Sellers & Stationers*
152, Budhwar Peth, Pune 411002, Maharashtra
Tel : (020) 2445 2254 / 6609 2463

### MUMBAI
*Pragati Book Corner*
Indira Niwas, 111 - A, Bhavani Shankar Road, Dadar (W), Mumbai 400028, Maharashtra
Tel : (022) 2422 3526 / 6662 5254, Email : pbcmumbai@pragationline.com

---

www.pragationline.com                                                                                              info@pragationline.com

*Dedicated to ...*

**My Father,
Late Shri Tatyasaheb Patil**

*...Dr. S. T. Patil*

# PREFACE

It gives us immense pleasure to present this book **'Microcontroller and Applications'** to the students of Third year Electronics and Electronics and Telecommunication Engineering of the University of Pune.

As per New Revised Examination Scheme which has been implemented from this academic year, In-semester assessment carries 30 Marks, over first three units and End Semester Examination carries 70 Marks over entire syllabus of which First Three Units will carry 20 Marks and Units 4, 5, 6 will carry 50 Marks.

Author has tried to introduce the subject to the average students, Brief details of MCS-8051 Microcontroller is prescribed. The subject matter has been developed in a logical and coherent manner with neat illustrations along with a fairly large number of embedded in C programs. Interfacing of many devices such as ADC, LED, LCD, DC motor control etc with PIC18f Microcontroller are also given in short but useful.

The objectives of this text are :

Unit I Covers : Introduction to 8-bit Microcontroller, software and hardware tools for development of microcontroller base systems.

Unit II Covers : Microcontroller MCS-8051 architecture, Instruction set.

Unit III Covers : PIC Microcontroller Architecture.

Unit IV Covers : Interfacing LED, LCD, Keypad with PIC18f Microcontroller with C-Programs.

Unit V Covers : Interfacing ADC, RTC, EEPROM with PIC18f Microcontroller with C-Programs.

Unit VI Covers : Case studies and design of DAS system, frequency counter, Digital Multmeter and DC Motor control with PIC18f Microcontroller with C-Programs.

I am very much thankful to **Dr. R. Jalnekar, Dr. D. S. Bormane, Dr. A. N. Gaikwad, Mr. Virendra** Pawar. I am indebted to all my family members, especially, my elder brother **Mr. Sanganna Patil** for providing me moral support. I also thankful to my wife **Vaishali**, Daughter **Ashwini** and My Son **Manjunath** without whose patience and understanding this work would not have seen the light of the day.

Publication of this book in such a short period required a very dedicated and active co-operation from the publisher.

I Shri Dineshbhai Furia, Shri Jignesh Furia and Shri M. P. Munde and team Miss. Mandakini Jadhavar, Mrs. Anita Kulkarni, Mrs. Pratibha Bele and Miss.Shilpa Zade.

The frontiers of knowledge are boundless and fathomless. Any suggestions and feedback shall be appreciated and acknowledged.

**Pune**                                                                                                       **Author**

**August 2014**

Dear Students,

It gives us great pleasure to introduce a New Series "**C**oncise **S**tudy **S**eries" for Second Year Engineering students. These "**CSS**" books are written by Experienced and Eminent Professors of respective subjects.

The specialty of this new Series "**CSS**" is that it:

- Covers full syllabus of University of Pune.
- Contains Matter written in Simple and Lucid language.
- Includes "To the Point" Topics and well arranged articles.
- Includes Most Likely Questions.
- Includes Previous Years University Question Papers.
- Available in all leading stores at Affordable Price.

**Happy Studying and Best of Luck!!!**

*Nirali Prakashan*

# SYLLABUS

### Unit I : Introduction to Microcontrollers

8 bit Microprocessor and Microcontroller architecture, comparison, advantages and applications of each Harward and Von Neumann architecture, RISC and CISC comparison. Survey of 8 bit controllers and its features Definition of embedded system and its characteristics. Role of microcontroller in embedded System. Limitation of 8 bit microcontrollers. Study of RS232, RS 485, I2C, SPI protocols. Software and hardware tools for development of microcontroller based system such as assembler, compiler, IDÉ, Emulators, debugger, programmer, development board, DSO, Logic Analyzer.

### Unit II : 8051 Architecture

MCS-51 architecture, family devices & its derivatives. Port architecture, memory organization, Interrupt structure, timers and its modes & serial communication and modes. Overview of Instruction set.

### Unit III : PIC Microcontroller Architecture

PIC 10, PIC12, PIC16, PIC18 series architectures, comparison, features and selection as per application. PIC18f architecture, registers, memory Organization and types, stack, oscillator options, BOD, power down modes and configuration bit settings. Brief summary of Peripheral support Overview of instruction set, MPLAB IDE & C18 Compiler

### Unit IV : Real World Interfacing Part I

Port structure, interrupt structure & timers of PIC18F. Interfacing of switches. LED, LCD, Keypad, use of timers With interrupts, PWM generation. All programs in embedded C.

### Unit V : Real World Interfacing Part II

MSSP structure,UART,SPI,I2C,ADC,Comparators Interfacing serial port, ADC, RTC with I2C and EEPROM with SPI. All programs in embedded C.

### Unit VI : Case studies with PIC

Design of DAS system, Design of frequency counter with display on LCD, Design of Digital Multimeter, Design of DC Motor control using PWM Should cover necessary signal conditioning of input stage ,hardware interfacing with PIC Microcontroller and algorithm or flowchart.

# CONTENTS

## UNT I : Introduction to Microcontroller — 1.1-1.48

| | | |
|---|---|---|
| 1.1 | Introduction | 1.1 |
| 1.2 | 8051 Microcontroller Architecture | 1.1 |
| | 1.2.1 Schematic and Features | 1.1 |
| | 1.2.2 8051 Pin Diagram and Description | 1.3 |
| 1.3 | 8051 Internal Architecture | 1.4 |
| 1.4 | Memory Organization | 1.10 |
| | 1.4.1 Program Memory Organization | 1.11 |
| | 1.4.2 Data Memory Organization | 1.12 |
| 1.5 | 8051 System Clock | 1.13 |
| 1.6 | 8051 Reset Circuit | 1.14 |
| 1.7 | Need of Microcontroller | 1.14 |
| 1.8 | Microcontroller Chips | 1.16 |
| 1.9 | Harvard vs. Von Neumann Architecture | 1.17 |
| 1.10 | Micro-Coded And Hard-Coded Processors | 1.18 |
| | 1.10.1 Memory Types : | 1.20 |
| | 1.10.2 Data Memory | 1.21 |
| | 1.10.3 I/O Registers Space in Harvard Architecture | 1.23 |
| 1.11 | Advantages of Microcontrollers | 1.25 |
| 1.12 | Applications of Microcontrollers | 1.25 |
| 1.13 | Limiations of Microcontroller | 1.26 |
| 1.14 | Comparison between Microprocessor And Microcontroller | 1.26 |
| 1.15 | Comparison between CISCAnd RISC | 1.28 |
| 1.16 | Embedded System | 1.29 |
| 1.17 | Characteristics of Embedded Systems | 1.31 |
| 1.18 | Embedded System Tools | 1.32 |
| | 1.18.1 Debugger | 1.33 |
| | 1.18.2 Assembler | 1.36 |
| | 1.18.3 Compilers | 1.38 |
| | 1.18.4 IDE | 1.41 |
| | 1.18.5 Simulator | 1.42 |
| | 1.18.6 Emulator | 1.43 |
| | 1.18.7 DSO | 1.45 |
| | 1.18.8 Logic Analyzer | 1.46 |
| • | Questions | 1.48 |

## UNIT II : 8051 Architecture — 2.1-2.32

- 2.1 Basic 8051 Architecture — 2.1
- 2.2 8051 Addressing Modes — 2.5
- 2.3 I/O Port Configuration — 2.6
  - 2.3.1 Port-0 Pin Structure — 2.6
  - 2.3.2 Port-1 Pin Structure — 2.7
  - 2.3.3 Port-2 Pin Structure — 2.7
  - 2.3.4 Port-3 Pin Structure — 2.8
- 2.4 Accessing External Memory — 2.9
- 2.5 Timers/Counters — 2.11
- 2.6 Interrupts — 2.14
- 2.7 Interrupt Handling — 2.17
- 2.8 Serial Interface — 2.21
  - 2.8.1 Serial Data Transmission Modes — 2.22
- 2.9 8051 Instructions — 2.26
- • Questions — 2.32

## UNIT III : PIC Microcontroller Architecture — 3.1-3.38

- 3.1 Introduction — 3.1
- 3.2 CPU Architecture — 3.2
- 3.3 PIC Memory Organisation — 3.2
- 3.4 PIC Microcontroller Clock — 3.4
- 3.5 Architecture of PIC16C74A — 3.5
- 3.6 CPU Registers (Registers Commonly Used By The CPU) — 3.6
  - 3.6.1 STATUS Register — 3.6
  - 3.6.2 FSR Register — 3.6
  - 3.6.3 INDF Register — 3.6
  - 3.6.4 PCL Register — 3.7
  - 3.6.5 PCLATH Register — 3.7
- 3.7 Program Counter Stack — 3.7
- 3.8 Port Structure and Pin Configuration of PIC16C74A — 3.9
- 3.9 Instruction Set — 3.10
- 3.10 I/O Ports Of PIC16C74A — 3.13
  - 3.10.1 Port-A — 3.14
  - 3.10.2 Port-B — 3.15
- 3.11 Overview of Timer Modules — 3.16
- 3.12 Interrupt Logic in PIC 16C74A — 3.22

| 3.13 | Caputre/Compare/PWM (CCP) Modules | 3.22 |
|---|---|---|
| | 3.13.1 Capture Mode (CCP1) | 3.24 |
| | 3.13.2 Compare Mode (CCP1) | 3.24 |
| | 3.13.3 PWM Mode (CCP1) | 3.25 |
| | 3.13.4 PWM Period | 3.26 |
| | 3.13.5 PWM Duty Cycle | 3.26 |
| | 3.13.6 PWM Period and Duty Cycle Calculation | 3.27 |
| 3.14 | ADC Module | 3.28 |
| 3.15 | MPLAB IDE | 3.34 |
| 3.16 | MPLAB IDE Development Tools | 3.36 |
| • | Questions | 3.38 |
| **UNIT IV : Real World Interfacing Part I** | | **4.1-4.50** |
| 4.1 | Introduction | 4.1 |
| 4.2 | Architecture of PIC Microcontroller | 4.3 |
| 4.3 | Limitations of PIC Architecture | 4.7 |
| 4.4 | Advantages of PIC Controlled System | 4.7 |
| 4.5 | Input Output Ports | 4.8 |
| 4.6 | ULPWU Unit | 4.10 |
| 4.7 | PIC Interrupt Structure of PIC18F | 4.19 |
| 4.8 | Interrupt Vector | 4.21 |
| 4.9 | Handling Interrupt in C | 4.22 |
| 4.10 | Interfacing Timer with PIC18F | 4.26 |
| | 4.10.1 Timer TMR0 | 4.26 |
| 4.11 | Interfacing LCD | 4.28 |
| 4.12 | Interfacing LED | 4.34 |
| 4.13 | PRC18F Interfacing with Keypad | 4.37 |
| 4.14 | Interfacing PWM with PIC18F | 4.44 |
| | 4.14.1 Interfacing PWM with PIC16F877A | 4.46 |
| • | Questions | 4.50 |
| **UNIT V : Real World Interfacing Part II** | | **5.1-5.72** |
| 5.1 | Introduction | 5.1 |
| | 5.1.1 Steps to Read Register in MCP23017 | 5.4 |
| 5.2 | UART | 5.6 |
| | 5.2.1 Serial UART, an Introduction | 5.6 |
| | 5.2.2 Serial UART Types | 5.6 |
| | 5.2.3 Registers | 5.7 |

|   |   | 5.2.4 | Interfacing UART | 5.9 |
|---|---|---|---|---|
|   |   | 5.2.5 | Source Code | 5.10 |
| 5.3 | Testing The UART With PIC16F877A | | | 5.11 |
|   |   | 5.3.1 | Serial Peripheral Interface (SPI) | 5.11 |
|   |   | 5.3.2 | I2C Communication in PIC Microcontroller | 5.12 |
|   |   | 5.3.3 | Timing Diagram for Data Transfer in 'Master Mode' | 5.13 |
|   |   | 5.3.4 | Data Communication Protocol | 5.14 |
|   |   | 5.3.5 | Software for I2C Communication | 5.16 |
|   |   | 5.3.6 | I2C Subroutine | 5.16 |
|   |   | 5.3.7 | Example of I2C Interfacing | 5.20 |
| 5.4 | Parallel Slave Port (PSP) | | | 5.21 |
|   |   | 5.4.1 | Serial Peripheral Interface (SPI) with Microchip PIC18 Families Microcontroller | 5.22 |
|   |   | 5.4.2 | Implementation of SPI | 5.24 |
|   |   | 5.4.3 | The PIC18F14K22 Microcontroller | 5.26 |
|   |   | 5.4.4 | Microchip MCP23S17 SPI I/O Expander | 5.27 |
|   |   | 5.4.5 | The PIC18 SPI Peripheral | 5.29 |
| 5.5 | Comparators | | | 5.34 |
|   |   | 5.5.1 | Using PIC's Analog Comparator | 5.36 |
|   |   | 5.5.2 | Interfacing Serial Port | 5.38 |
|   |   | 5.5.3 | RS232 Communication with CCS C Compiler | 5.40 |
|   |   | 5.5.4 | Interfacing RTC with Microcontroller | 5.42 |
| 5.6 | I2C (Inter Integrated Circuit) | | | 5.46 |
|   |   | 5.6.1 | Source Code | 5.48 |
| 5.7 | EEPROM With PIC Microcontroller | | | 5.53 |
|   |   | 5.7.1 | Circuit Diagram for Demonstration | 5.59 |
|   |   | 5.7.2 | EEPROM | 5.60 |
|   |   | 5.7.3 | Source Code | 5.62 |
| 5.8 | RS-232 Interfacing with 8085 Microcontroller | | | 5.67 |
| • | Questions | | | 5.72 |
| **UNIT VI : Case Studies with PIC** | | | | **6.1-6.16** |
| 6.1 | Data Acquisition System (DAS) | | | 6.1 |
| 6.2 | Frequency Counter | | | 6.6 |
| 6.3 | Digital Multimeter | | | 6.8 |
| 6.4 | DC Motor Control | | | 6.13 |
| • | Questions | | | 6.16 |

# Unit - I
# INTRODUCTION TO MICROCONTROLLERS

## 1.1 INTRODUCTION

**Intel** first produced a microcontroller in **1976** under the name **MCS-48**, which was an **8 bit** microcontroller. Later in 1980 they released a further improved version (which is also 8 bit), under the name MCS-51. The most popular microcontroller 8051 belongs to the MCS-51 family of microcontrollers by Intel. Following the success of 8051, many other semiconductor manufacturers released microcontrollers under their own brand name but using the MCS-51 core. Global companies and giants in semiconductor industry like Microchip, **Zilog, Atmel, Philips, Siemens** released products under their brand name. The specialty was that all these devices could be programmed using the same MCS-51 instruction sets. They basically differed in support device configurations like improved memory, presence of an ADC or DAC etc. Intel then released its first 16 bit microcontroller in 1982, under name MCS-96

**8051 Microcontroller Packaging**

There is no need of explaining what each package means, you already know it. So I will skim through mainly used packaging for 8051. See, availability of various packages change from device to device. The most commonly used is Dual Inline Package (40 pins) – known popularly as DIP. 8051 is also available in QFP (Quad Flat Package), TQFP (Thin Quad Flat Package), PQFP (Plastic Quad Flat Package) etc. For explaining the pin diagram, we have used a 40 pin DIP IC as model.

## 1.2 8051 MICROCONTROLLER ARCHITECTURE

Its possible to explain microcontroller architecture to a great detail, but we are limiting scope of this article to internal architecture, pin configuration, program memory and data memory organization. The basic architecture remains same for the MCS-51 family. In general all microcontrollers in MCS- 51 family are represented by XX51, where XX can take values like 80, 89 etc.

### 1.2.1 Schematic and Features

The general schematic diagram of 8051 microcontroller is shown above. We can see 3 system inputs, 3 control signals and 4 ports (for external interfacing). A Vcc power supply and ground is also shown. Now lets explain and go through each in detail. System inputs are necessary to make the micro controller functional. So the first and most important of this is power, marked as Vcc with a GND (ground potential).

Without proper power supply, no electronic system would work. XTAL 1 and XTAL 2 are for the system clock inputs from crystal clock circuit. RESET input is required to initialize microcontroller to default/desired values and to make a new start.

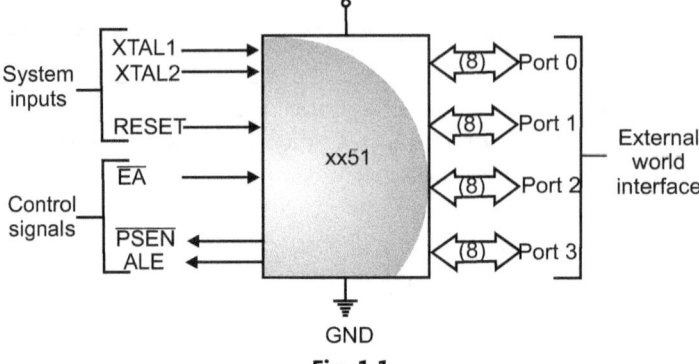

Fig. 1.1

There are 3 control signals, EA, PSEN and ALE. These signals known as External Access (EA), Program Store Enable (PSEN), and Address Latch Enable (ALE) are used for external memory interfacing.

Take a look at the **schematic diagram below** (a functional microcontroller)

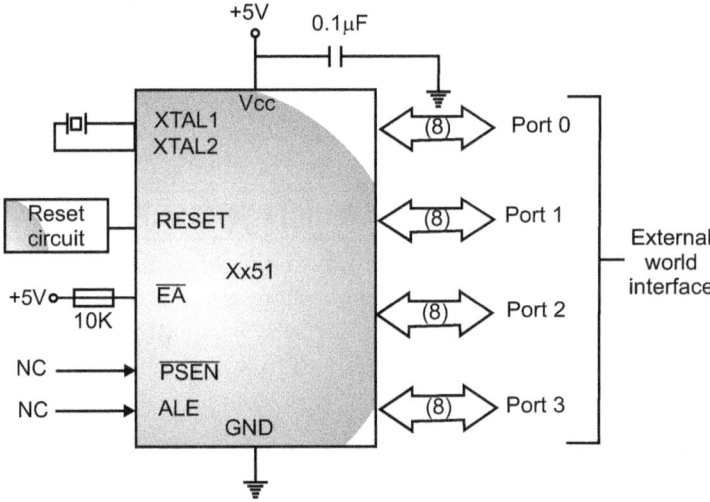

Fig. 1.2

As mentioned above, control signals are used for external memory interfacing. If there is no requirement of external memory interfacing then, EA pin is pulled high (connected to Vcc) and two others PSEN and ALE are left alone. You can also see a 0.1 micro farad decoupling capacitor connected to Vcc (to avoid HF oscillations at input).

There are four ports numbered 0,1,2,3 and called as Port 0, Port 1, Port 2 and Port 3 which are used for external interfacing of devices like DAC, ADC, 7 segment display, LED etc. Each port has 8 I/O lines and they all are bit programmable.

## 1.2.2 8051 Pin Diagram & Description

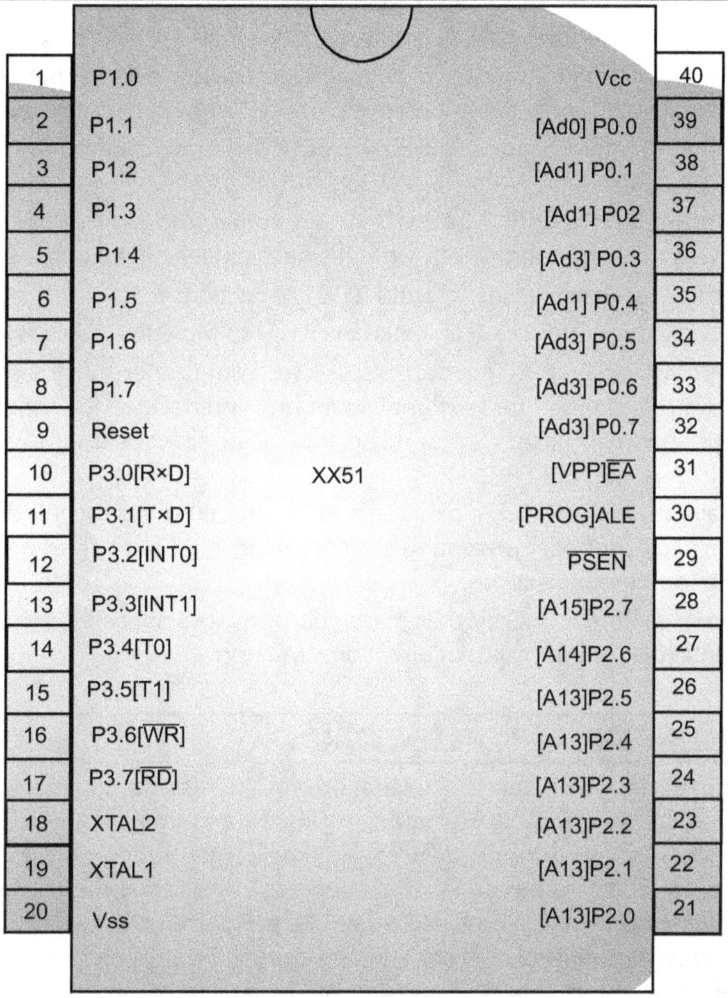

```
 1  P1.0                    Vcc        40
 2  P1.1                [Ad0] P0.0     39
 3  P1.2                [Ad1] P0.1     38
 4  P1.3                [Ad1] P02      37
 5  P1.4                [Ad3] P0.3     36
 6  P1.5                [Ad1] P0.4     35
 7  P1.6                [Ad3] P0.5     34
 8  P1.7                [Ad3] P0.6     33
 9  Reset               [Ad3] P0.7     32
10  P3.0[R×D]   XX51    [VPP]$\overline{EA}$  31
11  P3.1[T×D]           [PROG]ALE      30
12  P3.2[INT0]          $\overline{PSEN}$     29
13  P3.3[INT1]          [A15]P2.7      28
14  P3.4[T0]            [A14]P2.6      27
15  P3.5[T1]            [A13]P2.5      26
16  P3.6[$\overline{WR}$]  [A13]P2.4   25
17  P3.7[$\overline{RD}$]  [A13]P2.3   24
18  XTAL2               [A13]P2.2      23
19  XTAL1               [A13]P2.1      22
20  Vss                 [A13]P2.0      21
```

**Fig. 1.3**

For describing pin diagram and pin configuration of 8051, we are taking into consideration a 40 pin DIP (Dual inline package). Now lets go through pin configuration in detail.

**Pin-40 :** Named as Vcc is the main power source. Usually its +5V DC. You may note some pins are designated with two signals (shown in brackets).

**Pins 32-39:** Known as Port 0 (P0.0 to P0.7) – In addition to serving as I/O port, lower order address and data bus signals are multiplexed with this port (to serve the purpose of external memory interfacing). This is a bi directional I/O port (the only one in 8051) and external pull up resistors are required to function this port as I/O.

**Pin-31:-** ALE aka Address Latch Enable is used to demultiplex the address-data signal of port 0 (for external memory interfacing.) 2 ALE pulses are available for each machine cycle.

**Pin-30:-** EA/ External Access input is used to enable or disallow external memory interfacing. If there is no external memory requirement, this pin is pulled high by connecting it to Vcc.

**Pin- 29:-** PSEN or Program Store Enable is used to read signal from external program memory.

**Pins- 21-28:-** Known as Port 2 (P 2.0 to P 2.7) – in addition to serving as I/O port, higher order address bus signals are multiplexed with this quasi bi directional port.

**Pin 20:-** Named as Vss – it represents ground (0 V) connection.

**Pins 18 and 19:-** Used for interfacing an external crystal to provide system clock.

**Pins 10 – 17:-** Known as Port 3. This port also serves some other functions like interrupts, timer input, control signals for external memory interfacing RD and WR , serial communication signals RxD and TxD etc. This is a quasi bi directional port with internal pull up.

**Pin 9:-** As explained before RESET pin is used to set the 8051 microcontroller to its initial values, while the microcontroller is working or at the initial start of application. The RESET pin must be set high for 2 machine cycles.

**Pins 1 – 8:-** Known as Port 1. Unlike other ports, this port does not serve any other functions. Port 1 is an internally pulled up, quasi bi directional I/O port.

## 1.3 8051 INTERNAL ARCHITECTURE

There is no need of any detailed explanation to understand internal architecture of 8051 micro controller. Just look at the diagram above and you observer it carefully. The system bus connects all the support devices with the central processing unit. 8051 system bus composes of an 8 bit data bus and a 16 bit address bus and bus control signals. From the figure you can understand that all other devices like program memory, ports, data memory, serial interface, interrupt control, timers, and the central processing unit are all interfaced together through the system bus. RxD and TxD (serial port input and output) are interfaced with port 3. A complete computer system manufactured on a single chip is called a microcontroller. The features of a microcontroller are similar to that of a microprocessor like registers, ALU, program counter, flags, stack pointer, etc. Along with these common features, a microcontroller has some additional features such as a clock circuit, internal RAM, ROM, serial and parallel I/O counter.

Using a microcontroller provides a great advantage that a program is stored in ROM that has an important role in managing the system's operations and functions. Since the program written into ROM is fixed that is, it cannot be altered or changed; as a result the operation of the system remains constant (unchanged) regardless of the instructions given to it. Hence, a microcontroller can be thought of a device containing on-chip programme. A microcontroller can also be referred as a 'microcomputer'. Now let us see the architecture and block diagram of 8051 microcontroller. Major components of Intel 8051 microcontroller. The 8051 microcontroller is an 8-bit microcontroller. Let us see the major components of 8051 microcontroller and their functions.

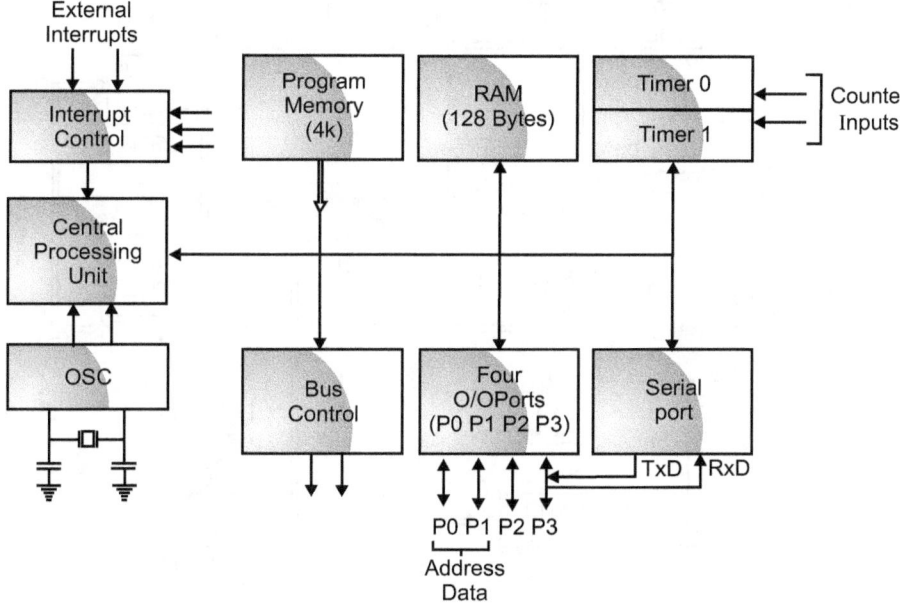

Fig. 1.4

**An 8051 microcontroller has the following 12 major components:**
1. ALU (Arithmetic and Logic Unit)
2. PC (Program Counter)
3. Registers
4. Timers and counters
5. Internal RAM and ROM
6. Four general purpose parallel input/output ports
7. Interrupt control logic with five sources of interrupt
8. Serial date communication
9. PSW (Program Status Word)
10. Data Pointer (DPTR)

11. Stack Pointer (SP)
12. Data and Address bus.

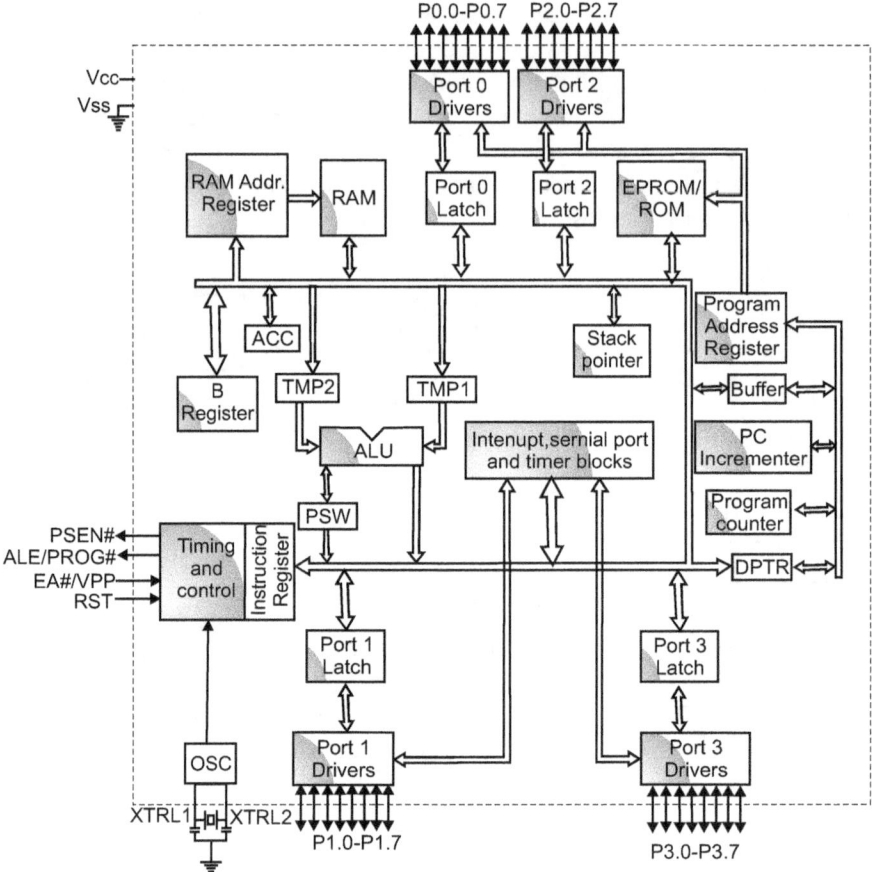

**Fig. 1.5**

Now let us see the functions of each of these components

### (1) ALU :

All arithmetic and logical functions are carried out by the ALU. Addition, subtraction with carry, and multiplication come under arithmetic operations. Logical AND, OR and exclusive OR (XOR) come under logical operations.

### (2) Program Counter (PC)

A program counter is a 16-bit register and it has no internal address. The basic function of program counter is to fetch from memory the address of the next instruction to be executed. The PC holds the address of the next instruction residing in memory and when a command is encountered, it produces that instruction. This way the PC increments automatically, holding the address of the next instruction.

### (3) Registers

Registers are usually known as data storage devices. 8051 microcontroller has 2 registers, namely Register A and Register B. Register A serves as an accumulator while Register B functions as a general purpose register. These registers are used to store the output of mathematical and logical instructions. The operations of addition, subtraction, multiplication and division are carried out by Register A. Register B is usually unused and comes into picture only when multiplication and division functions are carried out by Register A. Register A also involved in data transfers between the microcontroller and external memory. 8051 microcontroller also has 7 Special Function Registers (SFRs).

They are:
- Serial Port Data Buffer (SBUF)
- Timer/Counter Control (TCON)
- Timer/Counter Mode Control (TMOD)
- Serial Port Control (SCON)
- Power Control (PCON)
- Interrupt Priority (IP)
- Interrupt Enable Control (IE)

### (4) Timers and Counters

Synchronization among internal operations can be achieved with the help of clock circuits which are responsible for generating clock pulses. During each clock pulse a particular operation will be carried out, thereby, assuring synchronization among operations. For the formation of an oscillator, we are provided with two pins XTAL1 and XTAL2 which are used for connecting a resonant network in 8051 microcontroller device. In addition to this, circuit also consists of four more pins. They are, Internal operations can be synchronized using clock circuits which produce clock pulses. With each clock pulse, a particular function will be accomplished and hence synchronization is achieved. There are two pins XTAL1 and XTAL2 which form an oscillator circuit which connect to a resonant network in the microcontroller. The circuit also has 4 additional pins –

- EA: External enable
- ALE: Address latch enable
- PSEN: Program store enable and
- RST: Reset. Quartz crystal is used to generate periodic clock pulses.
- Internal RAM and ROM

## ROM

A code of 4K memory is incorporated as on-chip ROM in 8051. The 8051 ROM is a non-volatile memory meaning that its contents cannot be altered and hence has a similar range of data and program memory, i.e, they can address program memory as well as a 64K separate block of data memory.

## RAM

The 8051 microcontroller is composed of 128 bytes of internal RAM. This is a volatile memory since its contents will be lost if power is switched off. These 128 bytes of internal RAM are divided into 32 working registers which in turn constitute 4 register banks (Bank 0-Bank 3) with each bank consisting of 8 registers (R0 - R7). There are 128 addressable bits in the internal RAM.

### (6) Four General Purpose Parallel Input/Output Ports :

The 8051 microcontroller has four 8-bit input/output ports. These are: PORT P0: When there is no external memory present, this port acts as a general purpose input/output port. In the presence of external memory, it functions as a multiplexed address and data bus. It performs a dual role.

PORT P1: This port is used for various interfacing activities. This 8-bit port is a normal I/O port i.e. it does not perform dual functions.

PORT P2: Similar to PORT P0, this port can be used as a general purpose port when there is no external memory but when external memory is present it works in conjunction with PORT P0 as an address bus. This is an 8-bit port and performs dual functions.

PORT P3: PORT P3 behaves as a dedicated I/O port

### (7) Interrupt Control

An event which is used to suspend or halt the normal program execution for a temporary period of time in order to serve the request of another program or hardware device is called an interrupt. An interrupt can either be an internal or external event which suspends the microcontroller for a while and thereby obstructs the sequential flow of a program. There are two ways of giving interrupts to a microcontroller – one is by sending software instructions and the other is by sending hardware signals. The interrupt mechanism keeps the normal program execution in a "put on hold" mode and executes a subroutine program and after the subroutine is executed, it gets back to its normal program execution. This subroutine program is also called an interrupt handler. A subroutine is executed when a certain event occurs. In 8051, 5 sources of interrupts are provided. They are:

- 2 external interrupt sources connected through INT0 and INT1
- 3 external interrupt sources- serial port interrupt, Timer Flag 0 and Timer Flag 1.

The pins connected are as follows:

- ALE (Address Latch Enable) - Latches the address signals on Port P0
- EA (External Address) - Holds the 4K bytes of program memory.
- PSEN (Program Store Enable) - Reads external program memory.
- RST (Reset) - Reset the ports and internal registers upon start up

**(8) Serial Data Communication**

A method of establishing communication among computers is by transmitting and receiving data bits is a serial connection network. In 8051, the SBUF (Serial Port Data Buffer) register holds the data; the SCON (Serial Control) register manages the data communication and the PCON (Power Control) register manages the data transfer rates. Further, two pins - RXD and TXD, establish the serial network.

The SBUF register has 2 parts – one for storing the data to be transmitted and another for receiving data from outer sources. The first function is done using TXD pin and the second function is done using RXD pin.

There are 4 programmable modes in serial data communication. They are:
- Serial Data mode 0 (shift register mode).
- Serial Data mode 1 (standard UART).
- Serial Data mode 2 (multiprocessor mode).
- Serial Data mode 3

**(9) PSW (Program Status Word)**

Program Status Word or PSW is a hardware register which is a memory location which holds a program's information and also monitors the status of the program this is currently being executed. PSW also has a pointer which points towards the address of the next instruction to be executed. PSW register has 3 fields namely are instruction address field, condition code field and error status field.

We can say that PSW is an internal register that keeps track of the computer at every instant. Generally, the instruction of the result of a program is stored in a single bit register called a 'flag'. The are7 flags in the PSW of 8051. Among these 7 flags, 4 are math flags and 3 are general purpose or user flags. The 4 Math flags are:
- Carry (c)
- Auxiliary carry (AC)
- Overflow (OV)
- Parity (P)

The 3 General purpose flags or User flags are:
- FO
- GFO
- GF 1

### (10) Data Pointer (DPTR)

The data pointer or DPTR is a 16-bit register. It is made up of two 8-bit registers called DPH and DPL. Separate addresses are assigned to each of DPH and DPL. These 8-bit registers are used for the storing the memory addresses that can be used to access internal and external data/code.

### (11) Stack Pointer (SP)

The stack pointer (SP) in 8051 is an 8-bit register. The main purpose of SP is to access the stack. As it has 8-bits it can take values in the range 00 H to FF H. Stack is a special area of data in memory. The SP acts as a pointer for an address that points to the top of the stack.

### (12) Data and Address Bus

A bus is group of wires using which data transfer takes place from one location to another within a system. Buses reduce the number of paths or cables needed to set up connection between components. There are mainly two kinds of buses - Data Bus and Address Bus

Data Bus: The purpose of data bus is to transfer data. It acts as an electronic channel using which data travels. Wider the width of the bus, greater will be the transmission of data.

### (13) Address Bus:

The purpose of address bus is to transfer information but not data. The information tells from where within the components, the data should be sent to or received from. The capacity or memory of the address bus depends on the number of wires that transmit a single address bit.

## 1.4 MEMORY ORGANISATION

Before going deep into the memory architecture of 8051, lets talk a little bit about two variations available for the same. They are Princeton architecture and Harvard architecture. Princeton architecture treats address memory and data memory as a single unit (does not distinguish between two) where as Harvard architecture treats program memory and data memory as separate entities. Thus Harvard architecture demands address, data and control bus for accessing them separately where as Princeton architecture does not demand any such separate bus.

**Example :** 8051 micro controller is based on Harvard architecture and 8085 micro processor is based on Princeton architecture. Thus 8051 has two memories :- Program memory and Data memory

### 1.4.1 Program Memory Organization

Now lets dive into the program memory organization 0f 8051. It has an internal program of 4K size and if needed an external memory can be added (by interfacing ) of size 60K maximum. So in total 64K size memory is available for 8051 micro controller. By default, the External Access (EA) pin should be connected Vcc so that instructions are fetched from internal memory initially. When the limit of internal memory (4K) is crossed, control will automatically move to external memory to fetch remaining instructions. If the programmer wants to fetch instruction from external memory only (bypassing the internal memory), then he must connect External Access (EA) pin to ground (GND).

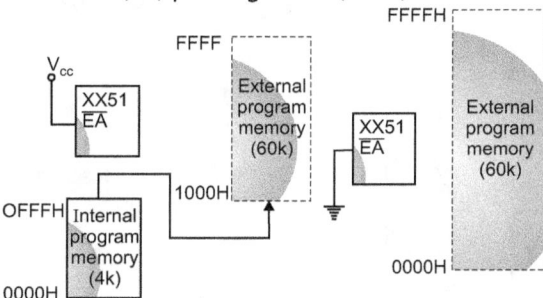

**Fig. 1.6**

You may already know that 8051 has a special feature of locking the program memory (internal) and hence protecting against software piracy. This feature is enable by program lock bits. Once these bits are programmed, contents of internal memory can not be accessed using an external circuitry. How ever locking the software is not possible if external memory is also used to store the software code. Only internal memory can be locked and protected. Once locked, these bits can be unlocked only by a memory-erase operation, which in turn will erase the programs in internal memory too. 8051 is capable of pipelining. Pipelining makes a processor capable of fetching the next instruction while executing previous instruction. Its some thing like multi tasking, doing more than one operation at a time. 8051 is capable of fetching first byte of the next instruction while executing the previous instruction.

## 1.4.2 Data Memory Organization

In the MCS-51 family, 8051 has 128 bytes of internal data memory and it allows interfacing external data memory of maximum size up to 64K. So the total size of data memory in 8051 can be upto 64K (external) + 128 bytes (internal). Observe the diagram carefully to get more understanding. So there are 3 separations/divisions of the data memory:- 1) Register banks 2) Bit addressable area 3) Scratch pad area.

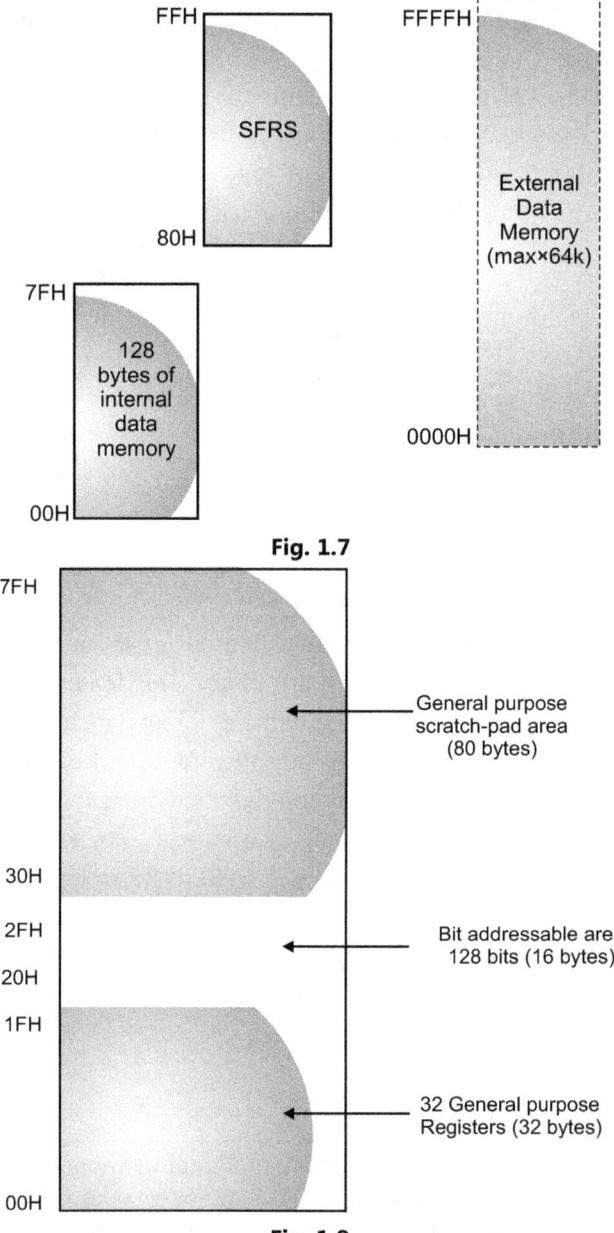

**Fig. 1.7**

**Fig. 1.8**

Register banks form the lowest 32 bytes on internal memory and there are 4 register banks designated bank #0,#1, #2 and #3. Each bank has 8 registers which are designated as

R0,R1...R7. At a time only one register bank is selected for operations and the registers inside the selected bank are accessed using mnemonics R0..R1.. etc. Other registers can be accessed simultaneously only by direct addressing. Registers are used to store data or operands during executions. By default register bank #0 is selected (after a system reset).

The bit addressable ares of 8051 is usually used to store bit variables. The bit addressable area is formed by the 16 bytes next to register banks. They are designated from address 20H to 2FH (total 128 bits). Each bits can be accessed from 00H to 7FH within this 128 bits from 20H to 2FH. Bit addressable area is mainly used to store bit variables from application program, like status of an output device like LED or Motor (ON/OFF) etc. We need only a bit to store this status and using a complete byte addressable area for storing this is really bad programming practice, since it results in wastage of memory.

The scratch pad area is the upper 80 bytes which is used for general purpose storage. Scratch pad area is from 30H to 7FH and this includes stack too.

## 1.5 8051 SYSTEM CLOCK

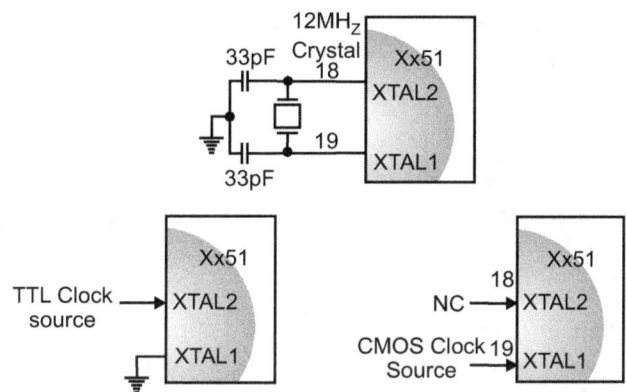

**Fig. 1.9**

An 8051 clock circuit is shown above. In general cases, a quartz crystal is used to make the clock circuit. The connection is shown in figure (a) and note the connections to XTAL 1 and XTAL 2. In some cases external clock sources are used and you can see the various connections above. Clock frequency limits (maximum and minimum) may change from device to device. Standard practice is to use 12MHz frequency. If serial communications are involved then its best to use 11.0592 MHz frequency. Okay, take a look at the above machine cycle waveform. One complete oscillation of the clock source is called a pulse. Two pulses forms a state and six states forms one machine cycle. Also note that, two pulses of ALE are available for 1 machine cycle.

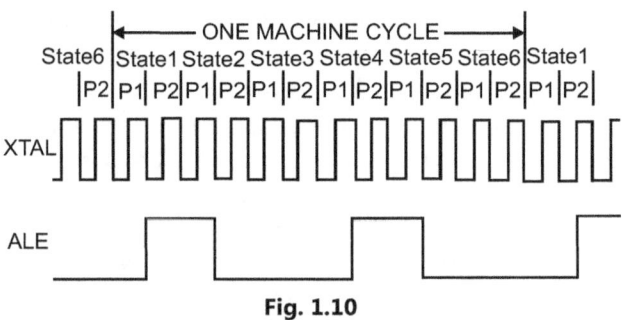

Fig. 1.10

## 1.6 8051 RESET CIRCUIT

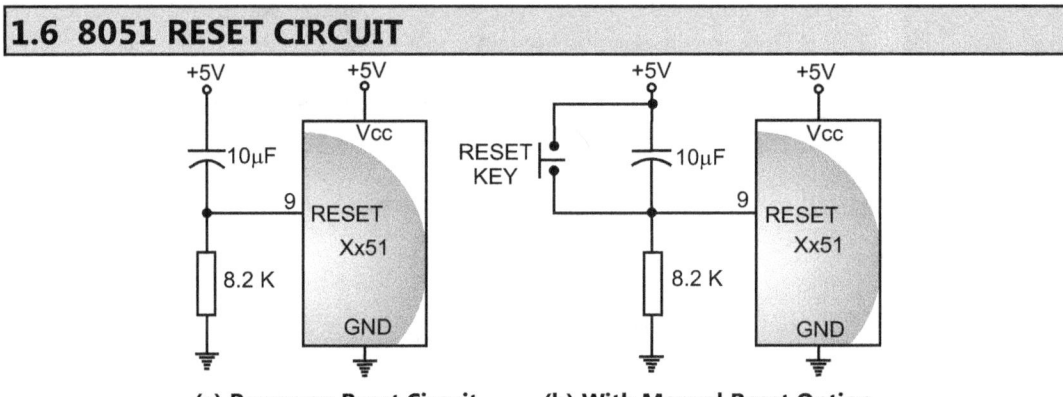

(a) Power-on Reset Circuit    (b) With Manual Reset Option

Fig. 1.11

8051 can be reset in two ways 1) is power-on reset – which resets the 8051 when power is turned ON and 2) manual reset – in which a reset happens only when a push button is pressed manually. Two different reset circuits are shown above. A reset doesn't affect contents of internal RAM. For reset to happen, the reset input pin (pin 9) must be active high for atleast 2 machine cycles. During a reset operation :- Program counter is cleared and it starts from 00H, register bank #0 is selected as default, Stack pointer is initialized to 07H, all ports are written with FFH.

## 1.7 NEED OF MICROCONTROLLER

A Microcontroller is a programmable digital processor with necessary peripherals. Both microcontrollers and microprocessors are complex sequential digital circuits meant to carry out job according to the program / instructions. Sometimes analog input/output interface makes a part of microcontroller circuit of mixed mode(both analog and digital nature).

A microcontroller can be compared to a Swiss knife with multiple functions incorporated in the same IC.

- A microprocessor requires an external memory for program/data storage. Instruction execution requires movement of data from the external memory to the microprocessor or vice versa. Usually, microprocessors have good computing power and they have higher clock speed to facilitate faster computation.
- A microcontroller has required on-chip memory with associated peripherals. A microcontroller can be thought of a microprocessor with inbuilt peripherals.
- A microcontroller does not require much additional interfacing ICs for operation and it functions as a stand alone system. The operation of a microcontroller is multipurpose, just like a Swiss knife.

Microcontrollers are also called embedded controllers. A microcontroller clock speed is limited only to a few tens of MHz. Microcontrollers are numerous and many of them are application specific.

**Development/Classification of Microcontrollers**

Microcontrollers have gone through a silent evolution (invisible). The evolution can be rightly termed as silent as the impact or application of a microcontroller is not well known to a common user, although microcontroller technology has undergone significant change since early 1970's. Development of some popular microcontrollers is given as follows.

| Intel 4004 | 4 bit (2300 PMOS trans, 108 kHz) | 1971 |
| Intel 8048 | 8 bit | 1976 |
| Intel 8031 | 8 bit (ROM-less) | – |
| Intel 8051 | 8 bit (Mask ROM) | 1980 |
| Microchip PIC16C64 | 8 bit | 1985 |
| Motorola 68HC11 | 8 bit (on chip ADC) | – |
| Intel 80C196 | 16 bit | 1982 |
| Atmel AT89C51 | 8 bit (Flash memory) | – |
| Microchip PIC 16F877 | 8 bit (Flash memory + ADC) | – |

**Development of Microprocessors**

Microprocessors have undergone significant evolution over the past four decades. This development is clearly perceptible to a common user, especially, in terms of phenomenal growth in capabilities of personal computers. Development of some of the microprocessors can be given as follows :

| Intel 4004 | 4 bit (2300 PMOS transistors) | 1971 |
|---|---|---|
| Intel 8080 8085 | 8 bit (NMOS) 8 bit | 1974 |
| Intel 8088 8086 | 16 bit 16 bit | 1978 |
| Intel 80186 80286 | 16 bit 16 bit | 1982 |
| Intel 80386 | 32 bit (275000 transistors) | 1985 |
| Intel 80486 SX DX | 32 bit 32 bit (built in floating point unit) | 1989 |
| Intel 80586 I MMX Celeron II III IV | 64 bit | 1993 1997 1999 2000 |
| Z-80 (Zilog) | 8 bit | 1976 |
| Motorola Power PC 601 602 603 | 32-bit | 1993 1995 |

We use more number of microcontrollers compared to microprocessors. Microprocessors are primarily used for computational purpose, whereas microcontrollers find wide application in devices needing real time processing / control. Application of microcontrollers is numerous. Starting from domestic applications such as in washing machines, TVs, air conditioners, microcontrollers are used in automobiles, process control industries, cell phones, electrical drives, robotics and in space applications.

## 1.8 MICROCONTROLLER CHIPS

**Microcontroller Chips**
Broad Classification of different microcontroller chips could be as follows:
- Embedded (Self -Contained) 8 - bit Microcontroller
- 16 to 32 Microcontrollers

Digital Signal Processors

**Features of Modern Microcontrollers**
- Built-in Monitor Program
- Built-in Program Memory
- Interrupts
- Analog I/O
- Serial I/O
- Facility to Interface External Memory

At times, a microcontroller can have external memory also (if there is no internal memory or extra memory interface is required). Early microcontrollers were manufactured using bipolar or NMOS technologies. Most modern microcontrollers are manufactured with CMOS technology, which leads to reduction in size and power loss. Current drawn by the IC is also reduced considerably from 10mA to a few micro Amperes in sleep mode(for a microcontroller running typically at a clock speed of 20MHz).

**Internal Structure of a Microcontroller**

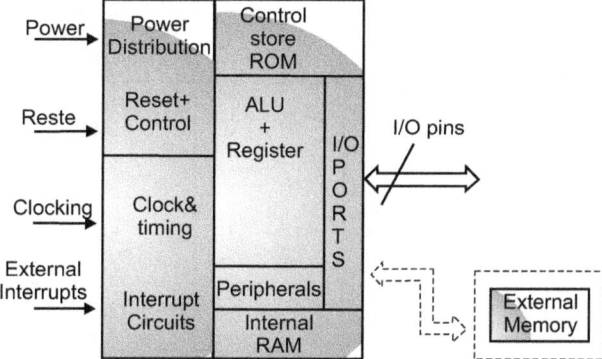

Fig. 1.12 : Internal Structure of a Micro Control

## 1.9 HARVARD VS. VON NEUMANN ARCHITECTURE

Many years ago, in the late 1940's, the US Government asked Harvard and Von Neumann universities to come up with a computer architecture to be used in computing distances of Naval artillery shell for defense applications. Von Neumann suggested computer architecture with a single memory interface.

It is also known as Von Neumann architecture after the name of the chief scientist of the project in Princeton University John Von Neumann (1903 - 1957 Born in Budapest, Hungary). Harvard suggested a computer with two different memory interfaces, one for the data / variables and the other for program / instructions. Although Princeton architecture was accepted for simplicity and ease of implementation, Harvard architecture became popular later, due to the parallelism of instruction execution.

**Princeton Architecture (Single memory interface)**

Example : An instruction "Read a data byte from memory and store it in the accumulator" is executed as follows :

**Cycle 1 :**

Read Instruction

**Cycle 2 :** Read Data out of RAM and put into Accumulator

## Harvard Architecture (Separate Program and Data Memory interfaces)

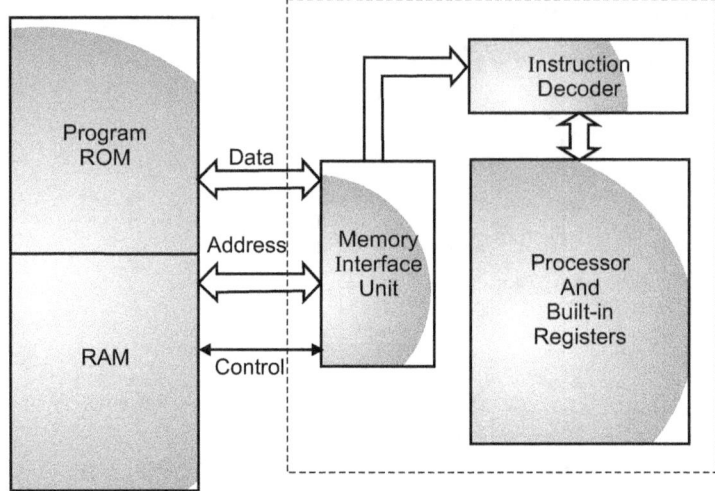

**Fig. 1.13 : VoN Neumann Architecture**

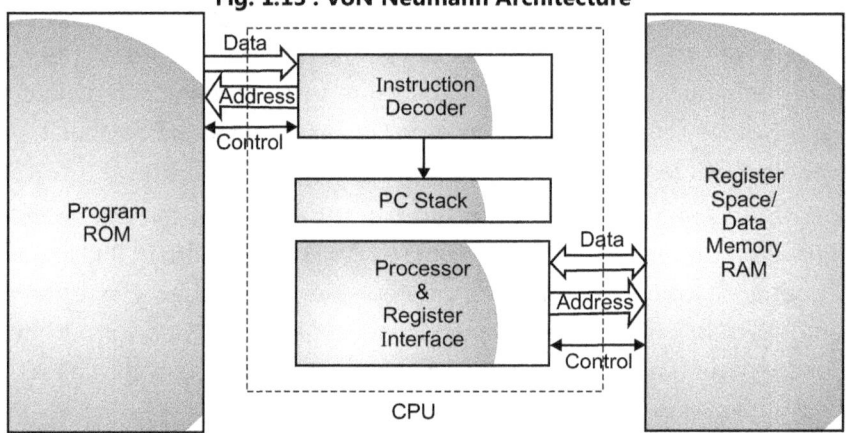

**Fig. 1.14 : Harvard Architecture**

The same instruction (as shown under Princeton Architecture) would be executed as follows:

**Cycle 1 : Complete previous instruction**

Read the "Move Data to Accumulator" instruction

**Cycle 2 : Execute "Move Data to Accumulator" instruction**

Read next instruction. Hence each instruction is effectively executed in one instruction cycle, except for the ones that modify the content of the program counter. For example, the "jump" (or call) instructions takes 2 cycles. Thus, due to parallelism, Harvard architecture executes more instructions in a given time compared to Princeton Architecture.

## 1.10 MICRO-CODED AND HARD-CODED PROCESSORS

The implementation of a computer architecture can be broadly achieved in two ways. A computer is a complex sequential digital circuit with both combinational and sequential circuit components. In a micro-coded processor, each instruction is realized by a number of steps that are implemented using small subroutines. These subroutines are called micro-codes stored within the instruction decode unit. Hence, a micro-coded processor can be called a processor within a processor.

**Micro-Coded Processor:**

Let us take an example. The instruction "Move Acc, Reg" can be executed in the following steps.

1. Output address to the data memory
2. Configure the internal bus for data memory value to be stored in accumulator.
3. Enable bus read.
4. Store the data into the accumulator.
5. Compare data read with zero or any other important condition and set bits in the STATUS register.
6. Disable data bus.

Each step of the instruction is realized by a subroutine (micro-code). A set of bits in the instruction points to the memory where the micro-code for the instruction is located.

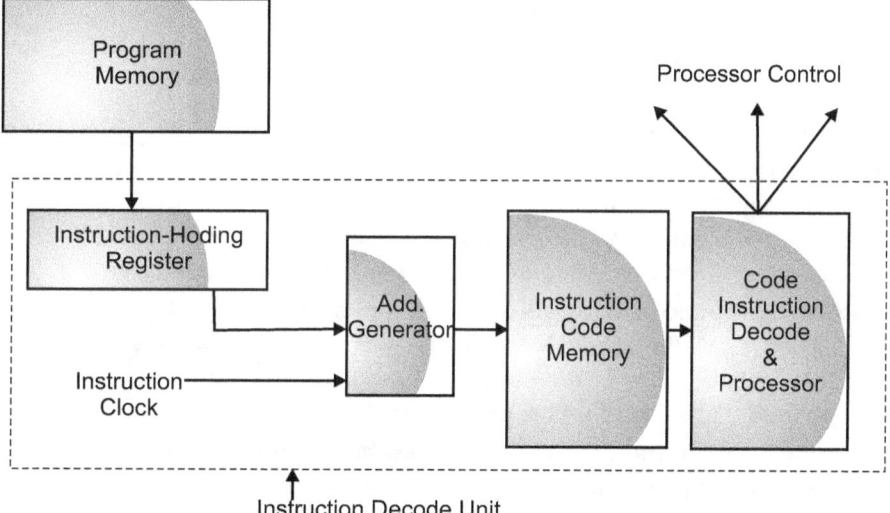

**Fig. 1.15 : Harvard Architecture of a Micro-Coded Processor**

**Advantages :**
- Ease of fabrication.
- Easy to debug.

**Disadvantages :**
- Program execution takes longer time.

**Hard Coded Processor :**

Each instruction is realized by combinational and/or sequential digital circuits. The design is complex, hard to debug.

However, the program execution is faster.

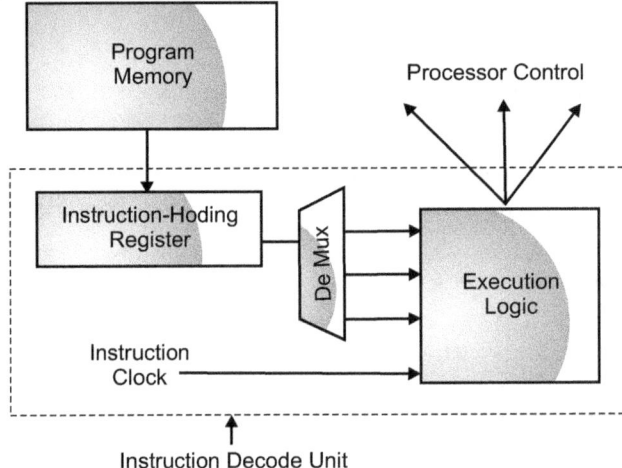

**Fig. 1.16 : Architecture of a Hard-Coded Processor**

## 1.10.1 Memory Types :

In a microcontroller, two types of memory are found. They are, program memory and data memory respectively. Program memory is also known as 'control store' and 'firm ware'. It is non-volatile i.e, the memory content is not lost when the power goes off. Non-volatile memory is also called Read Only Memory(ROM). There are various types of ROM.

**(1) Mask ROM :** Some microcontrollers with ROM are programmed while they are still in the factory. This ROM is called Mask ROM. Since the microcontrollers with Mask ROM are used for specific application, there is no need to reprogram them. Some times, this type of manufacturing reduces the cost for bulk production.

**(2) Reprogrammable program memory (or) Erasable PROM (EPROM):**

Microcontrollers with EPROM were introduced in late 1970's. These devices are electrically programmable but are erased with UV radiation. The construction of a EPROM memory cell is somewhat like a MOSFET but with a control and float semiconductor as shown in the figure.

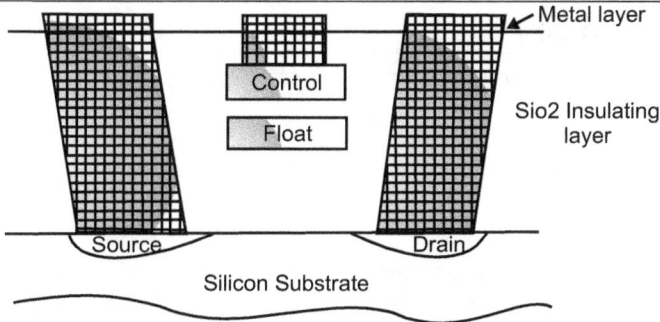

**Fig. 1.17 : Structure of an EPROM**

In the unprogrammed state, the 'float' does not have any charge and the MOSFET is in the OFF state. To program the cell, the 'control' above the 'float' is raised to a high enough potential such that a charge leaks to the float through $SiO_2$ insulating layer. Hence a channel is formed between 'Source' and 'Drain' in the silicon substrate and the MOSFET becomes 'ON'. The charge in the 'float' remains for a long time (typically over 30 years). The charge can be removed by exposing the float to UV radiation. For UV erasable version, the packaging is done in a ceramic enclosure with a glass window.

Usually, these versions of micro controllers are expensive.

**(3) OTP EPROM :** One time programmable (OTP) EPROM based microcontrollers do not have any glass window for UV erasing. These can be programmed only once. This type of packaging results in microcontroller that have the cost 10% of the microcontrollers with UV erase facility(i.e., 1/10th cost).

**(4) EEPROM** : (Electrically Erasable Programmable ROM): This is similar to EPROM but the float charge can be removed electrically.

**(5) FLASH (EEPROM Memory)** : FLASH memory was introduced by INTEL in late 1980's. This memory is similar to EEPROM but the cells in a FLASH memory are bussed so that they can be erased in a few clock cycles. Hence the reprogramming is faster.

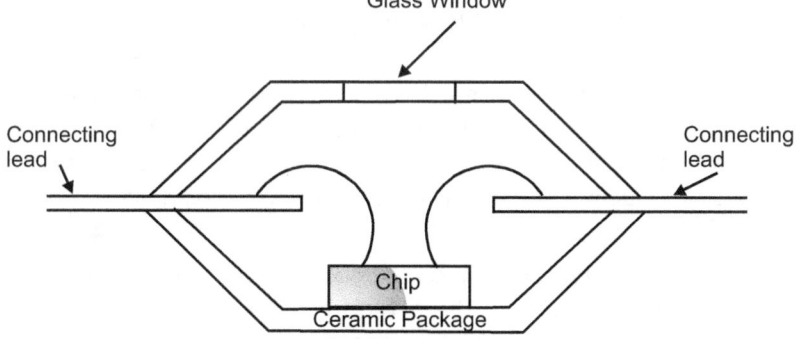

**Fig. 1.18 : UV Erasable Version of a EPROM**

## 1.10.2 DATA Memory

Data memory can be classified into the following categories
- Bits
- Registers
- Variable RAM

**Program Counter Stack :**

Microcontroller can have ability to perform manipulation of individual bits in certain registers(bit manipulation). This is a unique feature of a microcontroller, not available in a microprocessor. Eight bits make a byte. Memory bytes are known as file registers. Registers are some special RAM locations that can be accessed by the processor very easily.

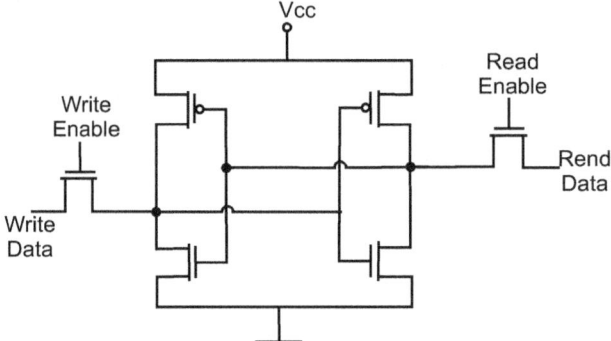

**Fig. 1.19 : Static Power (SRAM) Memory Cell**

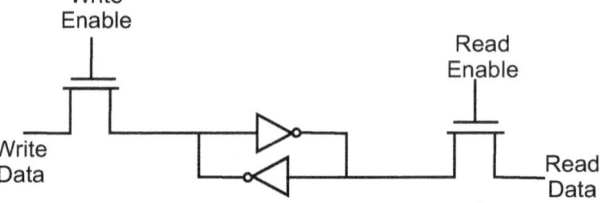

**Fig. 1.20 : SRAM Memory Cell Equivalent**

The figure of a single SRAM cell is shown above. This consists of two CMOS inverters connected back to front, so as to form a latch. Processor stacks store/save the data in a simple way during program execution. Processor stack is a part of RAM area where the data is saved in a Last In First Out (LIFO) fashion just like a stack of paper on a table. Data is stored by executing a 'push' instruction and data is read out using a 'pop' instruction.

**I/O Registers :**

In addition to the Data memory, some special purpose registers are required that are used in input/output and control operations. These registers are called I/O registers. These are important for microcontroller peripheral interface and control applications.

### Hardware interface registers (I/O Space) :

As we already know a microcontroller has some embedded peripherals and I/O devices. The data transfer to these devices takes place through I/O registers. In a microprocessor, input/output (I/O) devices are externally interfaced and are mapped either to memory address (memory mapped I/O) or a separate I/O address space (I/O mapped I/O).

In a microcontroller, two possible architectures can be used i.e., Princeton(Von Neumann) architecture and Harvard architecture.

### I/O Register space in Princeton Architecture :

In Princeton architecture we have only one memory interface for program memory (ROM) and data memory (RAM). One option is to map the I/O Register as a part of data memory or variable RAM area. This architecture is simple and straight forward. This is called memory mapped I/O. Alternatively a separate I/O register space can be assigned.

The drawback of memory mapped I/O is that a program which wrongly executed may overwrite I/O registers.

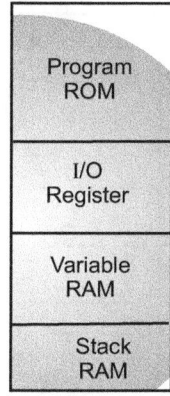
Memory mapped I/o

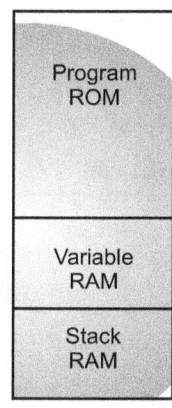

Separate I/O registers

**Fig. 1.21 : I/O Register in Von Neumann Architecture**

## 1.10.3 I/O Registers space in Harvard Architecture

These are the following options available for I/O register space in Harvard Architecture.
1. I/O registers in program ROM.
2. I/O registers in register space (Data Memory area).
3. I/O registers in separate space.

The first option is somewhat difficult to implement as there is no means to write to program ROM area. It is also complicated to have a separate I/O space as shown in (3). Hence the second option where I/O registers are placed in the register space is widely used.

Some of the microcontrollers of 8051 family are given as follows:

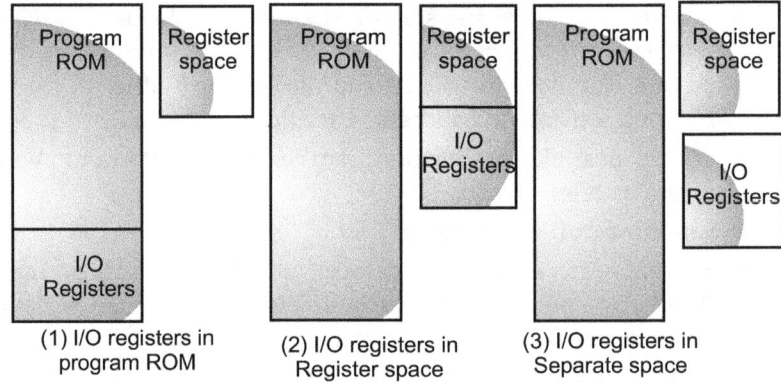

(1) I/O registers in program ROM

(2) I/O registers in Register space

(3) I/O registers in Separate space

**Fig. 1.22 : Organisation of I/O registers in Harward Architecture**

| DEVICE | ON-CHIP DATA MEMORY (bytes) | ON-CHIP PROGRAM MEMORY (bytes) | 16-BIT TIMER/COUNTER | NO. OF VECTORED INTERUPTS | FULL DUPLEX I/O |
|---|---|---|---|---|---|
| 8031 | 128 | None | 2 | 5 | 1 |
| 8032 | 256 | none | 2 | 6 | 1 |
| 8051 | 128 | 4k ROM | 2 | 5 | 1 |
| 8052 | 256 | 8k ROM | 3 | 6 | 1 |
| 8751 | 128 | 4k EPROM | 2 | 5 | 1 |
| 8752 | 256 | 8k EPROM | 3 | 6 | 1 |
| AT89C51 | 128 | 4k Flash Memory | 2 | 5 | 1 |
| AT89C52 | 256 | 8k Flash memory | 3 | 6 | 1 |

Microcontroller's use increased rapidly. Now these are used in almost every electronic equipment like Washing Machines, Mobile Phones and Microwave Oven. Following are the most important facts about Microcontrollers, which causes rapid growth of their use: You may also like: Difference Between Microcontroller & Microprocessor. Among the major manufacturers are:

| | |
|---|---|
| AMD | Enhanced 8051 parts (no longer producing 80x51 parts) |
| Atmel | FLASH and semi-custom parts |
| Dallas | Battery backed, program download, and fastest variants |
| Intel | 8051 through 80c51gb / 80c51sl |
| Matra | 80c154, low voltage static variants |
| OKI | 80c154, mask parts |
| Philips | 87c748 thru 89c588 - more variants than anyone else |
| Siemens | 80c501 through 80c517a, and SIECO cores |
| SMC | COM20051 with ARCNET token bus network engine |
| SSI | 80x52, 2 x HDLC variant for MODEM use |

## 1.11 ADVANTAGES OF MICROCONTROLLERS

- Microcontrollers are cheap and very small in size, therefore they can be embedded on any device.
- Programming of Microcontrollers is simple to learn. Its not much complicated.
- We can use simulators on Computers to see the practical results of our program. Thus we can work on a Embedded project without even buying the required Components and Chips. Thus we can virtually see the working of our project or program.
- Popular - readily available and widely supported, a full range of free and commercial support products is available.
- Fast and effective - the architecture correlates closely with the problem being solved (control systems), specialized instructions mean that fewer bytes of code need to be fetched and fewer conditional jumps are processed.
- High level of system integration within one component, only a handful of components needed to create a working system.
- Wide range - ONE set of tools covers the greatest horsepower range of any microcontroller family, other suppliers handle a number of DIFFERENT and INCOMPATIBLE (and often single-sourced) cores to cover the same power range as the 80x51, the 8051 provides a real cost savings in tools, training, and software support.
- Compatibility - opcodes and binaries are the SAME for all 80x51 variants (unlike most other microcontroller families)
- Multi-sourced - over 12 manufacturers, hundreds of varieties, something for everyone with the security of ready availability.
- Constant improvements - improvements in silicon/design increase speed and power annually, 16 bit models coming from several manufacturers,

## 1.12 APPLICATIONS OF MICROCONTROLLERS

**Microcontrollers are mostly used in following electronic equipments :**

- Mobile Phones
- Auto Mobiles
- CD/DVD Players
- Washing Machines
- Cameras
- In Computers-> Modems and Keyboard Controllers
- Security Alarms
- Electronic Measurement Instruments.
- Microwave Oven.

## 1.13 LIMIATIONS OF MICROCONTROLLER

- One accumulator.
- Register-bank switching is required to access the entire RAM of many devices.
- Operations and registers are not orthogonal; some instructions can address RAM and/or immediate constants, while others can use the accumulator only.
- The hardware call stack is not addressable, so preemptive task switching cannot be implemented.
- Software-implemented stacks are not efficient.

So it is difficult to generate reentrant code and support local variables.

With paged program memory, there are two page sizes to worry about: one for CALL and GOTO and another for computed GOTO (typically used for table lookups).

For example, on PIC16, CALL and GOTO have 11 bits of addressing, so the page size is 2048 instruction words. For computed GOTOs, where you add to PCL, the page size is 256 instruction words.

In both cases, the upper address bits are provided by the PCLATH register. This register must be changed every time control transfers between pages. PCLATH must also be preserved by any interrupt handler.

## 1.14 COMPARISON BETWEEN MICROPROCESSOR AND MICROCONTROLLER

| Microprocessor | Micro Controller |
|---|---|
| 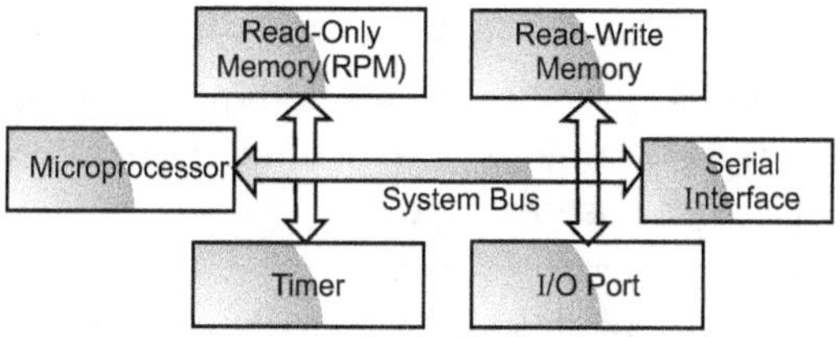 Fig. 1.23 | 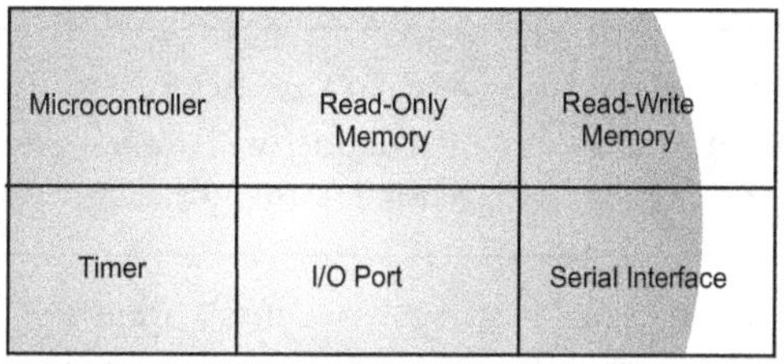 Fig. 1.24 |
| Microprocessor is heart of Computer system. | Micro Controller is a heart of embedded system. |
| It is just a processor. Memory and I/O components have to be connected externally | Micro controller has external processor along with internal memory and I/O components |
| Since memory and I/O has to be connected externally, the circuit becomes large. | Since memory and I/O are present internally, the circuit is small. |
| Cannot be used in compact systems and hence inefficient | Can be used in compact systems and hence it is an efficient technique |
| Cost of the entire system increases | Cost of the entire system is low |
| Due to external components, the entire power consumption is high. Hence it is not suitable to used with devices running on stored power like batteries. | Since external components are low, total power consumption is less and can be used with devices running on stored power like batteries. |

*(Contd.)*

| Microprocessor | Micro Controller |
|---|---|
| Most of the microprocessors do not have power saving features. | Most of the micro controllers have power saving modes like idle mode and power saving mode. This helps to reduce power consumption even further. |
| Since memory and I/O components are all external, each instruction will need external operation, hence it is relatively slower. | Since components are internal, most of the operations are internal instruction, hence speed is fast. |
| Microprocessor have less number of registers, hence more operations are memory based. | Micro controller have more number of registers, hence the programs are easier to write. |
| Microprocessors are based on von Neumann model/architecture where program and data are stored in same memory module | Micro controllers are based on Harvard architecture where program memory and Data memory are separate |
| Mainly used in personal computers | Used mainly in washing machine, MP3 players |

## 1.15 COMPARISON BETWEEN CISC AND RISC

| CISC Computer | RISC Computer |
|---|---|
| Computer that has a **C**omplex **I**nstruction**S**et **C**hip as its cpu. | Computer that has a **R**educed **I**nstruction**S**et **C**hip as its cpu. |
| Variable length instructions | fixed length instructions |
| Many complex instructions | Few simple instructions |
| Complexity in microcode | complexity in compiler |
| It is sometimes called a CISC "chip". This could have a tautology in the last two words, but it can | It is sometimes called a RISC "chip". This could have a tautology in the last two |

| | |
|---|---|
| be overcome by thinking of it as a **C**omplex **I**nstruction **S**et **C**omputer chip. | words, but it can be overcome by thinking of it as **R**educed **I**nstruction **S**et **C**omputer chip. |
| CISC chips have an increasing number of components and an ever increasing instruction set and so are always slower and less powerful at executing "common" instructions | RISC chips have fewer components and a smaller instruction set, allowing faster accessing of "common" instructions |
| CISC chips execute an instruction in two to ten machine cycles | RISC chips execute an instruction in one machine cycle |
| CISC chips do all of the processing themselves | RISC chips distribute some of their processing to other chips |
| CISC chips are more common in computers that have a wider range of instructions to execute | RISC chips are finding their way into components that need faster processing of a limited number of instructions, such as printers and games machines |
| Large set of instruction variable formats (16-64 bits/inst) | Small set of instruction with fixed (32 bit) format and most register based instruction |
| Addressing modes more :12-24 | Addressing modes less :3-5 |
| General purpose register and cache design: 8-24 GPRs , mostly with unified cache | General purpose register and cache design: 32-192 GPRs, with split cache(data and instruction) |
| Clock rate : 33-50 MHz,  CPI   2-15 | Clock rate :    50-150MHz, CPI <1.5 |
| CPU control: Micro programmed control unit | CPU control: Hardwired control unit |
| Many instructions can access memory | Only LOAD/STORE  instructions can access memory |
| Instructions are executed one at a time | Uses pipelining to execute instructions |
| Few general registers | Many general registers |

## 1.16 EMBEDDED SYSTEM

If we look around, we will find ourselves to be surrounded by computing systems. Every year millions of computing systems are built destined for desktop computers (Personal Computers, workstations, mainframes and servers) but surprisingly, billions of computing systems are built every year embedded within larger electronic devices and still goes unnoticed. Any device running on electric power either already has computing system or will soon have computing system embedded in it.

Today, **embedded systems** are found in cell phones, digital cameras, camcorders, portable video games, calculators, and personal digital assistants, microwave ovens, answering machines, home security systems, washing machines, lighting systems, fax machines, copiers, printers, and scanners, cash registers, alarm systems, automated teller machines, transmission control, cruise control, fuel injection, anti-lock brakes, active suspension and many other devices/ gadgets.

A precise ***definition of embedded systems*** is not easy. Simply stated, all computing systems other than general purpose computer (with monitor, keyboard, etc.) are embedded systems.

System is a way of working, organizing or performing one or many tasks according to a fixed set of rules, program or plan. In other words, an arrangement in which all units assemble and work together according to a program or plan. An embedded system is a system that has software embedded into hardware, which makes a system dedicated for an application (s) or specific part of an application or product or part of a larger system. It processes a fixed set of pre-programmed instructions to control electromechanical equipment which may be part of an even larger system (not a computer with keyboard, display, etc).

A general-purpose definition of embedded systems is that they are devices used to control, monitor or assist the operation of equipment, machinery or plant. "Embedded" reflects the fact that they are an integral part of the system. In many cases, their "embeddedness" may be such that their presence is far from obvious to the casual observer. *Block diagram of a typical embedded system* is shown in fig.

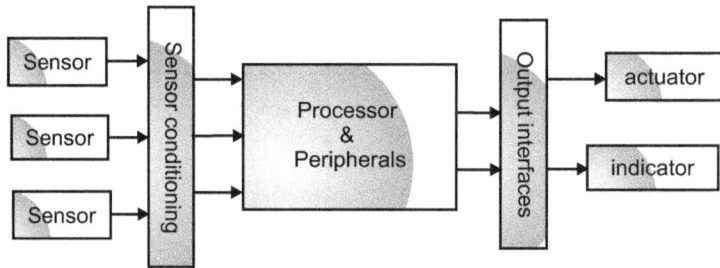

**Fig. 1.25**

An embedded system is an engineering artefact involving computation that is subject to physical constraints (reaction constraints and execution constraints) arising through interactions of computational processes with the physical world. Reaction constraints originate from the behavioural requirements & specify deadlines, throughput, and jitter whereas execution constraints originate from the implementation requirements & put bounds on available processor speeds, power, memory and hardware failure rates. The key to embedded systems design is to obtain desired functionality under both kinds of constraints.

An embedded system is a computer system with a dedicated function within a larger mechanical or electrical system, often with real-time computing constraints. It is *embedded* as part of a complete device often including hardware and mechanical parts. By contrast, a general-purpose computer, such as a personal computer (PC), is designed to be flexible and to meet a wide range of end-user needs. Embedded systems control many devices in common use today. Modern embedded systems are often based on microcontrollers (i.e. CPUs with integrated memory and/or peripheral interfaces) but ordinary microprocessors (using external chips for memory and peripheral interface circuits) are also still common, especially in more complex systems. In either case, the processor(s) used may be types ranging from rather general purpose to very specialized in certain class of computations, or even custom designed for the application at hand. A common standard class of dedicated processors is the digital signal processor (DSP). The key characteristic, however, is being dedicated to handle a particular task. Since the embedded system is dedicated to specific tasks, design engineers can optimize it to reduce the size and cost of the product and increase the reliability and performance.

Some embedded systems are mass-produced, benefiting from economies of scale. Physically, embedded systems range from portable devices such as digital watches and MP3 players, to large stationary installations like traffic lights, factory controllers, and largely complex systems like hybrid vehicles, MRI, and avionics. Complexity varies from low, with a single microcontroller chip, to very high with multiple units, peripherals and networks mounted inside a large chassis or enclosure.

## 1.17 CHARACTERISTICS OF EMBEDDED SYSTEMS

1. Embedded systems are application specific & single functioned; application is known apriori, the programs are executed repeatedly.
2. Efficiency is of paramount importance for embedded systems. They are optimized for energy, code size, execution time, weight & dimensions, and cost.
3. Embedded systems are typically designed to meet real time constraints; a real time system reacts to stimuli from the controlled object/ operator within the time interval dictated by the environment. For real time systems, right answers arriving too late (or even too early) are wrong.
4. Embedded systems often interact (sense, manipulate & communicate) with external world through sensors and actuators and hence are typically reactive systems; a

reactive system is in continual interaction with the environment and executes at a pace determined by that environment.

5. They generally have minimal or no user interface.
6. Embedded systems are designed to do some specific task, rather than be a general-purpose computer for multiple tasks. Some also have real-time performance constraints that must be met, for reasons such as safety and usability; others may have low or no performance requirements, allowing the system hardware to be simplified to reduce costs.
7. Embedded systems are not always standalone devices. Many embedded systems consist of small, computerized parts within a larger device that serves a more general purpose. For example, the Gibson Robot Guitar features an embedded system for tuning the strings, but the overall purpose of the Robot Guitar is, of course, to play music.[7] Similarly, an embedded system in an automobile provides a specific function as a subsystem of the car itself.
8. The program instructions written for embedded systems are referred to as firmware, and are stored in read-only memory or Flash memory chips. They run with limited computer hardware resources: little memory, small or non-existent keyboard or screen.

## 1.18 EMBEDDED SYSTEM TOOLS

As with other software, embedded system designers use compilers, assemblers, and debuggers to develop embedded system software. However, they may also use some more specific tools:

- In circuit debuggers or emulators (see next section).
- Utilities to add a checksum or CRC to a program, so the embedded system can check if the program is valid.
- For systems using digital signal processing, developers may use a math workbench such
as Scilab / Scicos, MATLAB / Simulink, EICASLAB, MathCad, Mathematica,orFlowStone DSP to simulate the mathematics. They might also use libraries for both the host and target which eliminates developing DSP routines as done in DSPnano RTOS.
- A model based development tool like VisSim lets you create and simulate graphical data flow and UML State chart diagrams of components like digital filters, motor controllers, communication protocol decoding and multi-rate tasks. Interrupt handlers can also be created graphically. After simulation, you can automatically generate C-code to theVisSim RTOS which handles the main control

task and preemption of background tasks, as well as automatic setup and programming of on-chip peripherals.
- Custom compilers and linkers may be used to optimize specialized hardware.
- An embedded system may have its own special language or design tool, or add enhancements to an existing language such as Forth or Basic.
- Another alternative is to add a real-time operating system or embedded operating system, which may have DSP capabilities like DSPnano RTOS.
- Modeling and code generating tools often based on state machines.

**Software Tools can come from Several Sources :**
- Software companies that specialize in the embedded market
- Ported from the GNU software development tools
- Sometimes, development tools for a personal computer can be used if the embedded processor is a close relative to a common PC processor

As the complexity of embedded systems grows, higher level tools and operating systems are migrating into machinery where it makes sense. For example, cellphones, personal digital assistants and other consumer computers often need significant software that is purchased or provided by a person other than the manufacturer of the electronics. In these systems, an open programming environment such as Linux, NetBSD, OSGi or Embedded Java is required so that the third-party software provider can sell to a large market.

## 1.18.1 Debugger

A special program used to find errors (*bugs*) in other programs. A debugger allows a programmer to stop a program at any point and examine and change the values of variables. Embedded debugging may be performed at different levels, depending on the facilities available. From simplest to most sophisticated they can be roughly grouped into the following areas:
- Interactive resident debugging, using the simple shell provided by the embedded operating system (e.g. Forth and Basic)
- External debugging using logging or serial port output to trace operation using either a monitor in flash or using a debug server like the Remedy Debugger which even works for heterogeneous multicore systems.
- An in-circuit debugger (ICD), a hardware device that connects to the microprocessor via a JTAG or Nexus interface. This allows the operation of the microprocessor to be controlled externally, but is typically restricted to specific debugging capabilities in the processor.
- An in-circuit emulator (ICE) replaces the microprocessor with a simulated equivalent, providing full control over all aspects of the microprocessor.

- A complete emulator provides a simulation of all aspects of the hardware, allowing all of it to be controlled and modified, and allowing debugging on a normal PC. The downsides are expense and slow operation, in some cases up to 100X slower than the final system.

For SoC designs, the typical approach is to verify and debug the design on an FPGA prototype board. Tools such as Certus [8] are used to insert probes in the FPGA RTL that make signals available for observation. This is used to debug hardware, firmware and software interactions across multiple FPGA with capabilities similar to a logic analyzer.

Unless restricted to external debugging, the programmer can typically load and run software through the tools, view the code running in the processor, and start or stop its operation. The view of the code may be as HLL source-code, assembly code or mixture of both.

Because an embedded system is often composed of a wide variety of elements, the debugging strategy may vary. For instance, debugging a software- (and microprocessor-) centric embedded system is different from debugging an embedded system where most of the processing is performed by peripherals (DSP, FPGA, co-processor). An increasing number of embedded systems today use more than one single processor core. A common problem with multi-core development is the proper synchronization of software execution. In such a case, the embedded system design may wish to check the data traffic on the busses between the processor cores, which requires very low-level debugging, at signal/bus level, with a logic analyzer, for instance.

A debugger or debugging tool is a computer program that is used to test and debug other programs (the "target" program). The code to be examined might alternatively be running on an *instruction set simulator* (ISS), a technique that allows great power in its ability to halt when specific conditions are encountered but which will typically be somewhat slower than executing the code directly on the appropriate (or the same) processor. Some debuggers offer two modes of operation—full or partial simulation—to limit this impact.

A "trap" occurs when the program cannot normally continue because of a programming bug or invalid data. For example, the program might have tried to use an instruction not available on the current version of the CPU or attempted to access unavailable or protectedmemory. When the program "traps" or reaches a preset condition, the debugger typically shows the location in the original code if it is asource-level debugger or symbolic debugger, commonly now seen in integrated development environments. If it is a low-level debugger or a machine-language debugger it shows the line in the disassembly (unless it also has online access to the original source code and can display the appropriate section of code from the assembly or compilation).

Typically, debuggers offer a query processor, symbol resolver, expression interpreter, and debug support interface at its top level.[1] Debuggers also offer more sophisticated functions such as running a program step by step (single-stepping or program animation), stopping (breaking) (pausing the program to examine the current state) at some event or specified instruction by means of a breakpoint, and tracking the values of variables.[2] Some debuggers have the ability to modify program state while it is running. It may also be possible to continue execution at a different location in the program to bypass a crash or logical error.

The same functionality which makes a debugger useful for eliminating bugs allows it to be used as a software cracking tool to evade copy protection, digital rights management, and other software protection features. It often also makes it useful as a general verification tool, fault coverage, and performance analyzer, especially if instruction path lengthsare shown.[3]

Most mainstream debugging engines, such as gdb and dbx, provide console-based command line interfaces. Debugger front-ends are popular extensions to debugger engines that provide IDE integration, program animation, and visualization features. Some early mainframe debuggers such as Oliver and SIMON provided this same functionality for theIBM System/360 and later operating systems, as long ago as the 1970s.

**Language Dependency**

Some debuggers operate on a single specific language while others can handle multiple languages transparently. For example if the main target program is written in COBOL but calls assembly language subroutines and PL/1 subroutines, the debugger may have to dynamically switch modes to accommodate the changes in language as they occur.

**Memory Protection**

Some debuggers also incorporate memory protection to avoid storage violations such as buffer overflow. This may be extremely important in transaction processing environments where memory is dynamically allocated from memory 'pools' on a task by task basis.

**Hardware support for Debugging**

Most modern microprocessors have at least one of these features in their CPU design to make debugging easier:

Hardware support for single-stepping a program, such as the trap flag.

An instruction set that meets the Popek and Goldberg virtualization requirements makes it easier to write debugger software that runs on the same CPU as the software being debugged; such a CPU can execute the inner loops of the program under test at full speed, and still remain under debugger control.

In-System Programming allows an external hardware debugger to reprogram a system under test (for example, adding or removing instruction breakpoints). Many systems with such ISP support also have other hardware debug support.

Hardware support for code and data breakpoints, such as address comparators and data value comparators or, with considerably more work involved, page fault hardware.[6]

JTAG access to hardware debug interfaces such as those on ARM architecture processors or using the Nexus command set. Processors used in embedded systems typically have extensive JTAG debug support.

Microcontrollers with as few as six pins need to use low pin-count substitutes for JTAG, such as BDM, Spy-Bi-Wire, or debugWIRE on the Atmel AVR. DebugWIRE, for example, uses bidirectional signaling on the RESET pin.

**Debugger Front-Ends**

Some of the most capable and popular debuggers implement only a simple command line interface (CLI) often to maximize portability and minimize resource consumption. Developers typically consider debugging via a graphical user interface (GUI) easier and more productive. This is the reason for visual front-ends, that allow users to monitor and control subservient CLI-only debuggers via graphical user interface. Some GUI debugger front-ends are designed to be compatible with a variety of CLI-only debuggers, while others are targeted at one specific debugger.

**List of Debuggers**

Some widely used debuggers are :
- GNU Debugger (GDB)
- Intel Debugger (IDB)
- LLDB
- Microsoft Visual Studio Debugger
- Valgrind
- WinDbg
- Eclipse debugger
- API used in a range of IDEs: Eclipse IDE (Java) Nodeclipse (JavaScript)

## 1.18.2 Assembler

An assembler directive is a message to the assembler that tells the assembler something it needs to know in order to carry out the assembly process; for example, an assemble directive tess the assembler where a program is to be located in memory.

An assembler is a program which creates object code by translating combinations of mnemonics and syntax for operations and addressing modes into their numerical equivalents. This representation typically includes an *operation code* ("opcode") as well as other control bits.[1] The assembler also calculates constant expressions and resolvessymbolic names for memory locations and other entities.[2] The use of symbolic references is a key feature of assemblers, saving tedious calculations and manual address updates after program modifications. Most assemblers also include macro facilities for performing textual substitution e.g., to generate common short sequences of instructions as inline, instead of *called* subroutines.

Some assemblers may also be able to perform some simple types of instruction set-specific optimizations. One concrete example of this may be the ubiquitous x86 assemblers from various vendors. Most of them are able to perform jump-instruction replacements (long jumps replaced by short or relative jumps) in any number of passes, on request. Others may even do simple rearrangement or insertion of instructions, such as some assemblers for RISC architectures that can help optimize a sensible instruction scheduling to exploit the CPU pipeline as efficiently as possible.

Like early programming languages such as Fortran, Algol, Cobol and Lisp, assemblers have been available since the 1950s and the first generations of text based computer interfaces. However, assemblers came first as they are far simpler to write than compilers for high-level languages. This is because each mnemonic along with the addressing modes and operands of an instruction translates rather directly into the numeric representations of that particular instruction, without much context or analysis. There have also been several classes of translators and semi automatic code generators with properties similar to both assembly and high level languages, with speed code as perhaps one of the better known examples.

There are two types of assemblers based on how many passes through the source are needed to produce the executable program.

One-pass assemblers go through the source code once. Any symbol used before it is defined will require "errata" at the end of the object code (or, at least, no earlier than the point where the symbol is defined) telling the linker or the loader to "go back" and overwrite a placeholder which had been left where the as yet undefined symbol was used.

Multi-pass assemblers create a table with all symbols and their values in the first passes, then use the table in later passes to generate code.

The A51 Assembler Kit for the 8051 microcontroller family enables you to write assembler programs for practically any 8051 derivatives including those from Analog Devices, Atmel, Cypress Semiconductor, Dallas Semiconductor, Goal, Hynix, Infineon, Intel, NXP (founded by Philips), OKI, Silicon Labs, SMSC, STMicroelectronics, Synopsis, TDK, Temic, Texas Instruments, and Winbond. Examples of common assembler directives are ORG (origin), EQU (equate), and DS.B (define space for a byte). Equate The EQU assembler directive simply equates a symbolic name to a numeric value. Consider: Sunday EQU 1 Monday EQU 2 The assembler substitutes the equated value for the symbolic name; for example, if you write the instruction ADD.B #Sunday,D2, the assembler treats it as if it were ADD.B #1,D2. You could also write Sunday EQU 1 Monday EQU Sunday + 1

In this case, the assembler evaluates "Sunday + 1" as 1 + 1 and assigns the value 2 to the symbolic name "Monday".

Assembler directives are instructions that direct the assembler to do something

Directives do many things; some tell the assembler to set aside space for variables, others tell the assembler to include additional source files, and others establish the start address for your program. The directives available are shown below:

=

Assigns a value to a symbol (same as EQU)

**EQU**
Assigns a value to a symbol (same as =)

**ORG**
Sets the current origin to a new value. This is used to set the program or register address during assembly. For example, ORG 0100h tells the assembler to assemble all subsequent code starting at address 0100h.

**DS**
Defines an amount of free space. No code is generated. This is sometimes used for allocating variable space.

**ID**
Sets the PIC's identification bytes. PIC16C5x chips have two ID bytes, which can be set to a 2-byte value. Newer PICs have four 7-bit ID locations, which can be filled with a 4-character text string.

**INCLUDE**
Loads another source file during assembly. This allows you to insert an additional source file into your code during assembly. Included source files usually contain common routines or data. By using an INCLUDE directive at the beginning of your program, you can avoid re-typing common information. Included files may not contain other included files. NOTE: The Device Include directive (i.e. INCLUDE 'C:\PicTools\16F877.inc' ) for the targeted device MUST be at the beginning of your source code.

**FUSES**
NOTE that FUSE CONFIGURATIONs can be '&' together on a single line and/or spread between multiple lines. ALL FUSES directives are ANDed together to create the composite FUSE CONFIGURATION. (view the device "include" file for specific fuse syntax)

**IF** <expression>
Assembles code if expression evaluates to TRUE.

**IFNOT** <expression>
Assembles code if expression evaluates to FALSE.

**ELSE**
Assembles code if preceeding evaluation is rejected.

**ENDIF**
Ends conditional evaluation.

**RESET**
Sets the reset start address. This address is where program execution will start following a reset. A jump to the given address is inserted at the last location in memory. After the PIC is reset, it starts executing code at the last location, which holds the jump to the given address. RESET is only available for PIC16C5x chips.

**EEORG**

Sets the current data EEPROM origin to a new value. This is used to set the data EEPROM address during assembly. This directive usually precedes EEDATA. EEORG is only available for PICs that have EEPROM memory.

**EEDATA**

Loads data EEPROM with given values. This provides a means of automatically storing values in the data EEPROM when the PIC is programmed. This is handy for storing configuration or start-up information. EEDATA is only available for PICs that have EEPROM memory.

## 1.18.3 Compilers

A **compiler** is a computer program (or set of programs) that transforms source code written in a programming language (the source language) into another computer language (the target language, often having a binary form known as object code).[1] The most common reason for wanting to transform source code is to create an executable program.

The name "compiler" is primarily used for programs that translate source code from a high-level programming language to a lower level language (e.g., assembly language or machine code). If the compiled program can run on a computer whose CPU or operating system is different from the one on which the compiler runs, the compiler is known as a cross-compiler.

A program that translates from a low level language to a higher level one is a decompiler. A program that translates between high-level languages is usually called asource-to-source compiler or transpiler. A language rewriter is usually a program that translates the form of expressions without a change of language. More generally, compilers are sometimes called translators. A compiler is likely to perform many or all of the following operations: lexical analysis, preprocessing, parsing, semantic analysis (Syntax-directed translation), code generation, and code optimization.

Program faults caused by incorrect compiler behavior can be very difficult to track down and work around; therefore, compiler implementers invest significant effort to ensure compiler correctness.

The term compiler-compiler is sometimes used to refer to a parser generator, a tool often used to help create the lexer and parser.

Compilers bridge source programs in high-level languages with the underlying hardware. A compiler verifies code syntax, generates efficient object code, performs run-time organization, and formats the output according to assembler and linker conventions. A compiler consists of:

**The front end:** Verifies syntax and semantics, and generates an *intermediate representation* or *IR* of the source code for processing by the middle-end. Performs type checking by collecting type information. Generates errors and warning, if any, in a useful way. Aspects of the front end include lexical analysis, syntax analysis, and semantic analysis.

**The middle end:** Performs optimizations, including removal of useless or unreachable code, discovery and propagation of constant values, relocation of computation to a less frequently executed place (e.g., out of a loop), or specialization of computation based on the context. Generates another IR for the backend.

**The back end:** Generates the assembly code, performing register allocation in process. (Assigns processor registers for the program variables where possible.) Optimizes target code utilization of the hardware by figuring out how to keep parallel execution units busy, filling delay slots. Although most algorithms for optimization are in NP, heuristic techniques are well-developed.

- One classification of compilers is by the platform on which their generated code executes. This is known as the *target platform*.
- A *native* or *hosted* compiler is one which output is intended to directly run on the same type of computer and operating system that the compiler itself runs on. The output of across compiler is designed to run on a different platform. Cross compilers are often used when developing software for embedded systems that are not intended to support a software development environment.
- The output of a compiler that produces code for a virtual machine (VM) may or may not be executed on the same platform as the compiler that produced it. For this reason such compilers are not usually classified as native or cross compilers.
- The lower level language that is the target of a compiler may itself be a high-level programming language. C, often viewed as some sort of portable assembler, can also be the target language of a compiler. E.g.: Cfront, the original compiler for C++ used C as target language. The C created by such a compiler is usually not intended to be read and maintained by humans. So indent style and pretty C intermediate code are irrelevant. Some features of C turn it into a good target language. E.g.: C code with #line directives can be generated to support debugging of the original source.

List with C or C++ compilers and support for 8051 microcontroller series.

- SDCC – C compiler for a wide series of microcontrollers including the 8051 models;
- mikroC PRO for 8051 – C compiler with friendly interface and support for Atmel and Silicon Labs microcontrollers;
- Keil – powerful and efficient C simulator for 8051;
- TASKING – compiler compatible with 8, 16 and 32-bit microcontrollers;
- IAR Embedded Workbench for 8051 – C and C++ compiler for 8051;
- 8051 C Compiler – based on ANSI standard, the Crossware 8051 C compiler is designed for 8051 microcontroller series;
- 8051 C++ Compiler – C++ simulator with support for object oriented programs;

- Ceibo 8051 C++ – C++ compiler with support for Object Oriented Programming and used for debugging and code maintenance;
- 8051 C-Compiler uC51 – a friendly interface tool based on ANSI C standard;

## 1.18.4 IDE

- An **integrated development environment (IDE)** or **interactive development environment** is a software application that provides comprehensive facilities to computer programmers for software development. An IDE normally consists of a source code editor, build automation tools and a debugger. Most modern IDEs offer Intelligent code completion features.
- Some IDEs contain a compiler, interpreter, or both, such as Net Beans and Eclipse; others do not, such as SharpDevelop and Lazarus. The boundary between an integrated development environment and other parts of the broader *software development environment* is not well-defined. Sometimes a version control system and various tools are integrated to simplify the construction of a GUI. Many modern IDEs also have a class browser, an object browser, and a class hierarchy diagram, for use in object-oriented software development.
- Integrated development environments are designed to maximize programmer productivity by providing tight-knit components with similar user interfaces. IDEs present a single program in which all development is done. This program typically provides many features for authoring, modifying, compiling, deploying and debugging software. This contrasts with software development using unrelated tools, such as vi, GCC or make.
- One aim of the IDE is to reduce the configuration necessary to piece together multiple development utilities, instead providing the same set of capabilities as a cohesive unit. Reducing that setup time can increase developer productivity, in cases where learning to use the IDE is faster than manually integrating all of the individual tools. Tighter integration of all development tasks has the potential to improve overall productivity beyond just helping with setup tasks. For example, code can be continuously parsed while it is being edited, providing instant feedback when syntax errors are introduced. That can speed learning a new programming language and its associated libraries.
- Some IDEs are dedicated to a specific programming language, allowing a feature set that most closely matches the programming paradigms of the language.
- However, there are many multiple-language IDEs, such as Eclipse, ActiveState Komodo, IntelliJ IDEA, Oracle JDeveloper, NetBeans, Codenvy and Microsoft Visual Studio. Xcode, Xojo and Delphi are dedicated to a closed language or set of programming languages.

- While most modern IDEs are graphical, text-based IDEs such as Turbo Pascal were in popular use before the widespread availability of windowing systems like Microsoft Windows and the X Window System (X11). They commonly use function keys or hotkeys to execute frequently used commands or macros.

**MCU 8051 IDE** is a free software integrated development environment for microcontrollers based on 8051. MCU 8051 IDE has its own simulator and assembler (support for some external assemblers is also available). This IDE supports 2 programming languages: C and Assembly language. For C language it uses SDCC.

**Key features**
- MCU simulator with many debugging features: register status, step by step, interrupt viewer, external memory viewer, code memory viewer, etc.
- Simulator for certain electronic peripherals like leds, LED displays, LED matrices, LCD displays, etc.
- Support for C language
- Native macro-assembler
- Support for ASEM-51 and other assemblers
- Advanced text editor with syntax highlighting and validation
- Support for vim and nano embedded in the IDE
- Simple hardware programmer for certain AT89Sxx MCUs
- Scientific calculator: time delay calculation and code generation, base converter, etc.
- Hexadecimal editor

**Similar software**
- Keil C51
- MIDE-51 Studio
- MikroElektronika

## 1.18.5 Simulator

Sometimes you just haven't ability to flash microcontroller in order to test program functionality in development phase. For this there may be many reasons like you don't have a prototype ready or you need to test parts of code and so on. For this there are software simulators used which simulates microcontroller work without microcontroller itself. Simulators usually don't have connection to real world all operations are simulated in software. Microcontroller simulator is a program model which imitates its work. Modern simulators now simulates not only arithmetic operations but also I/O operations and even peripherals like timers, ADC, USART, I2C and so on. In many cases there is possible to prepare whole project jus using simulator and then burn compiled code to real microcontroller.

Simulators usually allow:

- Debugging at source code level;
- Follow operation time in slow motion but with real world values;
- Connect stimulus signals like they are real world signals.

This is basic illustration because many moder simulators may have much more blocks.
- Memory block imitates work of real memory. Microcontroller program has to be loaded to this memory. O course this memory can be split in several modules like Flash, RAM, EEPROM or even External memory;
- Processor model imitates all operations of real processor like accessing memory contents, doing arithmetic operations, storing results back to memory;
- I/O model usually reads signals from file where prepared real world signals are stored or it is connected to external circuit model which generates required signals.

Processor model is a core of simulator, because it controls all operations including interrupts. Working with simulator gives many benefits because you can see all parameters just in one window. You can stop processor at any point, change memory contents at any time jus by clicking on screen. But one disadvantage is that simulator is totally isolated from real world. So another option is to use **Emulator**.

## 1.18.6 Emulator

Emulator is much closer to real world conditions, because software is emulated in real hardware while results are seen in special emulator software. In order to emulate target microcontroller special adapteris needed which interacts between host computer and target board. Usually Jtag interface is used to emulate. As a result of using emulator you can precisely emulate microcontroller work even more you don't need to take care on input signals from sensors as they come from real circuits.

An **in-circuit emulator** (ICE) is a hardware device used to debug the software of an embedded system. It was historically in the form of bond-out processor which has many internal signals brought out for the purpose of debugging. These signals provide information about the state of the processor.

More recently the term also covers JTAG based hardware debuggers which provide equivalent access using on-chip debugging hardware with standard production chips. Using standard chips instead of custom bond-out versions makes the technology ubiquitous and low cost, and eliminates most differences between the development and runtime environments. In this common case, the **in-circuit emulator** term is a misnomer, sometimes confusingly so, because emulation is no longer involved.

Embedded systems present special problems for a programmer because they usually lack keyboards, monitors, disk drives and other user interfaces that are present on computers. These shortcomings make in-circuit software debugging tools essential for many common development tasks.

**In-circuit emulation** can also refer to the use of hardware emulation, when the emulator is plugged into a system (not always embedded) in place of a yet-to-be-built chip (not always a processor). These in-circuit emulators provide a way to run the system with "live" data while still allowing relatively good debugging capabilities. It can be useful to compare this with an in-target probe (ITP) sometimes used on enterprise servers.

An in-circuit emulator provides a window into the embedded system. The programmer uses the emulator to load programs into the embedded system, run them, step through them slowly, and view and change data used by the system's software.

An "emulator" gets its name because it emulates (imitates) the central processing unit of the embedded system's computer. Traditionally it had a plug that inserts into the socket where the CPU chip would normally be placed. Most modern systems use the target system's CPU directly, with special JTAG-based debug access. Emulating the processor, or direct JTAG access to it, lets the ICE do anything that the processor can do, but under the control of a software developer.

ICEs attach a terminal or PC to the embedded system. The terminal or PC provides an interactive user interface for the programmer to investigate and control the embedded system. For example, it is routine to have asource code level debugger with a graphical windowing interface that communicates through a JTAG adapter ("emulator") to an embedded target system which has no graphical user interface.

Notably, when their program fails, most embedded systems simply become inert lumps of nonfunctioning electronics. Embedded systems often lack basic functions to detect signs of software failure, such as an MMU to catch memory access errors. Without an ICE, the development of embedded systems can be extremely difficult, because there is usually no way to tell what went wrong. With an ICE, the programmer can usually test pieces of code, then isolate the fault to a particular section of code, and then inspect the failing code and rewrite it to solve the problem.

In usage, an ICE provides the programmer with execution breakpoints, memory display and monitoring, and input/output control. Beyond this, the ICE can be programmed to look for any range of matching criteria to pause at, in an attempt to identify the origin of the failure.

Most modern microcontrollers utilize resources provided on the manufactured version of the microcontroller for device programming, emulation and debugging features, instead of needing another special emulation-version (that is, bond-out) of the target microcontroller.[1] Even though it is a cost-effective method, since the ICE unit only manages the emulation instead of actually emulating the target microcontroller, trade-offs have to be made in order to keep the prices low at manufacture time, yet provide enough emulation features for the (relatively few) emulation applications.

### Advantages

Virtually all embedded systems have a hardware element and a software element, which are separate but tightly interdependent. The ICE allows the software element to be run and tested on the actual hardware on which it is to run, but still allows programmer conveniences to help isolate faulty code, such as "source-level debugging" (which shows the program the way the programmer wrote it) and single-stepping (which lets the programmer run the program step-by-step to find errors).

Most ICEs consist of an adaptor unit that sits between the ICE host computer and the system to be tested. A header and cable assembly connects the adaptor to a socket where the actual CPU or microcontroller mounts within the embedded system. Recent ICEs enable a programmer to access the on-chip debug circuit that is integrated into the CPU via JTAG or BDM (Background Debug Mode) in order to debug the software of an embedded system. These systems often use a standard version of the CPU chip, and can simply attach to a debug port on a production system. They are sometimes called in-circuit debuggers or ICDs, to distinguish the fact that they do not replicate the functionality of the CPU, but instead control an already existing, standard CPU. Since the CPU does not have to be replaced, they can operate on production units where the CPU is soldered in and cannot be replaced. On x86 Pentiums, a special 'probe mode' is used by ICEs to aid in debugging.[2]

In the context of embedded systems, the ICE is not emulating hardware. Rather, it is providing direct debug access to the actual CPU. The system under test is under full control, allowing the developer to load, debug and test code directly.

Most host systems are ordinary commercial computers unrelated to the CPU used for development - for example, a Linux PC might be used to develop software for a system using a Freescale 68HC11 chip, which itself could not run Linux. The programmer usually edits and compiles the embedded system's code on the host system, as well. The host system will have special compilers that produce executable code for the embedded system. These are called cross compilers/cross assemblers.

## 1.18.7 DSO

A **digital storage oscilloscope** is an oscilloscope which stores and analyses the signal digitally rather than using analogue techniques. It is now the most common type of oscilloscope in use because of the advanced trigger, storage, display and measurement features which it typically provides

The input analogue signal is sampled and then converted into a digital record of the amplitude of the signal at each sample time. The sampling frequency should be not less than the Nyquist rate to avoid aliasing. These digital values are then turned back into an analogue signal for display on a cathode ray tube (CRT), or transformed as needed for the various possible types of output—liquid crystal display, chart recorder, plotter or network interface.

The principal advantage over analog storage is that the stored traces are as bright, as sharply defined, and written as quickly as non-stored traces. Traces can be stored indefinitely or written out to some external data storage device and reloaded. This allows, for example, comparison of an acquired trace from a system under test with a standard trace acquired from a known-good system. Many models can display the waveform prior to the trigger signal. Digital oscilloscopes usually analyze waveforms and provide numerical values as well as visual displays. These values typically include averages, maxima and minima, root mean square (RMS) and frequencies. They may be used to capture transient signals when operated in a single sweep mode, without the brightness and writing speed limitations of an analog storage oscilloscope.

The displayed trace can be manipulated after acquisition; a portion of the display can be magnified to make fine detail more visible, or a long trace can be examined in a single display to identify areas of interest. Many instruments allow a stored trace to be annotated by the user. Many digital oscilloscopes use flat panel displays similar to those made in high volumes for computers and television displays.

An **oscilloscope**, previously called an oscillograph, and informally known as a **scope**, **CRO** (for cathode-ray oscilloscope), or **DSO** (for the more modern digital storage oscilloscope), is a type of electronic test instrument that allows observation of constantly varying signal voltages, usually as a two-dimensional plot of one or more signals as a function of time. Non-electrical signals (such as sound or vibration) can be converted to voltages and displayed. Oscilloscopes are used to observe the change of an electrical signal over time, such that voltage and time describe a shape which is continuously graphed against a calibrated scale. The observed waveform can be analyzed for such properties as amplitude, frequency, rise time, time interval, distortion and others. Modern digital instruments may calculate and display these properties directly. Originally, calculation of these values required manually measuring the waveform against the scales built into the screen of the instrument.

The oscilloscope can be adjusted so that repetitive signals can be observed as a continuous shape on the screen. A storage oscilloscope allows single events to be captured by the instrument and displayed for a relatively long time, allowing human observation of events too fast to be directly perceptible.

Oscilloscopes are used in the sciences, medicine, engineering, and telecommunications industry. General-purpose instruments are used for maintenance of electronic equipment and laboratory work. Special-purpose oscilloscopes may be used for such purposes as analyzing an automotive ignition system or to display the waveform of the heartbeat as an electrocardiogram. Before the advent of digital electronics, oscilloscopes used cathode ray tubes (CRTs) as their display element (hence were commonly referred to as CROs) and linear amplifiers for signal processing. Storage oscilloscopes used special storage CRTs to maintain a steady display of a single brief signal. CROs were later largely superseded by digital storage oscilloscopes (DSOs) with thin panel displays, fastanalog-to-digital converters and digital signal processors. DSOs without integrated displays (sometimes known as digitisers) are available at lower cost and use a general-purpose digital computer to process and display waveforms.

## 1.18.8 Logic Analyzer

It is an electronic instrument that captures and displays multiple signals from a digital system or digital circuit. A logic analyzer may convert the captured data into timing diagrams, protocol decodes, state machine traces, assembly language, or may correlate assembly with source-level software. Logic Analyzers have advanced triggering capabilities, and are useful when a user needs to see the timing relationships between many signals in a digital system. Presently, there are three distinct categories of logic analyzers available on the market:

**Modular** LAs, which consist of both a chassis or mainframe and logic analyzer modules. The mainframe/chassis contains the display, controls, control computer, and multiple slots into which the actual data-capturing hardware is installed. The modules each have a specific number of channels, and multiple modules may be combined to obtain a very high channel count. While modular logic analyzers are typically more expensive, the ability to combine multiple modules to obtain a high channel count and the generally higher performance of modular logic analyzers often justifies the price.

For the very high end modular logic analyzers, the user often must provide their own host PCor purchase an embedded controller compatible with the system.[3]

**Portable** LAs, sometimes referred to as standalone LAs. Portable logic analyzers integrate everything into a single package, with options installed at the factory. While portable logic analyzers generally have lower performance than their modular counterparts, they are often used for general purpose debugging by cost conscious users.

**PC-based** LAs. The hardware connects to a computer through a USB or Ethernet connection and relays the captured signals to the software on the computer. These devices are typically much smaller and less expensive because they make use of a PC's existing keyboard, display and CPU, as compared to portable logic analyzers which must provide their own versions of all of that hardware. A logic analyzer can be triggered on a complicated sequence of digital events, then capture a large amount of digital data from the system under test (SUT).

When logic analyzers first came into use, it was common to attach several hundred "clips" to a digital system. Later, specialized connectors came into use. The evolution of logic analyzer probes has led to a common footprint that multiple vendors support, which provides added freedom to end users. Introduced in April, 2002, connectorless technology (identified by several vendor-specific trade names: Compression Probing; Soft Touch; D-Max) has become popular. These probes provide a durable, reliable mechanical and electrical connection between the probe and the circuit board with less than 0.5 to 0.7 pF loading per signal.

Once the probes are connected, the user programs the analyzer with the names of each signal, and can group several signals together for easier manipulation. Next, a capture mode is chosen, either "timing" mode, where the input signals are sampled at regular intervals based on an internal or external clock source, or "state" mode, where one or more of the signals are defined as "clocks", and data are taken on the rising or falling edges of these clocks, optionally using other signals to qualify these clocks. After the mode is chosen, a *trigger condition* must be set.

A trigger condition can range from simple (such as triggering on a rising or falling edge of a single signal) to the very complex (such as configuring the analyzer to decode the higher levels of the TCP/IP stack and triggering on a certain HTTP packet). At this point, the user sets the analyzer to "run" mode, either triggering once, or repeatedly triggering. Once the data are captured, they can be displayed several ways, from the simple (showing waveforms or state listings) to the complex (showing decoded Ethernet protocol traffic).

Some analyzers can also operate in a "compare" mode, where they compare each captured data set to a previously recorded data set, and halt capture or visually notify the operator when this data set is either matched or not. This is useful for long-term empirical testing. Recent analyzers can even be set to email a copy of the test data to the engineer on a successful trigger. Many digital designs, including those of ICs, are simulated to detect defects before the unit is constructed. The simulation usually provides logic analysis displays. Often, complex discrete logic is verified by simulating inputs and testing outputs using boundary scan. Logic analyzers can uncover hardware defects that are not found in simulation. These problems are typically too difficult to model in simulation, or too time consuming to simulate and often cross multiple clock domains. Field-programmable gate arrays have become a common measurement point for logic analyzers.

## QUESTIONS

1. What is microcontroller? State features of microcontroller.
2. Compare microprocessor and microprocessor
3. Compare RISC and CISC
4. Compare Harward and Von Meumann architecture
5. Explain advantages and applications of 8-bit microcontroller
6. What is embedded systems? State characteristics
7. How microcontroller is used in embedded systems?
8. What are the limitations if microcontroller?
9. Draw, explain operation and application of RS232.
10. Draw, explain operation and application of RS485.
11. Write short notes on assembler, compiler, IDE, emulator, debugger, DSO and logic analyzer.
12. What are the selection criteria for microcontroller for a particular application.

# Unit - II
# 8051 ARCHITECTURE

## 2.1 BASIC 8051 ARCHITECTURE

8051 employs Harvard architecture. It has some peripherals such as 32 bit digital I/O, Timers and Serial I/O. The basic architecture of 8051 is given in Fig. 2.1

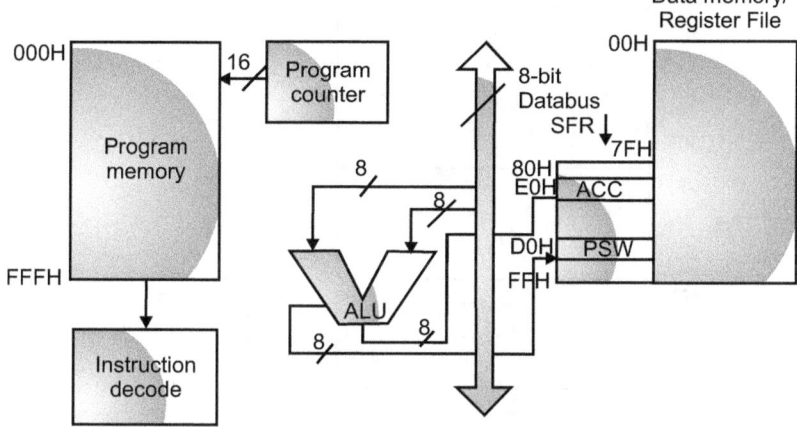

**Fig. 2.1 : Basic 8051 Architecture**

Various features of 8051 microcontroller are given as follows.
- 8-bit CPU
- 16-bit Program Counter
- 8-bit Processor Status Word (PSW)
- 8-bit Stack Pointer
- Internal RAM of 128bytes
- Special Function Registers (SFRs) of 128 bytes
- 32 I/O pins arranged as four 8-bit ports (P0 - P3)
- Two 16-bit timer/counters : T0 and T1
- Two external and three internal vectored interrupts
- One full duplex serial I/O

**8051 Clock and Instruction Cycle**

In 8051, one instruction cycle consists of twelve (12) clock cycles. Instruction cycle is sometimes called as Machine cycle by some authors.

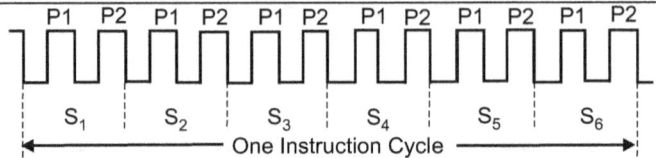

**Fig. 2.2 : Instruction cycle of 8051**

In 8051, each instruction cycle has six states ($S_1$ - $S_6$). Each state has two pulses (P1 and P2)

## 128 bytes of Internal RAM Structure (lower address space)

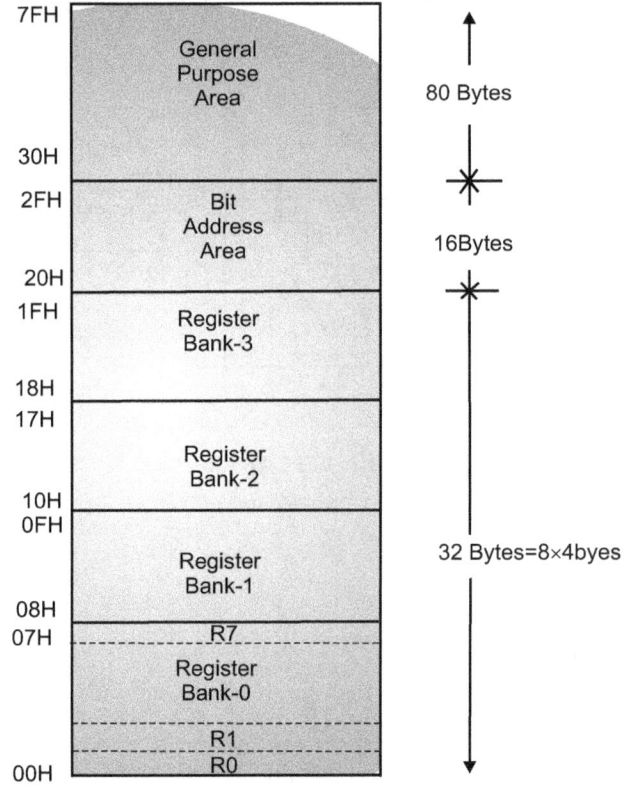

**Fig 2.3 : Internal RAM Structure**

The lower 32 bytes are divided into 4 separate banks. Each register bank has 8 registers of one byte each. A register bank is selected depending upon two bank select bits in the PSW register. Next 16bytes are bit addressable. In total, 128bits (16X8) are available in bitaddressable area. Each bit can be accessed and modified by suitable instructions. The bit addresses are from 00H (LSB of the first byte in 20H) to 7FH (MSB of the last byte in 2FH). Remaining 80bytes of RAM are available for general purpose.

## Internal Data Memory and Special Function Register (SFR) Map :

The special function registers (SFRs) are mapped in the upper 128 bytes of internal data memory address. Hence there is an address overlap between the upper 128 bytes of data RAM and SFRs. Please note that the upper 128 bytes of data RAM are present only in the 8052 family. The lower128 bytes of RAM (00H - 7FH) can be accessed both by direct or indirect addressing while the upper 128 bytes of RAM (80H - FFH) are accessed by indirect addressing. The SFRs (80H - FFH) are accessed by direct addressing only. This feature distinguishes the upper 128 bytes of memory from the SFRs, as shown in Fig. 2.4.

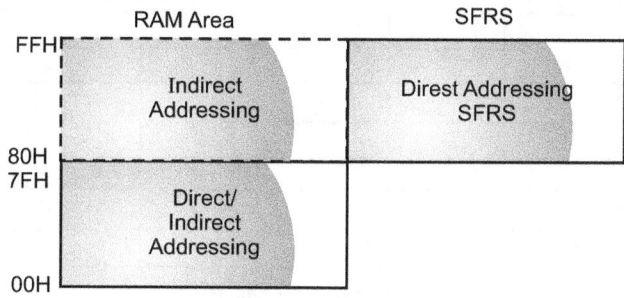

**Fig. 2.4 : Internal Data Memory Map**

### SFR Map

The set of Special Function Registers (SFRs) contains important registers such as Accumulator, Register B, I/O Port latch registers, Stack pointer, Data Pointer, Processor Status Word (PSW) and various control registers. Some of these registers are bit addressable (they are marked with a * in the diagram below). The detailed map of various registers is shown in the Fig. 2.6.

It should be noted hat all registers appearing in the first column are bit addressable. The bit address of a bit in the register is calculated as follows.

Bit address of 'b' bit of register 'R' is
        Address of register 'R' + b
        where $0 \leq b \leq 7$

### Processor Status Word (PSW)    Address=D0H

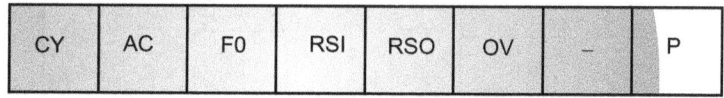

**Fig. 2.5 : Processor Status Word**

PSW register stores the important status conditions of the microcontroller. It also stores the bank select bits (RS1 & RS0) for register bank selection.

| | 0 | 1 | 2 | 3 | 4 | 5 | 6 | 7 |
|---|---|---|---|---|---|---|---|---|
| F8H | | | | | | | | |
| F0H | B* | | | | | | | |
| E8H | | | | | | | | |
| E0H | ACC* | | | | | | | |
| D8H | | | | | | | | |
| D0H | PSW* | | | | | | | |
| C8H | (T2CON)* | | (RCAP2L) | (RCAP2H) | (TL2) | (TH2) | | |
| C0H | | | | | | | | |
| B8H | IP* | | | | | | | |
| B0H | P3* | | | | | | | |
| A8H | IE* | | | | | | | |
| A0H | P2* | | | | | | | |
| 98H | SCON* | SBUF | | | | | | |
| 90H | P1* | | | | | | | |
| 88H | TCON* | TMOD | TI0 | TL1 | TH0 | TH1 | | |
| 80H | P0* | SP | DPL | DPH | | | | PCON |

**Fig. 2.6 : SFR Map**

### Interfacing External Memory

If external program/data memory are to be interfaced, they are interfaced in the following way.

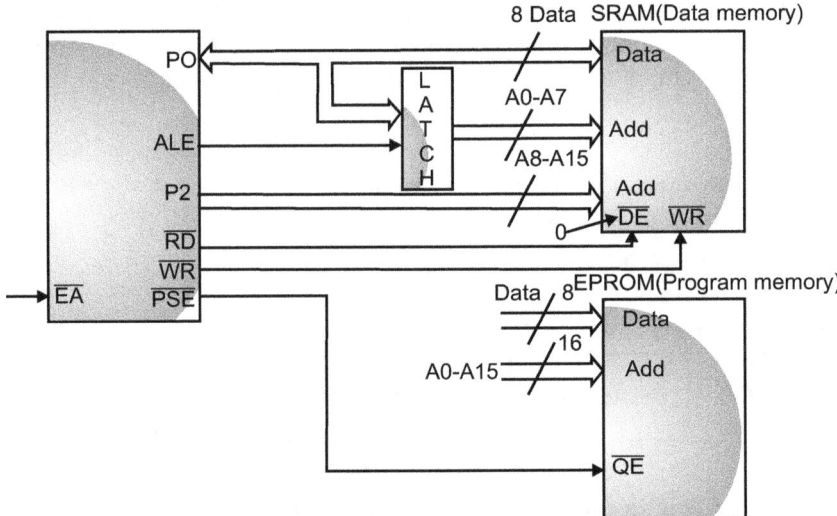

**Fig. 2.7 : Circuit Diagram for Interfacing of External Memory**

External program memory is fetched if either of the following two conditions are satisfied.

1. $\overline{EA}$ (Enable Address) is low. The microcontroller by default starts searching for program from external program memory.
2. PC is higher than FFFH for 8051 or 1FFFH for 8052.

$\overline{PSEN}$ tells the outside world whether the external memory fetched is program memory or data memory. $\overline{EA}$ is user configurable. $\overline{PSEN}$ is processor controlled.

## 2.2 8051 ADDRESSING MODES

8051 has four addressing modes.

### 1. Immediate Addressing :
Data is immediately available in the instruction.
For example -
ADD A, #77; Adds 77 (decimal) to A and stores in A
ADD A, #4DH; Adds 4D (hexadecimal) to A and stores in A
MOV DPTR, #1000H; Moves 1000 (hexadecimal) to data pointer

### 2. Bank Addressing or Register Addressing :
This way of addressing accesses the bytes in the current register bank. Data is available in the register specified in the instruction. The register bank is decided by 2 bits of Processor Status Word (PSW).
For example-
ADD A, R0; Adds content of R0 to A and stores in A

### 3. Direct Addressing :
The address of the data is available in the instruction.
For example -
MOV A, 088H; Moves content of SFR TCON (address 088H)to A

### 4. Register Indirect Addressing :
The address of data is available in the R0 or R1 registers as specified in the instruction.
For example -
MOV A, @R0 moves content of address pointed by R0 to A

### 5. External Data Addressing :
Pointer used for external data addressing can be either R0/R1 (256 byte access) or DPTR (64kbyte access).
For example -
MOVX A, @R0; Moves content of 8-bit address pointed by R0 to A
MOVX A, @DPTR; Moves content of 16-bit address pointed by DPTR to A

### 6. External Code Addressing :

Sometimes we may want to store non-volatile data into the ROM e.g. look-up tables. Such data may require reading the code memory. This may be done as follows -

MOVC A, @A+DPTR; Moves content of address pointed by A+DPTR to A

MOVC A, @A+PC; Moves content of address pointed by A+PC to A.

## 2.3 I/O PORT CONFIGURATION

Each port of 8051 has bidirectional capability. Port 0 is called 'true bidirectional port' as it floats (tristated) when configured as input. Port-1, 2, 3 are called 'quasi bidirectional port'.

### 2.3.1 Port-0 Pin Structure

Port -0 has 8 pins (P0.0-P0.7). The structure of a Port-0 pin is shown in Fig. 2.8.

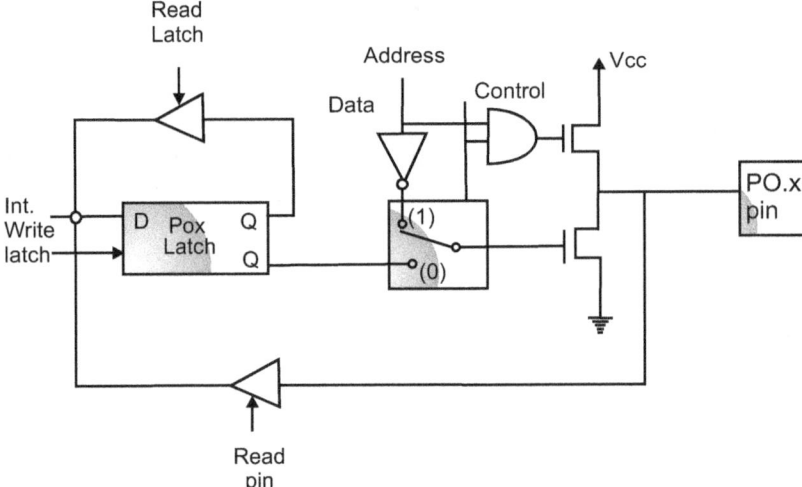

**Fig. 2.8 : Port-0 Structure**

Port-0 can be configured as a normal bidirectional I/O port or it can be used for address/data interfacing for accessing external memory. When control is '1', the port is used for address/data interfacing. When the control is '0', the port can be used as a normal bidirectional I/O port. Let us assume that control is '0'. When the port is used as an input port, '1' is written to the latch. In this situation both the output MOSFETs are 'off'. Hence the output pin floats. This high impedance pin can be pulled up or low by an external source. When the port is used as an output port, a '1' written to the latch again turns 'off' both the output MOSFETs and causes the output pin to float. An external pull-up is required to output a '1'. But when '0' is written to the latch, the pin is pulled down by the lower MOSFET. Hence the output becomes zero.

When the control is '1', address/data bus controls the output driver MOSFETs. If the address/data bus (internal) is '0', the upper MOSFET is 'off' and the lower MOSFET is 'on'. The output becomes '0'. If the address/data bus is '1', the upper transistor is 'on' and the lower transistor is 'off'. Hence the output is '1'. Hence for normal address/data interfacing (for external memory access) no pull-up resistors are required.

Port-0 latch is written to with 1's when used for external memory access.

## 2.3.2 Port-1 Pin Structure

Port-1 has 8 pins (P1.1-P1.7). The structure of a port-1 pin is shown in Fig. 2.9.

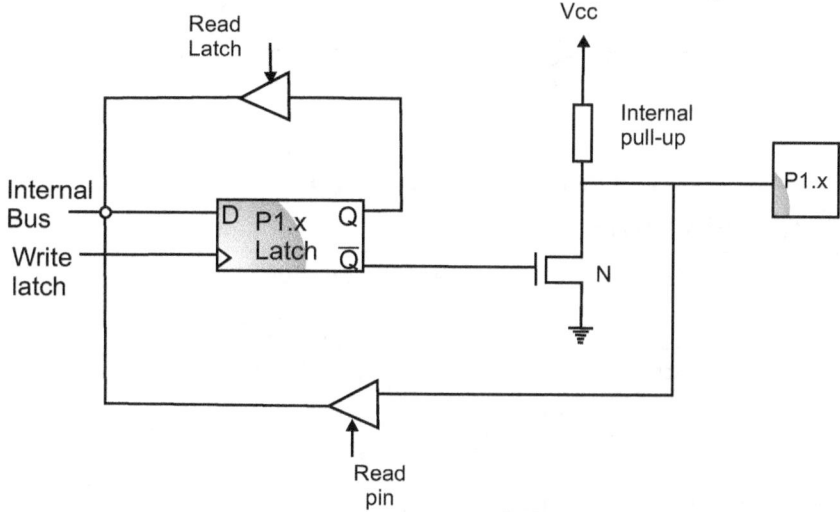

**Fig. 2.9 : Port 1 Structure**

Port-1 does not have any alternate function i.e. it is dedicated solely for I/O interfacing. When used as output port, the pin is pulled up or down through internal pull-up. To use port-1 as input port, '1' has to be written to the latch. In this input mode when '1' is written to the pin by the external device then it read fine. But when '0' is written to the pin by the external device then the external source must sink current due to internal pull-up. If the external device is not able to sink the current the pin voltage may rise, leading to a possible wrong reading.

## 2.3.3 PORT 2 Pin Structure

Port-2 has 8-pins (P2.0-P2.7). The structure of a port-2 pin is shown in Fig. 2.10.

Port-2 is used for higher external address byte or a normal input/output port. The I/O operation is similar to Port-1. Port-2 latch remains stable when Port-2 pin are used for external memory access. Here again due to internal pull-up there is limited current driving capability.

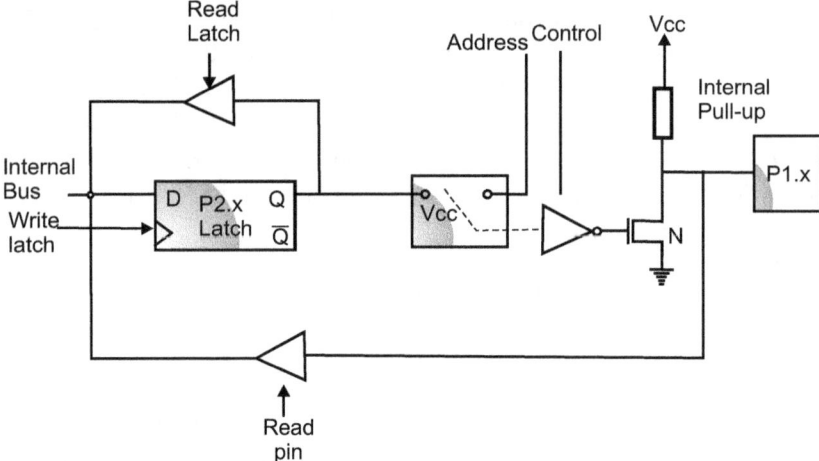

**Fig. 2.10 : Port 2 Structure**

## 2.3.4 PORT 3 Pin Structure

Port-3 has 8 pin (P3.0-P3.7) . Port-3 pins have alternate functions. The structure of a port-3 pin is shown in Fig. 2.11.

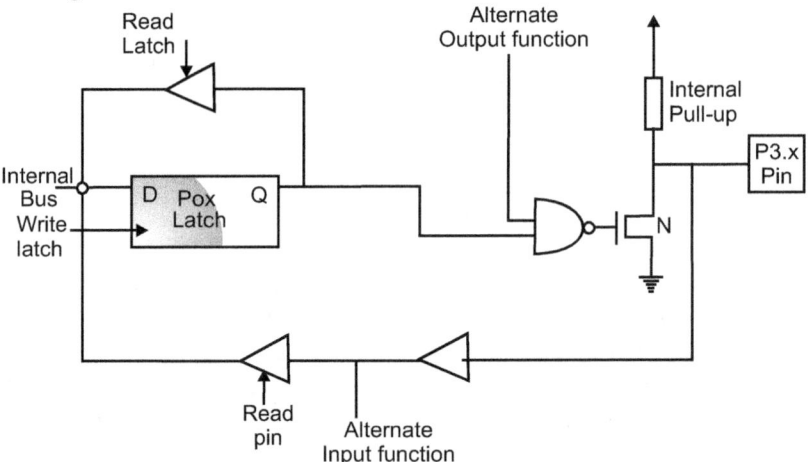

**Fig. 2.11 : Port 3 Structure**

Each pin of Port-3 can be individually programmed for I/O operation or for alternate function. The alternate function can be activated only if the corresponding latch has been written to '1'. To use the port as input port, '1' should be written to the latch. This port also has internal pull-up and limited current driving capability.

Alternate functions of Port-3 pins are :

| P3.3 | $\overline{INT1}$ |
|---|---|
| P3.4 | T0 |
| P3.5 | T1 |
| P3.6 | $\overline{WR}$ |

Note:
1. Port 1, 2, 3 each can drive 4 LS TTL inputs.
2. Port-0 can drive 8 LS TTL inputs in address /data mode. For digital output port, it needs external pull-up resistors.
3. Ports-1,2and 3 pins can also be driven by open-collector or open-drain outputs.
4. Each Port 3 bit can be configured either as a normal I/O or as a special function bit.

**Reading a Port (port-pins) versus Reading a Latch**

There is a subtle difference between reading a latch and reading the output port pin.

The status of the output port pin is sometimes dependant on the connected load. For instance if a port is configured as an output port and a '1' is written to the latch, the output pin should also show '1'. If the output is used to drive the base of a transistor, the transistor turns 'on'.

If the port pin is read, the value will be '0' which is corresponding to the base-emitter voltage of the transistor.

**Reading a Latch :** Usually the instructions that read the latch, read a value, possibly change it, and then rewrite it to the latch. These are called "read-modify-write" instructions. Examples of a few instructions are-

ORL P2, A; P2 <-- P2 or A

MOV P2.1, C; Move carry bit to PX.Y bit.

In this the latch value of P2 is read, is modified such that P2.1 is the same as Carry and is then written back to P2 latch.

**Reading a Pin :** Examples of a few instructions that read port pin, are-

MOV A, P0 ; Move port-0 pin values to A

MOV A, P1; Move port-1 pin values to A

## 2.4 ACCESSING EXTERNAL MEMORY

Access to external program memory uses the signal $\overline{PSEN}$ (Program store enable) as the read strobe. Access to external data memory uses $\overline{RD}$ $\overline{WR}$ (alternate function of P3.7 and P3.6).

For external program memory, always 16 bit address is used. For example -

MOVC A, @ A+DPTR

MOVC A, @ A+PC

Access to external data memory can be either 8-bit address or 16-bit address -

**8-bit address :** MOVX A, @Rp where Rp is either R0 or R1

MOVX @Rp, A

**16 bit address :** MOVX A,@DPTR

MOV X @DPTR, A

The external memory access in 8051 can be shown by a schematic diagram as given in Fig. 2.12.

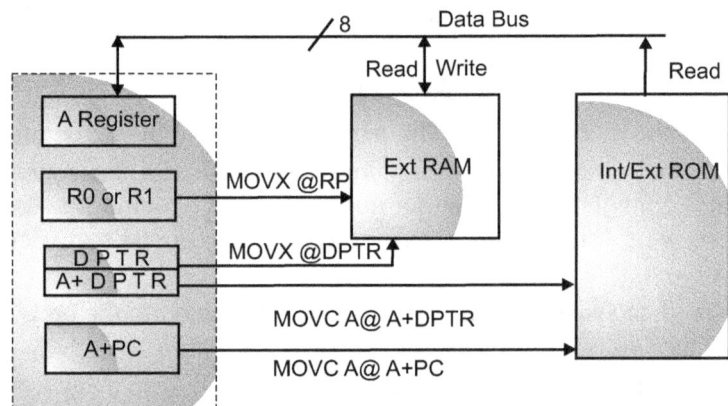

**Fig. 2.12 : Schematic diagram of external memory access**

If an 8-bit external address is used for data memory (i.e. MOVX @Rp) then the content of Port-2 SFR remains at Port-2 pins throughout the external memory cycle. This facilitates memory paging as the upper 8 bit address remains fixed.

During any access to external memory, the CPU writes FFH to Port-0 latch (SFR). If the user writes to Port-0 during an external memory fetch, the incoming byte is corrupted.

External program memory is accessed under the following condition.

1. Whenever $\overline{EA}$ is low, or

2. Whenever $\overline{PC}$ contains a number higher than 0FFFH (for 8051) or 1FFF (for 8052).

Some typical use of code/program memory access:

External program memory can be not only used to store the code, but also for lookup table of various functions required for a particular application. Mathematical functions such as Sine, Square root, Exponential, etc. can be stored in the program memory (Internal or eternal) and these functions can be accessed using MOVC instruction.

Program Memory

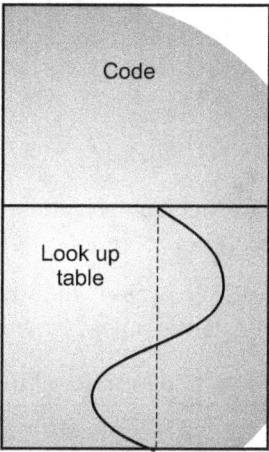

Fig. 2.13 : Program memory showing the storage of lookup table

## 2.5 TIMERS/COUNTERS

8051 has two 16-bit programmable UP timers/counters. They can be configured to operate either as timers or as event counters. The names of the two counters are T0 and T1 respectively. The timer content is available in four 8-bit special function registers, viz, TL0,TH0,TL1 and TH1 respectively.

In the "timer" function mode, the counter is incremented in every machine cycle. Thus, one can think of it as counting machine cycles. Hence the clock rate is $1/12^{th}$ of the oscillator frequency.

In the "counter" function mode, the register is incremented in response to a 1 to 0 transition at its corresponding external input pin (T0 or T1). It requires 2 machine cycles to detect a high to low transition. Hence maximum count rate is $1/24^{th}$ of oscillator frequency.

The operation of the timers/counters is controlled by two special function registers, TMOD and TCON respectively.

**Timer Mode control (TMOD) Special Function Register:**

TMOD register is not bit addressable.
TMOD
Address: 89 H
Various bits of TMOD are described as follows :

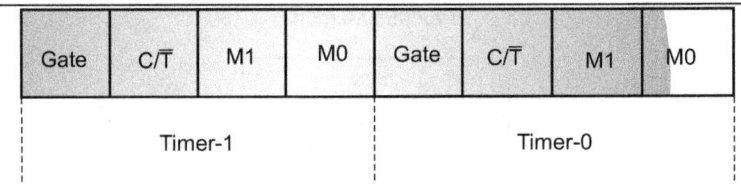

Fig. 2.14

**Gate:** This is an OR Gate enabled bit which controls the effect of $\overline{INT1/0}$ on START/STOP of Timer. It is set to one ('1') by the program to enable the interrupt to start/stop the timer. If TR1/0 in TCON is set and signal on $\overline{INT1/0}$ pin is high then the timer starts counting using either internal clock (timer mode) or external pulses (counter mode).

$C\overline{T}$ It is used for the selection of Counter/Timer mode. Mode Select Bits:

| M1 | M0 | Mode |
|---|---|---|
| 0 | 0 | Mode 0 |
| 0 | 1 | Mode 1 |
| 1 | 0 | Mode 2 |
| 1 | 1 | Mode 3 |

M1 and M0 are mode select bits.

**Timer/ Counter control logic:**

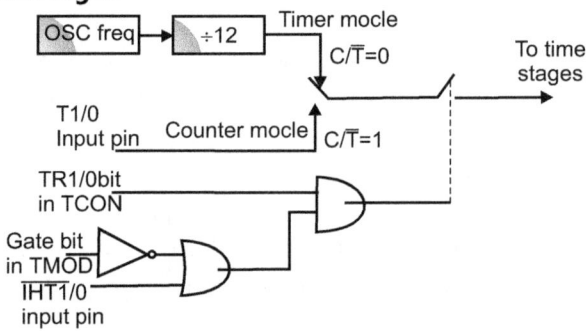

Fig. 2.15 : Timer/Counter Control Logic

**Timer control (TCON) Special function register:**

TCON is bit addressable. The address of TCON is 88H. It is partly related to Timer and partly to interrupt.

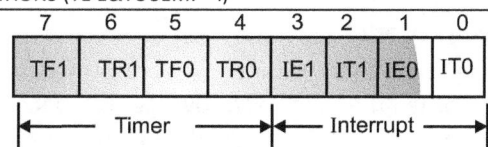

**Fig. 2.16 : TCON Register**

The various bits of TCON are as follows.

**TF1 :** Timer1 overflow flag. It is set when timer rolls from all 1s to 0s. It is cleared when processor vectors to execute ISR located at address 001BH.

**TR1 :** Timer1 run control bit. Set to 1 to start the timer / counter.

**TF0 :** Timer0 overflow flag. (Similar to TF1)

**TR0 :** Timer0 run control bit.

**IE1 :** Interrupt1 edge flag. Set by hardware when an external interrupt edge is detected. It is cleared when interrupt is processed.

**IE0 :** Interrupt0 edge flag. (Similar to IE1)

**IT1 :** Interrupt1 type control bit. Set/ cleared by software to specify falling edge / low level triggered external interrupt.

**IT0 :** Interrupt0 type control bit. (Similar to IT1)

As mentioned earlier, Timers can operate in four different modes. They are as follows

**Timer Mode-0:**

In this mode, the timer is used as a 13-bit UP counter as follows.

**Fig. 2.17 : Operation of Timer on Mode 0**

The lower 5 bits of TLX and 8 bits of THX are used for the 13 bit count. Upper 3 bits of TLX are ignored. When the counter rolls over from all 0's to all 1's, TFX flag is set and an interrupt is generated.

The input pulse is obtained from the previous stage. If TR1/0 bit is 1 and Gate bit is 0, the counter continues counting up. If TR1/0 bit is 1 and Gate bit is 1, then the operation of the counter is controlled by $\overline{INTX}$ input. This mode is useful to measure the width of a given pulse fed to $\overline{INTX}$ input.

**Timer Mode-1:**

**Fig. 2.18 : Operation of Timer on Mode-1**

This mode is similar to mode-0 except for the fact that the Timer operates in 16-bit mode.

## Timer Mode-2: (Auto-Reload Mode)

This is a 8 bit counter/timer operation. Counting is performed in TLX while THX stores a constant value. In this mode when the timer overflows i.e. TLX becomes FFH, it is fed with the value stored in THX. For example if we load THX with 50H then the timer in mode 2 will count from 50H to FFH. After that 50H is again reloaded. This mode is useful in applications like fixed time sampling.

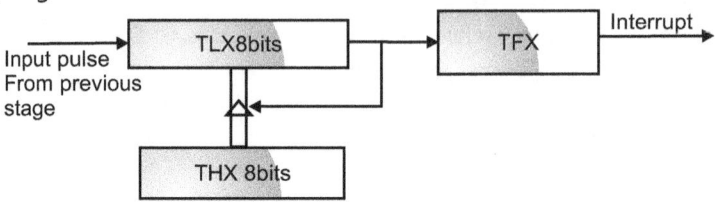

**Fig. 2.19 : Operation of Timer in Mode 2**

## Timer Mode-3:

Timer 1 in mode-3 simply holds its count. The effect is same as setting TR1=0. Timer0 in mode-3 establishes TL0 and TH0 as two separate counters.

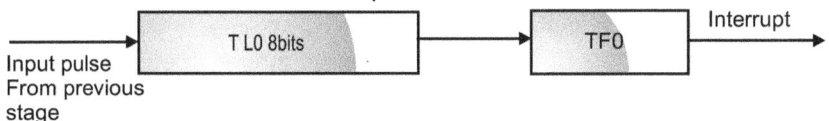

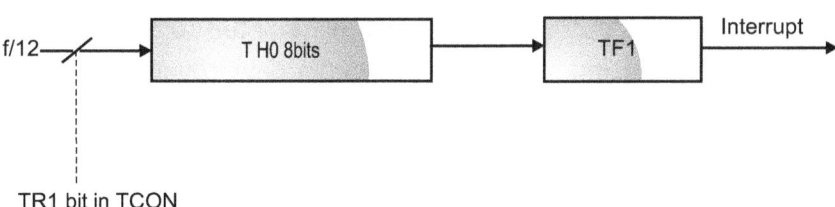

**Fig. 2.20 : Operation of Timer in Mode 3**

Control bits TR1 and TF1 are used by Timer-0 (higher 8 bits) (TH0) in Mode-3 while TR0 and TF0 are available to Timer-0 lower 8 bits(TL0).

# 2.6 INTERRUPTS

**Interrupts**

8051 provides 5 vectored interrupts. They are -

1. $\overline{INT0}$

2. TF0
3. $\overline{INT1}$
4. TF1
5. RI/TI

Out of these, $\overline{INT0}$ and $\overline{INT1}$ are external interrupts whereas Timer and Serial port interrupts are generated internally. The external interrupts could be negative edge triggered or low level triggered. All these interrupt, when activated, set the corresponding interrupt flags. Except for serial interrupt, the interrupt flags are cleared when the processor branches to the Interrupt Service Routine (ISR). The external interrupt flags are cleared on branching to Interrupt Service Routine (ISR), provided the interrupt is negative edge triggered. For low level triggered external interrupt as well as for serial interrupt, the corresponding flags have to be cleared by software by the programmer.

The schematic representation of the interrupts is as follows :

**Interrupt Location**

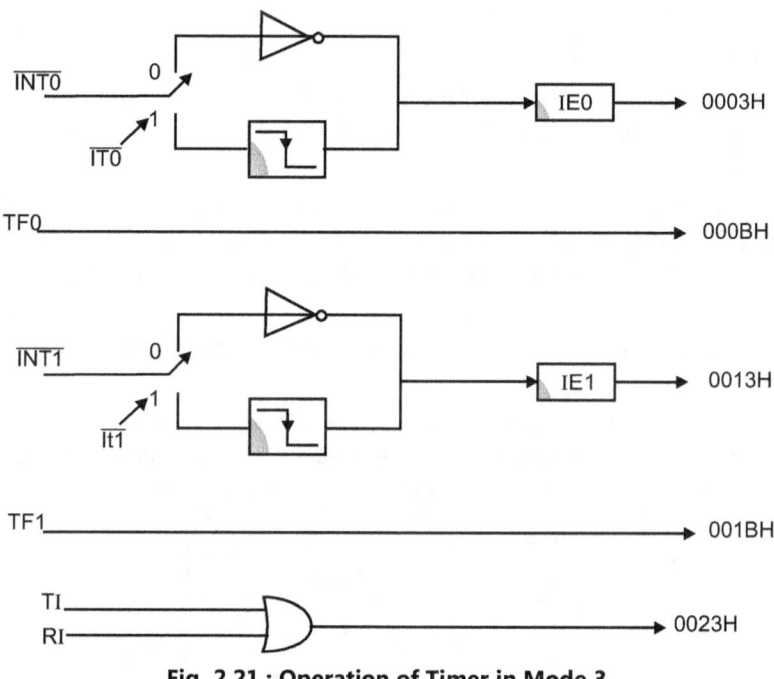

Fig. 2.21 : Operation of Timer in Mode 3

Each of these interrupts can be individually enabled or disabled by 'setting' or 'clearing' the corresponding bit in the IE (Interrupt Enable Register) SFR. IE contains a global enable bit EA which enables/disables all interrupts at once.

**Interrupt Enable Register (IE):** Address: A8H

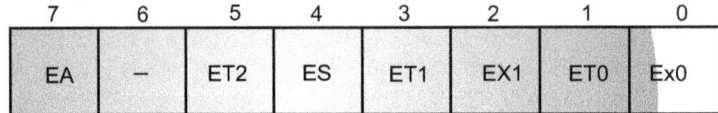

**Fig. 2.22 : 8051 Interrupt Details**

EX0 ⟶ $\overline{INT0}$ interrupt (External) enable bit

ET0 ⟶ Timer-0 interrupt enable bit

EX1 ⟶ $\overline{INT1}$ interrupt (External) enable bit

ET1 ⟶ Timer-1 interrupt enable bit

ES ⟶ Serial port interrupt enable bit

ET2 ⟶ Timer-2 interrupt enable bit

EA ⟶ Enable/Disable all

Setting ⟶ '1' Enable the corresponding interrupt

Setting ⟶ '0' Disable the corresponding interrupt

**Priority level structure:**

Each interrupt source can be programmed to have one of the two priority levels by setting (high priority) or clearing (low priority) a bit in the IP (Interrupt Priority) Register. A low priority interrupt can itself be interrupted by a high priority interrupt, but not by another low priority interrupt.

If two interrupts of different priority levels are received simultaneously, the request of higher priority level is served.

If the requests of the same priority level are received simultaneously, an internal polling sequence determines which request is to be serviced. Thus, within each priority level, there is a second priority level determined by the polling sequence, as follows :

| Source | Priority Level |
|---|---|
| IE0 | Highest |
| TF0 | |
| IE1 | ↓ |
| TF1 | |
| RI + TI | Lowest |

**Interrupt Priority register (IP)**

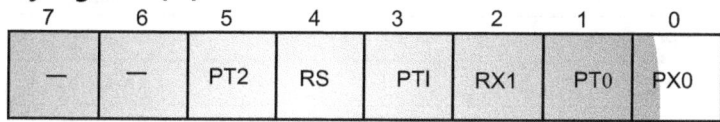

Fig. 2.23

'0' ⟶ low priority
'1' ⟶ high priority

## 2.7 INTERRUPT HANDLING

The interrupt flags are sampled at P2 of S5 of every instruction cycle (Note that every instruction cycle has six states each consisting of P1 and P2 pulses). The samples are polled during the next machine cycle (or instruction cycle).

If one of the flags was set at S5P2 of the preceding instruction cycle, the polling detects it and the interrupt process generates a long call (LCALL) to the appropriate vector location of the interrupt. The LCALL is generated provided this hardware generated LCALL is not blocked by any one of the following conditions.

1. An interrupt of equal or higher priority level is already in progress.
2. The current polling cycle is not the final cycle in the execution of the instruction in progress.
3. The instruction in progress is RETI or any write to IE or IP registers.

When an interrupt comes and the program is directed to the interrupt vector address, the Program Counter (PC) value of the interrupted program is stored (pushed) on the stack. The required Interrupt Service Routine (ISR) is executed. At the end of the ISR, the instruction RETI returns the value of the PC from the stack and the originally interrupted program is resumed.

**Reset** is a non-maskable interrupt. A reset is accomplished by holding the RST pin high for at least two machine cycles. On resetting the program starts from 0000H and some flags are modified as follows :

| Register | Value (Hex) on Reset |
|---|---|
| PC | 0000H |
| DPTR | 0000H |
| A | 00H |
| B | 00H |
| SP | 07H |
| PSW | 00H |

*(Contd.)*

| Ports P0-3 Latches | FFH |
|---|---|
| IP | XXX 00000 b |
| IE | 0 XX 00000 b |
| TCON | 00H |
| TMOD | 00H |
| TH0 | 00H |
| TL0 | 00H |
| TH1 | 00H |
| TL1 | 00H |
| SCON | 00 H |
| SBUF | 00 H |
| PCON | 0 XXXX XXX b |

The schematic diagram of the detection and processing of interrupts is given as follows.

**Instruction Cycles :**

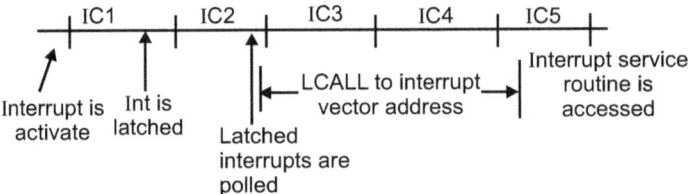

**Fig. 2.24 : Interrupt Handling in 8051**

It should be noted that the interrupt which is blocked due to the three conditions mentioned before is not remembered unless the flag that generated interrupt is not still active when the above blocking conditions are removed, i.e. ,every polling cycle is new.

**Jump and Call Instructions**

There are 3 types of jump instructions. They are:-

1. Relative Jump
2. Short Absolute Jump
3. Long Absolute Jump

**(1) Relative Jump**

Jump that replaces the PC (program counter) content with a new address that is greater than (the address following the jump instruction by 127 or less) or less than (the address following the jump by 128 or less) is called a relative jump. Schematically, the relative jump can be shown as follows: -

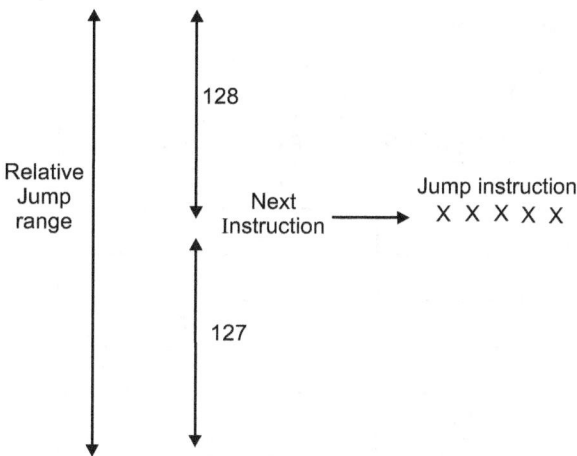

**Fig. 2.25 : Relative Jump**

**The advantages of the relative jump are as follows :**

- Only 1 byte of jump address needs to be specified in the 2's complement form, ie. For jumping ahead, the range is 0 to 127 and for jumping back, the range is −1 to −128.
- Specifying only one byte reduces the size of the instruction and speeds up program execution.
- The program with relative jumps can be relocated without reassembling to generate absolute jump addresses.

**Disadvantages of the Absolute Jump :**

- Short jump range (-128 to 127 from the instruction following the jump instruction)

**Instructions that use Relative Jump :**

SJMP <relative address>
(The remaining relative jumps are conditional jumps)
JC <relative address>
JNC <relative address>
JB bit, <relative address>
JNB bit, <relative address>
JBC bit, <relative address>
CJNE <destination byte>, <source byte>, <relative address>
DJNZ <byte>, <relative address>
JZ <relative address>
JNZ <relative address>

## (2) Short Absolute Jump

In this case only 11bits of the absolute jump address are needed. The absolute jump address is calculated in the following manner.

In 8051, 64 kbyte of program memory space is divided into 32 pages of 2 kbyte each. The hexadecimal addresses of the pages are given as follows: :

| Page (Hex) | Address (Hex) |
|---|---|
| 00 | 0000 - 07FF |
| 01 | 0800 - 0FFF |
| 02 | 1000 - 17FF |
| 03 | 1800 - 1FFF |
| . | . |
| 1E | F000 - F7FF |
| 1F | F800 - FFFF |

It can be seen that the upper 5bits of the program counter(PC) hold the page number and the lower 11bits of the PC hold the address within that page. Thus, an absolute address is formed by taking page numbers of the instruction (from the program counter) following the jump and attaching the specified 11bits to it to form the 16-bit address.

**Advantage :**

The instruction length becomes 2 bytes.

However, difficulty is encountered when the next instruction following the jump instruction begins from a fresh page (at X000H or at X800H). This does not give any problem for the forward jump, but results in an error for the backward jump. In such a case the assembler prompts the user to relocate the program suitably.

Example of short absolute jump : ACALL <address 11> AJMP   <address 11>

## (3) Long Absolute Jump/Call

Applications that need to access the entire program memory from 0000H to FFFFH use long absolute jump. Since the absolute address has to be specified in the op-code, the instruction length is 3 bytes (except for JMP @ A+DPTR). This jump is not re-locatable.

Example: -

LCALL <address 16>
LJMP   <address 16>
JMP @A+DPTR

## 2.8 SERIAL INTERFACE

The serial port of 8051 is full duplex, i.e., it can transmit and receive simultaneously.

The register SBUF is used to hold the data. The special function register SBUF is physically two registers. One is, write-only and is used to hold data to be transmitted out of the 8051 via TXD. The other is, read-only and holds the received data from external sources via RXD. Both mutually exclusive registers have the same address 099H.

**Serial Port Control Register (SCON)**

Register     SCON   controls serial data communication.

Address: 098H (Bit addressable)

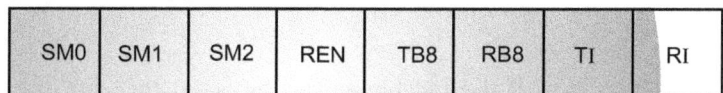

Fig. 2.26

Mode select bits

| SM0 | SM1 | Mode |
|---|---|---|
| 0 | 0 | Mode 0 |
| 0 | 1 | Mode 1 |
| 1 | 0 | Mode 2 |
| 1 | 1 | Mode 3 |

**SM2** : Multi processor communication bit.
**REN** : Receive Enable Bit.
**TB8** : Transmitted bit 8 (Normally we have 0 – 7)
**RB8** : Received Bit 8
**TI** : Transmit interrupt flag
**RI** : Receive Interrupt flag

**Power Mode control Register**

Register PCON controls processor powerdown, sleep modes and serial data bandrate. Only one bit of PCON is used with respect to serial communication. The seventh bit (b7)(SMOD) is used to generate the baud rate of serial communication.

Address: 87H

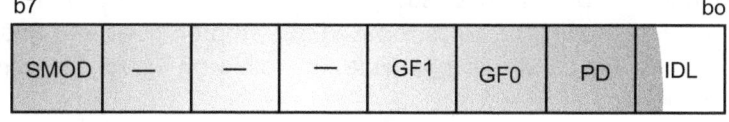

Fig. 2.27

| | | |
|---|---|---|
| **SM0D** | : | Serial band rate modify bit. |
| **GF1** | : | General purpose user flag bit 1 |
| **GF0** | : | General purpose user flag bit 0 |
| **PD** | : | Power down bit |
| **ID2** | : | Idle mode bit |

**Data Transmission**

Transmission of serial data begins at any time when data is written to SBUF. Pin P3.1 (Alternate function bit TXD) is used to transmit data to the serial data network. TI is set to 1 when data has been transmitted. This signifies that SBUF is empty so that another byte can be sent.

**Data Reception**

Reception of serial data begins if the receive enable bit is set to 1 for all modes. Pin P3.0 (Alternate function bit RXD) is used to receive data from the serial data network. Receive interrupt flag, RI, is set after the data has been received in all modes. The data gets stored in SBUF register from where it can be read.

## 2.8.1 Serial Data Transmission Modes

**Mode-0 :** In this mode, the serial port works like a shift register and the data transmission works synchronously with a clock frequency of $f_{osc}/12$. Serial data is received and transmitted through RXD. 8 bits are transmitted/ received aty a time. Pin TXD outputs the shift clock pulses of frequency $f_{osc}/12$, which is connected to the external circuitry for synchronization. The shift frequency or baud rate is always 1/12 of the oscillator frequency.

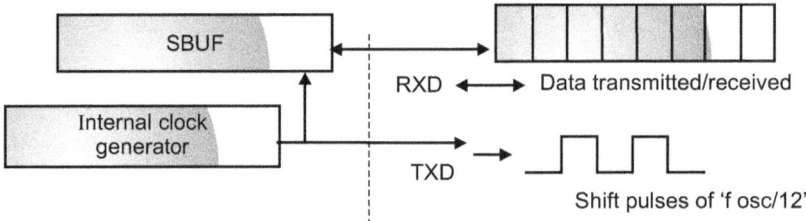

**Fig. 2.28 : Data transmission/reception in Mode-0**

**Mode-1 (standard UART mode) :**

In mode-1, the serial port functions as a standard Universal Asynchronous Receiver Transmitter (UART) mode. 10 bits are transmitted through TXD or received through RXD. The 10 bits consist of one start bit (which is usually '0'), 8 data bits (LSB is sent first/received first), and a stop bit (which is usually '1'). Once received, the stop bit goes into RB8 in the special function register SCON. The baud rate is variable. The following figure shows the way the bits are transmitted/ received.

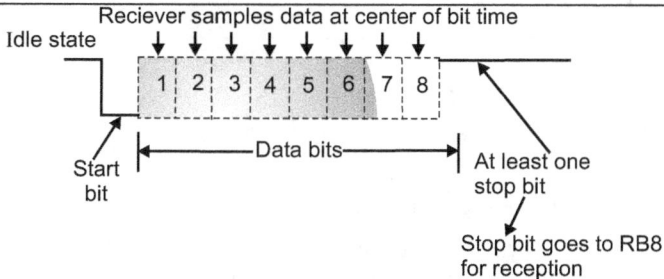

**Fig. 2.29 : Data transmission format in UART mode**

Bit time= $1/f_{baud}$

In receiving mode, data bits are shifted into the receiver at the programmed baud rate. The data word (8-bits) will be loaded to SBUF if the following conditions are true.

1. RI must be zero. (i.e., the previously received byte has been cleared from SBUF)
2. Mode bit SM2 = 0 or stop bit = 1.

After the data is received and the data byte has been loaded into SBUF, RI becomes one.

**Mode-1 Baud Rate Generation :**

Timer-1 is used to generate baud rate for mode-1 serial communication by using overflow flag of the timer to determine the baud frequency. Timer-1 is used in timer mode-2 as an auto-reload 8-bit timer. The data rate is generated by timer-1 using the following formula.

$$f_{band} = \frac{2^{SMOD}}{32} \times \frac{f_{osc}}{12 \times [256 - (TH1)]}$$

Where,

SMOD is the 7$^{th}$ bit of PCON register $f_{osc}$ is the crystal oscillator frequency of the microcontroller

It can be noted that $f_{osc}/ (12 \times [256- (TH1)])$ is the timer overflow frequency in timer mode-2, which is the auto-reload mode.

If timer-1 is not run in mode-2, then the baud rate is,

$$f_{band} = \frac{2^{SMOD}}{32} \times (timer - 1 \text{ overflow frequency})$$

Timer-1 can be run using the internal clock, fosc/12 (timer mode) or from any external source via pin T1 (P3.5) (Counter mode).

**Example 2 :** If standard baud rate is desired, then 11.0592 MHz crystal could be selected. To get a standard 9600 baud rate, the setting of TH1 is calculated as follows.

Assuming SMOD to be '0'

$$9600 = \frac{2^0}{32} \times \frac{11.0592 \times 10^6}{12 \times (256 - TH1)}$$

Or, $\quad 256 - TH1 = \dfrac{1}{32} \times \dfrac{11.0592 \times 10^6}{12 \times 9600} = 3$

Or, $\quad TH1 = 256 - 3 = 253 - FDH$

In mode-1, if SM2 is set to 1, no receive interrupt (RI) is generated unless a valid stop bit is received.

**Serial Data Mode-2 - Multiprocessor Mode :**

In this mode 11 bits are transmitted through TXD or received through RXD. The various bits are as follows: a start bit (usually '0'), 8 data bits (LSB first), a programmable 9 th (TB8 or RB8)bit and a stop bit (usually '1').

While transmitting, the 9 th data bit (TB8 in SCON) can be assigned the value '0' or '1'. For example, if the information of parity is to be transmitted, the parity bit (P) in PSW could be moved into TB8. On reception of the data, the 9 th bit goes into RB8 in 'SCON', while the stop bit is ignored. The baud rate is programmable to either 1/32 or 1/64 of the oscillator frequency.

f baud = (2 SMOD /64) fosc.

**Mode-3 - Multi processor mode with variable baud rate :**

In this mode 11 bits are transmitted through TXD or received through RXD. The various bits are: a start bit (usually '0'), 8 data bits (LSB first), a programmable 9 th bit and a stop bit (usually '1').

Mode-3 is same as mode-2, except the fact that the baud rate in mode-3 is variable (i.e., just as in mode-1).

f baud = (2 SMOD /32) * ( fosc / 12 (256-TH1)) .

This baudrate holds when Timer-1 is programmed in Mode-2.

Operation in Multiprocessor mode :

8051 operates in multiprocessor mode for serial communication Mode-2 and Mode-3. In multiprocessor mode, a Master processor can communicate with more than one slave processors. The connection diagram of processors communicating in Multiprocessor mode is given in Fig. 2.30.

The Master communicates with one slave at a time. 11 bits are transmitted by the Master, viz, One start bit (usually '0'), 8 data bits (LSB first), TB8 and a stop bit (usually '1'). TB8 is '1' for an address byte and '0' for a data byte.

If the Master wants to communicate with certain slave, it first sends the address of the slave with TB8=1. This address is received by all the slaves. Slaves initially have their SM2 bit set to '1'. All slaves check this address and the slave who is being addressed, responds by clearing its SM2 bit to '0' so that the data bytes can be received.

It should be noted that in Mode 2&3, receive interrupt flag RI is set if REN=1, RI=0 and the following condition is true.

1. SM2=1 and RB8=1 and a valid stop bit is received. Or
2. SM2=0 and a valid stop bit is received.

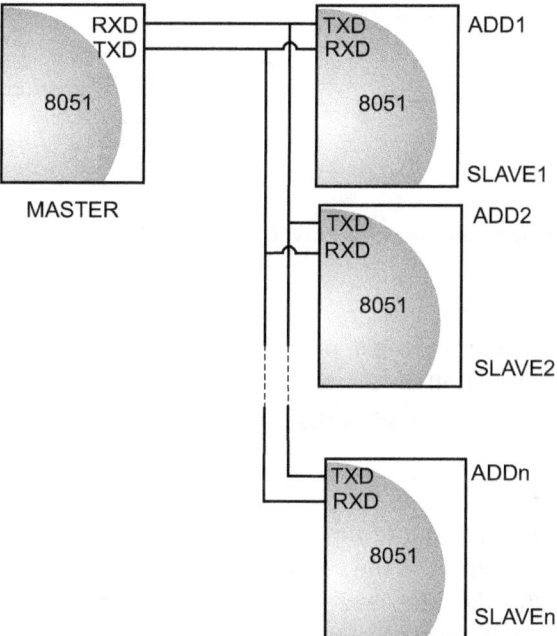

**Fig. 2.30 : 8051 in Multiprocessor Communication**

After the communication between the Master and a slave has been established, the data bytes are sent by the Master with TB8=0. Hence other slaves do not respond /get interrupted by this data as their SM2 is pulled high (1).

Power saving modes of operation :

8051 has two power saving modes. They are :
1. Idle Mode
2. Power Down mode.

The two power saving modes are entered by setting two bits IDL and PD in the special function register (PCON) respectively.

The structure of PCON register is as follows.

PCON:         Address 87H

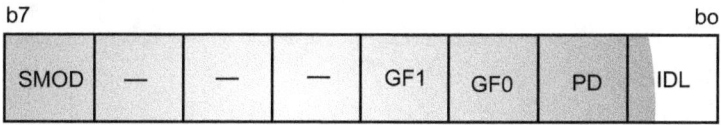

**Fig. 2.31**

The schematic diagram for 'Power down' mode and 'Idle' mode is given as follows:

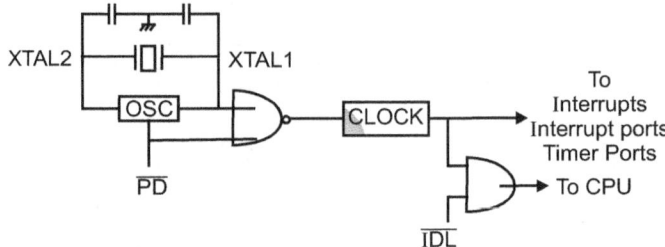

**Fig. 2.32 : Schematic diagram for Power Down and Idle mode implementation**

### Idle Mode

Idle mode is entered by setting IDL bit to 1 (i.e., $\overline{IDL}$ =0). The clock signal is gated off to CPU, but not to the interrupt, timer and serial port functions. The CPU status is preserved entirely. SP, PC, PSW, Accumulator and other registers maintain their data during IDLE mode. The port pins hold their logical states they had at the time Idle was initiated. ALE and $\overline{PSEN}$ are held at logic high levels.

**Ways to exit Idle Mode:**

1. Activation of any enabled interrupt will clear PCON.0 bit and hence the Idle Mode is exited. The program goes to the Interrupt Service Routine (ISR). After RETI is executed at the end of the ISR, the next instruction will start from the one following the instruction that enabled Idle Mode.
2. A hardware reset exits the idle mode. The CPU starts from the instruction following the instruction that invoked the 'Idle' mode.

**Power Down Mode:**

The Power down Mode is entered by setting the PD bit to 1. The internal clock to the entire microcontroller is stopped (frozen). However, the program is not dead. The Power down Mode is exited (PCON.1 is cleared to 0) by Hardware Reset only. The CPU starts from the next instruction where the Power down Mode was invoked. Port values are not changed/ overwritten in power down mode. Vcc can be reduced to as low as 2V in Power Down mode. However, Vcc has to be restored to normal value before Power Down mode is exited.

## 2.9 8051 INSTRUCTIONS

**8051 Instructions**

8051 has about 111 instructions. These can be grouped into the following categories

1. Arithmetic Instructions
2. Logical Instructions
3. Data Transfer instructions

4. Boolean Variable Instructions
5. Program Branching Instructions

The following nomenclatures for register, data, address and variables are used while write instructions.

A: Accumulator

B: "B" register

C: Carry bit

Rn: Register R0 - R7 of the currently selected register bank

Direct: 8-bit internal direct address for data. The data could be in lower 128bytes of RAM (00 - 7FH) or it could be in the special function register (80 - FFH).

@Ri: 8-bit external or internal RAM address available in register R0 or R1. This is used for indirect addressing mode.

#data8: Immediate 8-bit data available in the instruction.

#data16: Immediate 16-bit data available in the instruction.

Addr11: 11-bit destination address for short absolute jump. Used by instructions AJMP & ACALL. Jump range is 2 kbyte (one page).

Addr16: 16-bit destination address for long call or long jump.

Rel: 2's complement 8-bit offset (one - byte) used for short jump (SJMP) and all conditional jumps.

bit: Directly addressed bit in internal RAM or SFR

**Arithmetic Instructions**

| Mnemonics | Description | Bytes | Instruction Cycles |
|---|---|---|---|
| ADD A, Rn | A ← A + Rn | 1 | 1 |
| ADD A, direct | A ← A + (direct) | 2 | 1 |
| ADD A, @Ri | A ← A + @Ri | 1 | 1 |
| ADD A, #data | A ← A + data | 2 | 1 |
| ADDC A, Rn | A ← A + Rn + C | 1 | 1 |
| ADDC A, direct | A ← A + (direct) + C | 2 | 1 |
| ADDC A, @Ri | A ← A + @Ri + C | 1 | 1 |
| ADDC A, #data | A ← A + data + C | 2 | 1 |
| DA A | Decimal adjust accumulator | 1 | 1 |
| DIV AB | Divide A by B | 1 | 4 |

| Mnemonics | Description | Bytes | Instruction Cycles |
|---|---|---|---|
| | A ← quotient<br>B ← remainder | | |
| DEC A | A ← A -1 | 1 | 1 |
| DEC Rn | Rn ← Rn - 1 | 1 | 1 |
| DEC direct | (direct) ← (direct) - 1 | 2 | 1 |
| DEC @Ri | @Ri ← @Ri - 1 | 1 | 1 |
| INC A | A ← A+1 | 1 | 1 |
| INC Rn | Rn ← Rn + 1 | 1 | 1 |
| INC direct | (direct) ← (direct) + 1 | 2 | 1 |
| INC @Ri | @Ri ← @Ri +1 | 1 | 1 |
| INC DPTR | DPTR ← DPTR +1 | 1 | 2 |
| MUL AB | Multiply A by B<br>A ← low byte (A*B)<br>B ← high byte (A* B) | 1 | 4 |
| SUBB A, Rn | A ← A - Rn - C | 1 | 1 |
| SUBB A, direct | A ← A - (direct) - C | 2 | 1 |
| SUBB A, @Ri | A ← A - @Ri - C | 1 | 1 |
| SUBB A, #data | A ← A - data - C | 2 | 1 |

**Logical Instructions**

| Mnemonics | Description | Bytes | Instruction Cycles |
|---|---|---|---|
| ANL A, Rn | A ← A AND Rn | 1 | 1 |
| ANL A, direct | A ← A AND (direct) | 2 | 1 |
| ANL A, @Ri | A ← A AND @Ri | 1 | 1 |
| ANL A, #data | A ← A AND data | 2 | 1 |
| ANL direct, A | (direct) ← (direct) AND A | 2 | 1 |
| ANL direct, #data | (direct) ← (direct) AND data | 3 | 2 |
| CLR A | A ← 00H | 1 | 1 |
| CPL A | A ← A | 1 | 1 |
| ORL A, Rn | A ← A OR Rn | 1 | 1 |

| Mnemonics | Description | Bytes | Instruction Cycles |
|---|---|---|---|
| ORL A, direct | A ← A OR (direct) | 1 | 1 |
| ORL A, @Ri | A ← A OR @Ri | 2 | 1 |
| ORL A, #data | A ← A OR data | 1 | 1 |
| ORL direct, A | (direct) ← (direct) OR A | 2 | 1 |
| ORL direct, #data | (direct) ← (direct) OR data | 3 | 2 |
| RL A | Rotate accumulator left | 1 | 1 |
| RLC A | Rotate accumulator left through carry | 1 | 1 |
| RR A | Rotate accumulator right | 1 | 1 |
| RRC A | Rotate accumulator right through carry | 1 | 1 |
| SWAP A | Swap nibbles within Acumulator | 1 | 1 |
| XRL A, Rn | A ← A EXOR Rn | 1 | 1 |
| XRL A, direct | A ← A EXOR (direct) | 1 | 1 |
| XRL A, @Ri | A ← A EXOR @Ri | 2 | 1 |
| XRL A, #data | A ← A EXOR data | 1 | 1 |
| XRL direct, A | (direct) ← (direct) EXOR A | 2 | 1 |
| XRL direct, #data | (direct) ← (direct) EXOR data | 3 | 2 |

**Data Transfer Instructions**

| Mnemonics | Description | Bytes | Instruction Cycles |
|---|---|---|---|
| MOV A, Rn | A ← Rn | 1 | 1 |
| MOV A, direct | A ← (direct) | 2 | 1 |
| MOV A, @Ri | A ← @Ri | 1 | 1 |
| MOV A, #data | A ← data | 2 | 1 |
| MOV Rn, A | Rn ← A | 1 | 1 |
| MOV Rn, direct | Rn ← (direct) | 2 | 2 |

*(Contd.)*

| Mnemonics | Description | Bytes | Instruction Cycles |
|---|---|---|---|
| MOV Rn, #data | Rn ← data | 2 | 1 |
| MOV direct, A | (direct) ← A | 2 | 1 |
| MOV direct, Rn | (direct) ← Rn | 2 | 2 |
| MOV direct1, direct2 | (direct1) ← (direct2) | 3 | 2 |
| MOV direct, @Ri | (direct) ← @Ri | 2 | 2 |
| MOV direct, #data | (direct) ← #data | 3 | 2 |
| MOV @Ri, A | @Ri ← A | 1 | 1 |
| MOV @Ri, direct | @Ri ← (direct) | 2 | 2 |
| MOV @Ri, #data | @Ri ← data | 2 | 1 |
| MOV DPTR, #data16 | DPTR ← data16 | 3 | 2 |
| MOVC A, @A+DPTR | A ← Code byte pointed by A + DPTR | 1 | 2 |
| MOVC A, @A+PC | A ← Code byte pointed by A + PC | 1 | 2 |
| MOVC A, @Ri | A ← Code byte pointed by Ri 8-bit address) | 1 | 2 |
| MOVX A, @DPTR | A ← External data pointed by DPTR | 1 | 2 |
| MOVX @Ri, A | @Ri ← A (External data - 8bit address) | 1 | 2 |
| MOVX @DPTR, A | @DPTR ← A(External data - 16bit address) | 1 | 2 |
| PUSH direct | (SP) ← (direct) | 2 | 2 |
| POP direct | (direct) ← (SP) | 2 | 2 |
| XCH Rn | Exchange A with Rn | 1 | 1 |
| XCH direct | Exchange A with direct byte | 2 | 1 |
| XCH @Ri | Exchange A with indirect RAM | 1 | 1 |
| XCHD A, @Ri | Exchange least significant nibble of A with that of indirect RAM | 1 | 1 |

## Boolean Variable Instructions

| Mnemonics | Description | Bytes | Instruction Cycles |
|---|---|---|---|
| CLR C | C-bit ← 0 | 1 | 1 |
| CLR bit | bit ← 0 | 2 | 1 |
| SET C | C ← 1 | 1 | 1 |
| SET bit | bit ← 1 | 2 | 1 |
| CPL C | C ← $\overline{\text{C-bit}}$ | 1 | 1 |
| CPL bit | bit ← $\overline{\text{bit}}$ | 2 | 1 |
| ANL C, /bit | C ← C . $\overline{\text{bit}}$ | 2 | 1 |
| ANL C, bit | C ← C. bit | 2 | 1 |
| ORL C, /bit | C ← C + $\overline{\text{bit}}$ | 2 | 1 |
| ORL C, bit | C ← C + bit | 2 | 1 |
| MOV C, bit | C ← bit | 2 | 1 |
| MOV bit, C | bit ← C | 2 | 2 |

## Program Branching Instructions

| Mnemonics | Description | Bytes | Instruction Cycles |
|---|---|---|---|
| ACALL addr11 | PC + 2 → (SP) ; addr 11 → PC | 2 | 2 |
| AJMP addr11 | Addr11 → PC | 2 | 2 |
| CJNE A, direct, rel | Compare with A, jump (PC + rel) if not equal | 3 | 2 |
| CJNE A, #data, rel | Compare with A, jump (PC + rel) if not equal | 3 | 2 |
| CJNE Rn, #data, rel | Compare with Rn, jump (PC + rel) if not equal | 3 | 2 |
| CJNE @Ri, #data, rel | Compare with @Ri A, jump (PC + rel) if not equal | 3 | 2 |
| DJNZ Rn, rel | Decrement Rn, jump if not zero | 2 | 2 |
| DJNZ direct, rel | Decrement (direct), jump if not zero | 3 | 2 |
| JC rel | Jump (PC + rel) if C bit = 1 | 2 | 2 |
| JNC rel | Jump (PC + rel) if C bit = 0 | 2 | 2 |
| JB bit, rel | Jump (PC + rel) if bit = 1 | 3 | 2 |
| JNB bit, rel | Jump (PC + rel) if bit = 0 | 3 | 2 |
| JBC bit, rel | Jump (PC + rel) if bit = 1 | 3 | 2 |
| JMP @A+DPTR | A+DPTR → PC | 1 | 2 |
| JZ rel | If A=0, jump to PC + rel | 2 | 2 |
| JNZ rel | If A ≠ 0 , jump to PC + rel | 2 | 2 |
| LCALL addr16 | PC + 3 → (SP), addr16 → PC | 3 | 2 |
| LJMP addr 16 | Addr16 → PC | 3 | 2 |

| Mnemonics | Description | Bytes | Instruction Cycles |
|---|---|---|---|
| NOP | No operation | 1 | 1 |
| RET | (SP) ⟶ PC | 1 | 2 |
| RETI | (SP) ⟶ PC, Enable Interrupt | 1 | 2 |
| SJMP rel | PC + 2 + rel ⟶ PC | 2 | 2 |
| JMP @A+DPTR | A+DPTR ⟶ PC | 1 | 2 |
| JZ rel | If A = 0. jump PC+ rel | 2 | 2 |
| JNZ rel | If A ≠ 0, jump PC + rel | 2 | 2 |
| NOP | No operation | 1 | 1 |

## QUESTIONS

1. Draw and explain 8051 architecture.
2. What are the family devices and its derivatives of MCS-51 microcontroller.
3. Explain Port architecture of 8051 microcontroller with neat diagram.
4. Explain Memory organization of 8051 microcontroller with neat diagram.
5. Explain Interrupt structure of 8051 microcontroller with neat diagram.
6. Explain Timers used in 8051 microcontroller with neat diagram, and give one example of time delay using assembly language.
7. Describe different timer modes of 8051 microcontroller with neat diagram and example.
8. How serial communication is carried out in 8051 microcontroller.
9. What is instruction ? What is instruction set? what are the different types of instructions explain with two instructions in each type.
10. Explain the following instructions
    (i) MOVCA,@AA+DPTR    (ii) ADDC A, B(iii) ANL A,#data    (iv) CJNE A, B LABEL
11. Explain the following pins of 8051 microcontroller
    I. P3.6[WR]      BAR on WR
    II. PSEN         BAR on PSEN
    III. VPP[EA]     BAR on EA
    IV. PROG[ALE]

# Unit - III
# PIC MICROCONTROLLER ARCHITECTURE

## 3.1 INTRODUCTION

**PIC Microcontroller Architecture**

PIC stands for Peripheral Interface Controller given by Microchip Technology to identify its single-chip microcontrollers. These devices have been very successful in 8-bit microcontrollers. The main reason is that Microchip Technology has continuously upgraded the device architecture and added needed peripherals to the microcontroller to suit customers' requirements. The architectures of various PIC microcontrollers can be divided as follows.

**Low - end PIC Architectures :**

Microchip PIC microcontrollers are available in various types. When PIC microcontroller MCU was first available from General Instruments in early 1980's, the microcontroller consisted of a simple processor executing 12-bit wide instructions with basic I/O functions. These devices are known as low-end architectures. They have limited program memory and are meant for applications requiring simple interface functions and small program & data memories. Some of the low-end device numbers are

12C5XX
16C5X
16C505

**Mid Range PIC Architectures**

Mid range PIC architectures are built by upgrading low-end architectures with more number of peripherals, more number of registers and more data/program memory. Some of the mid-range devices are

16C6X
16C7X
16F87X

Program memory type is indicated by an alphabet.

C = EPROM

F = Flash

RC = Mask ROM

Popularity of the PIC microcontrollers is due to the following factors.

1. Speed: Harvard Architecture, RISC architecture, 1 instruction cycle = 4 clock cycles.
2. Instruction set simplicity: The instruction set consists of just 35 instructions (as opposed to 111 instructions for 8051).

3. Power-on-reset and brown-out reset. Brown-out-reset means when the power supply goes below a specified voltage (say 4V), it causes PIC to reset; hence malfunction is avoided.

   A watch dog timer (user programmable) resets the processor if the software/program ever malfunctions and deviates from its normal operation.
4. PIC microcontroller has four optional clock sources.
   - Low power crystal
   - Mid range crystal
   - High range crystal
   - RC oscillator (low cost).
5. Programmable timers and on-chip ADC.
6. Up to 12 independent interrupt sources.
7. Powerful output pin control (25 mA (max.) current sourcing capability per pin.)
8. EPROM/OTP/ROM/Flash memory option.
9. I/O port expansion capability.
10. Free assembler and simulator support from Microchip at www.microchip.com

## 3.2 CPU ARCHITECTURE

The CPU uses Harvard architecture with separate Program and Variable (data) memory interface. This facilitates instruction fetch and the operation on data/accessing of variables simultaneously.

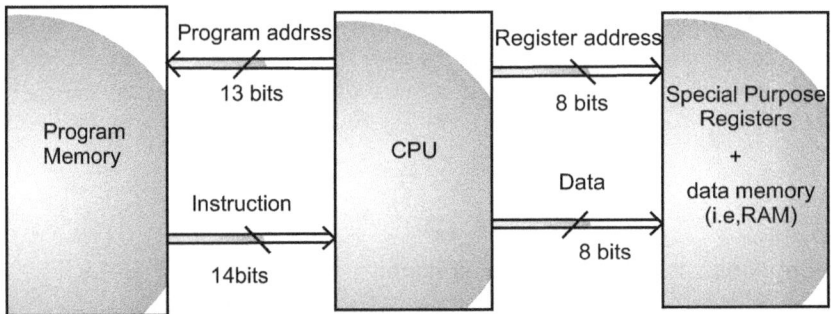

**Fig. 3.1 : CPU Architecture of PIC microcontroller**

## 3.3 PIC MEMORY ORGANISATION

PIC microcontroller has 13 bits of program memory address. Hence it can address up to 8k of program memory. The program counter is 13-bit. PIC 16C6X or 16C7X program memory is 2k or 4k. While addressing 2k of program memory, only 11- bits are required. Hence two most significant bits of the program counter are ignored. Similarly, while addressing 4k of memory, 12 bits are required. Hence the MSB of the program counter is ignored.

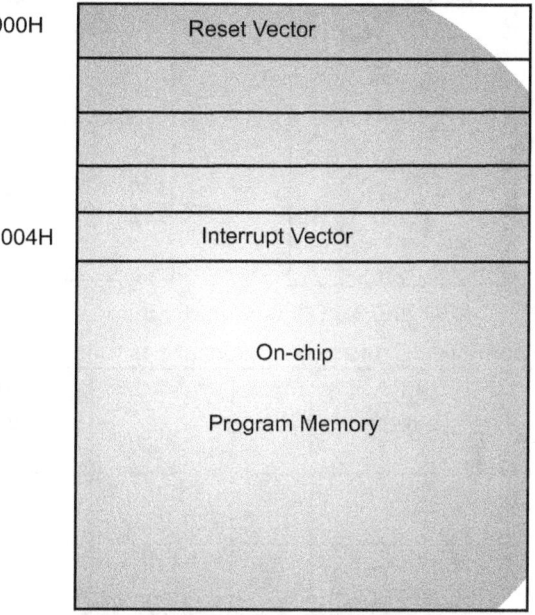

**Fig. 3.2 : Program Memory map**

The program memory map of PIC16C74A is shown in Fig 16.2. On reset, the program counter is cleared and the program starts at 00H. Here a 'goto' instruction is required that takes the processor to the mainline program.

When a peripheral interrupt, that is enabled, is received, the processor goes to 004H. A suitable branching to the interrupt service routine (ISR) is written at 004H.

**Data Memory (Register Files)**

Data Memory is also known as Register File. Register File consists of two components.

1. General purpose register file (same as RAM).
2. Special purpose register file (similar to SFR in 8051).

The special purpose register file consists of input/output ports and control registers. Addressing from 00H to FFH requires 8 bits of address.

However, the instructions that use direct addressing modes in PIC to address these register files use 7 bits of instruction only.

Therefore the register bank select (RP0) bit in the STATUS register is used to select one of the register banks. In indirect addressing FSR register is used as a pointer to anywhere from 00H to FFH in the data memory.

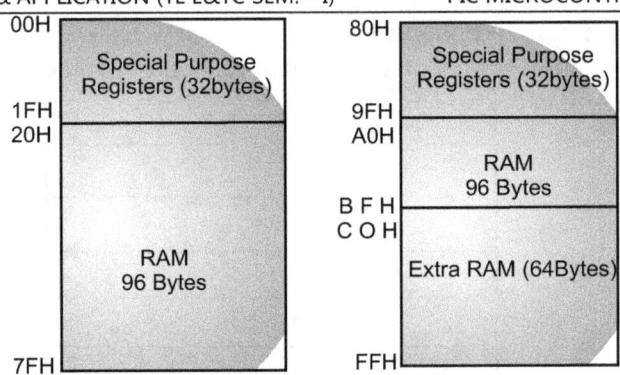

**Fig. 3.3 : Data Memory map**

Specifications of some popular PIC microcontrollers are as follows:

| Device | Program Memory (14bits) | Data RAM (bytes) | I/O Pins | ADC | Timers 8/16 bits | CCP (PWM) | USART SPI / I2C |
|---|---|---|---|---|---|---|---|
| 16C74A | 4K EPROM | 192 | 33 | 8 bits x 8 channels | 2/1 | 2 | USART SPI / $I^2C$ |
| 16F877 | 8K Flash | 368 (RAM) 256 (EEPROM) | 33 | 10 bits x 8 channels | 2/1 | 2 | USART SPI / $I^2C$ |

| Device | Interrupt Sources | Instruction Set |
|---|---|---|
| 16C74A | 12 | 35 |
| 16F877 | 15 | 35 |

## 3.4 PIC MICROCONTROLLER CLOCK

Most of the PIC microcontrollers can operate upto 20MHz. One instructions cycle (machine cycle) consists of four clock cycles.

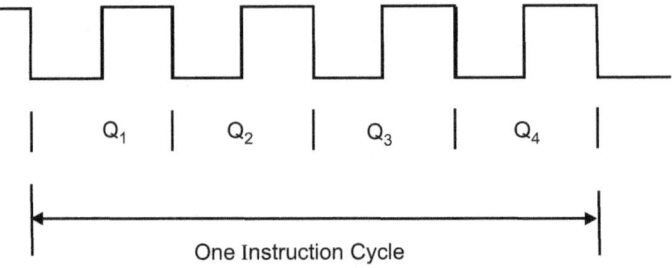

**Fig. 3.4 : Relation between instruction cycles and clock cycles for PIC microcontrollers**

Instructions that do not require modification of program counter content get executed in one instruction cycle. Although the architectures of various midrange 8 - bit PIC microcontroller are not the same, the variation is mostly interns of addition of memory and peripherals. We will discuss here the architecture of a standard mid-range PIC microcontroller, 16C74A. Unless mentioned otherwise, the information given here is for a PIC 16C74A microcontroller Chip.

## 3.5 ARCHITECTURE OF PIC16C74A

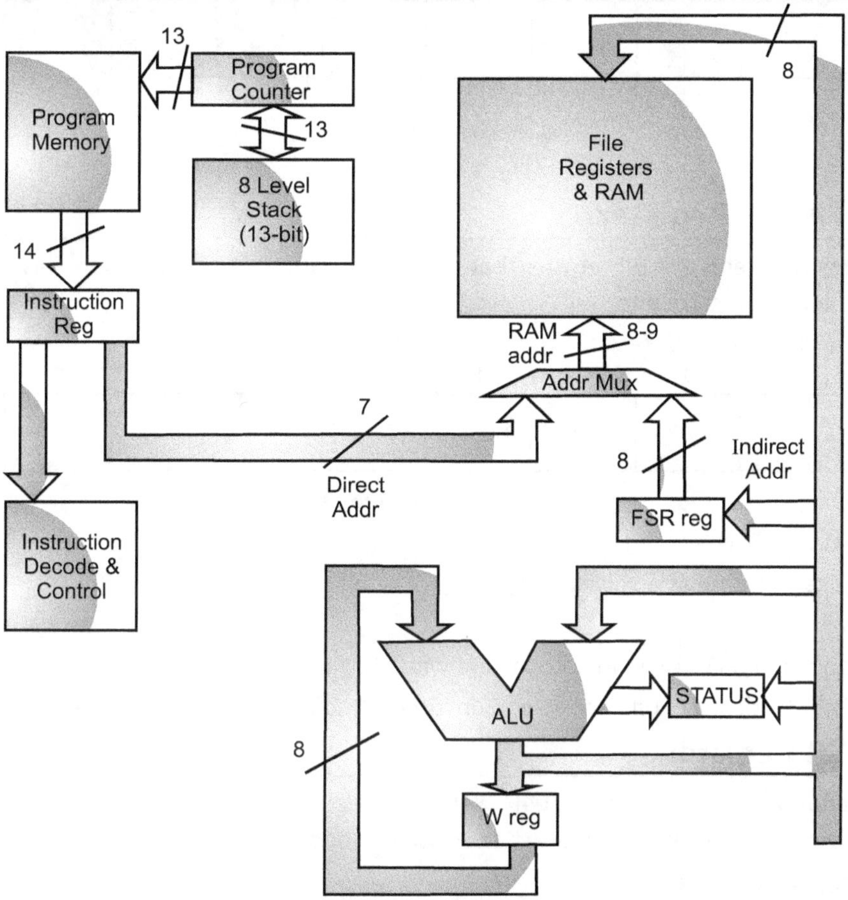

**Fig. 3.5 : Basic Architecture of PIC 16C74A**

The basic architecture of PIC16C74A is shown in Fig. 3.5. The architecture consists of Program memory, file registers and RAM, ALU and CPU registers. It should be noted that the program Counter is 13 - bit and the program memory is organised as 14 - bit word. Hence the program Memory capacity is 8k x 14 bit. Each instruction of PIC 16C74A is 14 - bit long. The various CPU registers are discussed here.

## 3.6 CPU REGISTERS (REGISTERS COMMONLY USED BY THE CPU)

W, the working register, is used by many instructions as the source of an operand. This is similar to accumulator in 8051. It may also serve as the destination for the result of the instruction execution. It is an 8 - bit register.

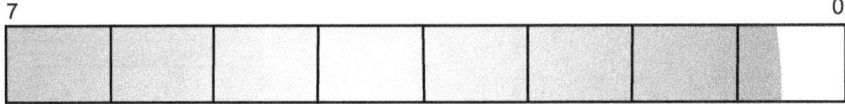

W ,Working register

**Fig. 3.6 : W register**

### 3.6.1 STATUS Register

The STATUS register is a 8-bit register that stores the status of the processor. This also stores carry, zero and digit carry bits.

STATUS - address 03H, 83H

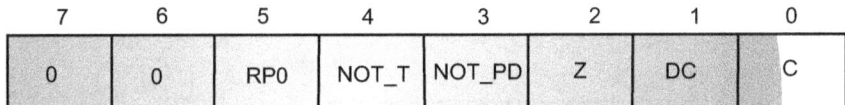

**Fig. 3.7 : STATUS register**

C = Carry bit

DC = Digit carry (same as auxiliary carry)

Z = Zero bit

NOT_TO and NOT_PD - Used in conjunction with PIC's sleep mode

RP0- Register bank select bit used in conjunction with direct addressing mode.

### 3.6.2 FSR Register

(File Selection Register, address = 04H, 84H) FSR is an 8-bit register used as data memory address pointer. This is used in indirect addressing mode.

### 3.6.3 INDF Register

(INDirect through FSR, address = 00H, 80H) INDF is not a physical register. Accessing INDF access is the location pointed to by FSR in indirect addressing mode.

## 3.6.4 PCL Register

(Program Counter Low Byte, address = 02H, 82H) PCL is actually the lower 8-bits of the 13-bit program counter. This is a both readable and writable register.

## 3.6.5 PCLATH Register

(Program Counter Latch, address = 0AH, 8AH) PCLATH is a 8-bit register which can be used to decide the upper 5bits of the program counter. PCLATH is not the upper 5bits of the program counter.

PCLATH can be read from or written to without affecting the program counter. The upper 3bits of PCLATH remain zero and they serve no purpose. When PCL is written to, the lower 5bits of PCLATH are automatically loaded to the upper 5 bits of the program counter, as shown in the Fig. 3.8.

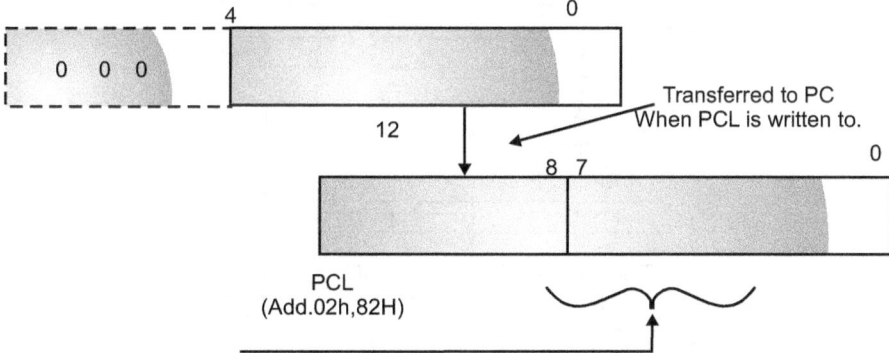

**Fig. 3.8 : Schematic of how PCL is loaded from PCLATH**

## 3.7 PROGRAM COUNTER STACK

An independent 8-level stack is used for the program counter. As the program counter is 13-bit, the stack is organized as 8x13bit registers. When an interrupt occurs, the program counter is pushed onto the stack. When the interrupt is being serviced, other interrupts remain disabled. Hence, other 7 registers of the stack can be used for subroutine calls within an interrupt service routine or within the mainline program.

**Register File Map :**

It can be noted that some of the special purpose registers are available both in Bank-0 and Bank-1. These registers have the same value in both banks. Changing the register content in one bank automatically changes its content in the other bank.

| Addr | Bank-0 | Bank-1 | Addr |
|---|---|---|---|
| 00 | INDF | INDF | 80 |
| 01 | TMR0 | OPTION | 81 |
| 02 | PCL | PCL | 82 |
| 03 | STATUS | STATUS | 82 |
| 04 | FSR | FSR | 84 |
| 05 | PORTA | TRISA | 85 |
| 06 | PORTB | TRISB | 86 |
| 07 | PORTC | TRISC | 87 |
| 08 | PORTD | TRISD | 88 |
| 09 | PORTE | TRISE | 89 |
| 0A | PCLATH | PCLATH | 8A |
| 0B | INTCON | INTCON | 8B |
| 0C | PIR1 | PIE1 | 8C |
| 0D | PIR2 | PIE2 | 8D |
| 0E | TMR1L | PCON | 8E |
| 0F | TMR1H | | 8F |
| 10 | T1CON | | 90 |
| 11 | TRM2 | | 91 |
| 12 | T2CON | PR2 | 92 |
| 13 | SSPBUF | SSPADD | 93 |
| 14 | SSPCON | SSPSTAT | 94 |
| 15 | CCPR1L | | 95 |
| 16 | OCPR1H | | 96 |
| 17 | CCP1CON | | 97 |
| 18 | RCSTA | TXSTA | 98 |
| 19 | TXREG | SPBRC | 99 |
| 1A | RCREC | | 9A |
| 1B | CCPR2L | | 9B |
| 1C | CCPR2H | | 9C |
| 1D | CCP2CON | | 9D |
| 1E | ADRES | | 9E |
| 1F | ADCON0 | ADCON1 | 9F |
| 20 | General Purpose RAM | General Purpose RAM | A0 |
| 7F | | | BFH |

**Fig. 3.9 : Register File Map**

## 3.8 PORT STRUCTURE AND PIN CONFIGURATION OF PIC 16C74A

As mentioned earlier, there is a large variety of PIC microcontrollers. However, the midrange architectures are widely used. Our discussion will mainly confine to PIC16C74A whose architecture has most of the required features of a mid-range PIC microcontroller. Study of any other mid-range PIC microcontroller will not cause much variation from the basic architecture of PIC 16C74A ..

PIC 16C74A has 5 I/O Ports. Each port is a bidirectional I/O port. In addition, they have the following alternate functions.

| Port | Alternative Uses of I/O Pins | No. of I/O Pins |
|---|---|---|
| Port A | A/D Converter Inputs | 6 |
| Port B | External Interrupt Inputs | 8 |
| Port C | Serial Port, Timer I/O | 8 |
| Port D | Parallel Slave Port | 8 |
| Port E | A/D Converter Inputs | 3 |
| | **Total I/O pins** | 33 |
| | **Total Pins** | 40 |

In addition to I/O pins, there is a Master clear pin (MCLR) which is equivalent to reset in 8051. However, unlike 8051, MCLR should be pulled low to reset the micro controller. Since PIC16C74Ahas inherent power-on reset, no special connection is required with MCLR pin to reset the micro controller on power-on.

There are two $V_{DD}$ pins and two $V_{SS}$ pins. There are two pins (OSC1 and OSC2) for connecting the crystal oscillator/ RC oscillator. Hence the total number of pins with a 16C74A is 33+7=40. This IC is commonly available in a dual-in-pin (DIP) package.

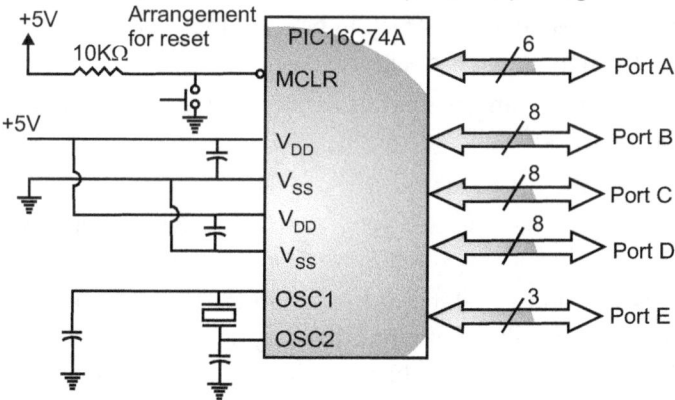

**Fig. 3.10 : Pin configuration of PIC 16C74A**

**Guidelines from Microchip Technology**

For writing assembly language program Microchip Technology has suggested the following guidelines.

1. Write instruction mnemonics in lower case. (e.g., movwf)
2. Write the special register names, RAM variable names and bit names in upper case. (e.g., PCL, RP0, etc.)
3. Write instructions and subroutine labels in mixed case. (e.g., Mainline, LoopTime)

## 3.9 INSTRUCTION SET

The instruction set for PIC16C74A consists of only 35 instructions. Some of these instructions are byte oriented instructions and some are bit oriented instructions.

The byte oriented instructions that require two parameters (For example, movf f, F(W)) expect the f to be replaced by the name of a special purpose register (e.g., PORTA) or the name of a RAM variable (e.g., NUM1), which serves as the source of the operand. 'f' stands for file register. The F(W) parameter is the destination of the result of the operation. It should be replaced by:

F, if the destination is to be the source register. W, if the destination is to be the working register (i.e., Accumulator or W register).

The bit oriented instructions also expect parameters (e.g., btfsc f, b). Here 'f' is to be replaced by the name of a special purpose register or the name of a RAM variable. The 'b' parameter is to be replaced by a bit number ranging from 0 to 7.

For example:

Z equ 2 btfsc STATUS, Z

Z has been equated to 2. Here, the instruction will test the Z bit of the STATUS register and will skip the next instruction if Z bit is clear.

The literal instructions require an operand having a known value (e.g., 0AH) or a label that represents a known value.

For example:

NUM equ 0AH ;                Assigns 0AH to the label NUM (a constant)
movlw NUM ;                  will move 0AH to the W register.

Every instruction fits in a single 14-bit word. In addition, every instruction also executes in a single cycle, unless it changes the content of the Program Counter. These features are due to the fact that PIC micro controller has been designed on the principles of RISC (Reduced Instruction Set Computer) architecture.

**Instruction set:**

| Mnemonics | Description | Instruction Cycles |
|---|---|---|
| bcf f, b | Clear bit b of register f | 1 |
| bsf f, b | Set bit b of register f | 1 |
| clrw | Clear working register W | 1 |
| clrf f | Clear f | 1 |
| movlw k | Move literal 'k' to W | 1 |
| movwf f | Move W to f | 1 |
| movf f, F(W) | Move f to F or W | 1 |
| swapf f, F(W) | Swap nibbles of f, putting result in F or W | 1 |
| andlw k | And literal value into W | 1 |
| andwf f, F(W) | And W with F and put the result in W or F | 1 |
| andwf f, F(W) | And W with F and put the result in W or F | 1 |
| iorlw k | inclusive-OR literal value into W | 1 |
| iorwf f, F(W) | inclusive-OR W with f and put the result in F or W | 1 |
| xorlw k | Exclusive-OR literal value into W | 1 |
| xorwf f, F(W) | Exclusive-OR W with f and put the result in F or W | 1 |
| addlw k | Add the literal value to W and store the result in W | 1 |
| addwf f, F(W) | Add W to f and store the result in F or W | 1 |
| sublw k | Subtract the literal value from W and store the result in W | 1 |
| subwf f, F(W) | Subtract f from W and store the result in F or W | 1 |
| rlf f, F(W) | Copy f into F or W; rotate F or W left through the carry bit | 1 |
| rrf f, F(W) | Copy f into F or W; rotate F or W right through the carry bit | 1 |
| btfsc f, b | Test 'b' bit of the register f and skip the next instruction if bit is clear | 1 / 2 |
| btfss f, b | Test 'b' bit of the register f and skip the next instruction if bit is set | 1 / 2 |

| Mnemonics | Description | Instruction Cycles |
|---|---|---|
| decfsz f, F(W) | Decrement f and copy the result to F or W; skip the next instruction if the result is zero | 1 / 2 |
| incfcz f, F(W) | Increment f and copy the result to F or W; skip the next instruction if the result is zero | 1 / 2 |
| goto label | Go to the instruction with the label "label" | 2 |
| call label | Go to the subroutine "label", push the Program Counter in the stack | 2 |
| retrun | Return from the subroutine, POP the Program Counter from the stack | 2 |
| retlw k | Retrun from the subroutine, POP the Program Counter from the stack; put k in W | 2 |
| retie | Return from Interrupt Service Routine and re-enable interrupt | 2 |
| clrwdt | Clear Watch Dog Timer | 1 |
| sleep | Go into sleep/ stand by mode | 1 |
| nop | No operation | 1 |

**Encoding of Instruction:**

As has been discussed, each instruction is of 14-bit long. These 14-bits contain both op-code and the operand. Some examples of instruction encoding are shown here.

*Example-1:*

**bcf f, b**        Clear 'b' bit of register 'f'

Operands:     0 ≤ f  ≤ 127  0 ≤ b ≤ 7

Encoding:

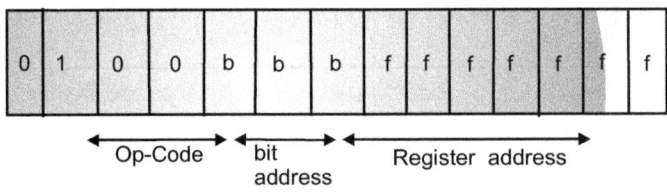

**Fig. 3.11**

The instruction is executed in one instruction cycle, i.e., 4 clock cycles. The activities in various clock cycles are as follows :

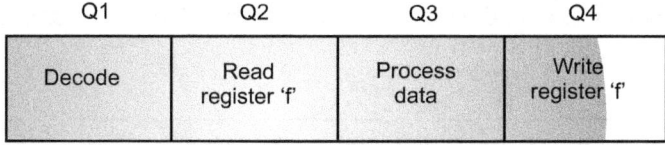

**Fig. 3.12**

*Example-2:*

**goto K**        Go to label 'k' instruction
Operand:         0 ≤ K ≤ 2047 (11-bit address is specified)
Operation:       K ⟶ PC <10:0>  PCLATH <4:3> ⟶ PC <12:11>
Encoding:

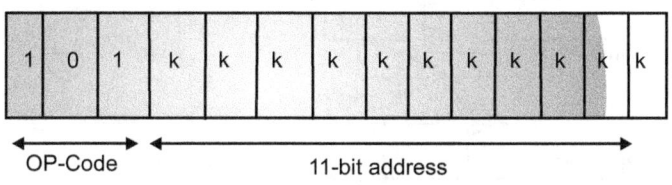

**Fig. 3.13**

Since this instruction requires modification of program Counter, it takes two instruction cycles for execution.

Q-Cycle activities are shown as follows :

|  | Q1 | Q2 | Q3 | Q4 |
|---|---|---|---|---|
| 1st instruction cycle | Decode | Read literal 'k' | Process data | Write to PC |
| 2nd Instruction cycle | No-Operation | No-Operation | No-Operation | No-Operation |

**Fig. 3.14**

## 3.10 I/O PORTS OF PIC16C74A

PIC16C74A has five I/O ports. Port-B, Port-C and Port-D have 8 pins each. Port-A and Port-E have 6 and 3 pins respectively. Each port has bidirectional digital I/O capability. In addition, these I/O ports are multiplexed with alternate functions for the peripheral devices on the microcontroller. In general, when a peripheral is enabled, that pin may not be used as a general purpose I/O pin.

Each port latch has a corresponding TRIS (Tri-state Enable) register for configuring the port either as an input or as an output. The port pins are designated by the alphabet R, followed by the respective port (viz. A, B, C, D or E) and the pin number. For example, Port-A pins are named as RA0, RA1, etc.

## 3.10.1 Port-A

Port-A pins RA0-RA3 and RA5 are similar. These pins function (alternate function) as analog inputs to the analog-to-digital converter.

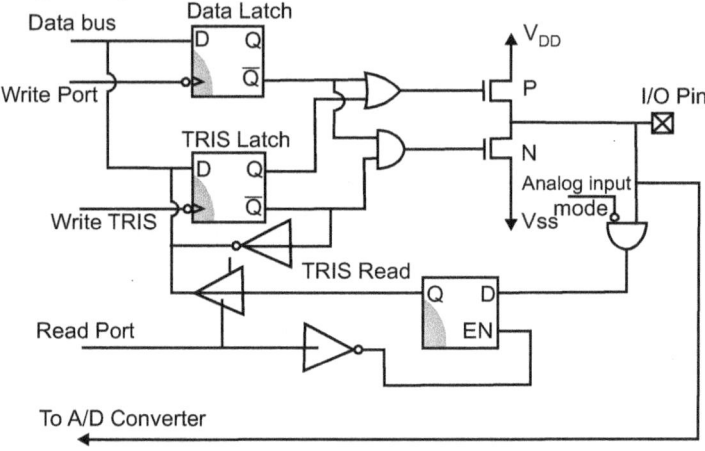

**Fig. 3.15 : RA0-RA3 and RA5 pin of Port-A**

The structure of Port-A pins RA0-RA3 and RA5 is shown in the figure. TRISA register decides whether the port-pin is configured as an input or as an output (digital) pin. Setting a TRISA register bit puts the corresponding output driver in high impedance mode. In this mode, the pin can be used as a digital or analog input. Clearing a bit in the TRISA register puts the contents of the data latch on the selected pins, i.e., the pin functions as a digital output. Pins RA0-RA and RA5 have current sourcing capability of 25mA. The alternate function of RA4 pin is Timer-0 clock input (T0CKI). RA4 pin is an open drain pin and hence requires external pull-up when configured as output pin. It is shown in the Fig. 3.16.

**Configuration of Port-A pins**

*Example* : Set RB0-RB3 as outputs, RB4-RB5 as inputs, RB7 as output.

| | | | | | |
|---|---|---|---|---|---|
| Bcf | STATUS, | RP0 | | select | band 0 |
| clrf | PORTA | | clears | the | data latch |
| bsf | STATUS, | RP0 | | select | band 1 |
| movlw | 30H | W ← 03H | (data direction) | | |
| movwf | TRISA | Set RA0-RA3 as outputs, RA4-RA5 as inputs | | | |

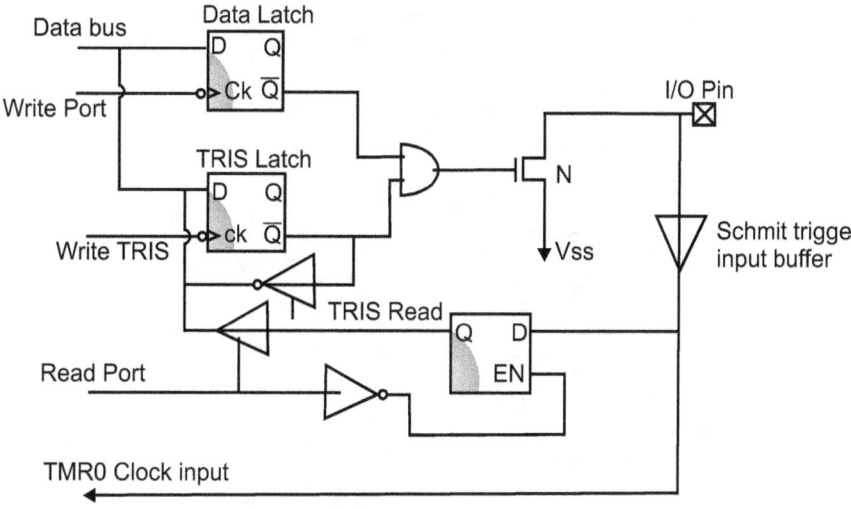

**Fig. 3.16 : RA4 pin Configuration**

## 3.10.2 Port-B

Port-B is an 8-bit bidirectional I/O port. The data direction in Port-B is controlled by TRISB register. Setting a bit in TRISB register puts the corresponding output in high impedance input mode. When a bit in TRISB is made zero, the corresponding pin in Port-B outputs the content of the latch (output mode).

Each port pin has a weak internal pull-up that can be enabled by clearing bit $\overline{RBPU}$ of OPTION register (bit-7). When a pin is configured in the output mode, the weak pull-up is automatically turned off. Internal pull-up is used so that we can directly drive a device from the pins.

**Configuration of Port-B pins :**

**Example :** Set RB0 : $RB_3$ as outputs, $RB_4$ : $RB_5$ as inputs, $RB_7$ as output.

| | |
|---|---|
| bcf | PoRTB |
| clrf | PoRTB |
| bsf | STATUS, RPo |
| Mov/w | 70 H |
| Mov/wf | TRISB |

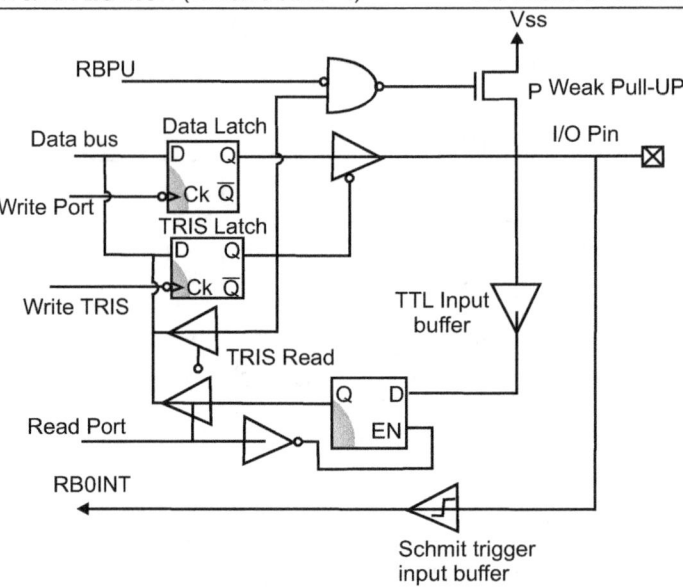

**Fig. 3.17 : Pins RB0-RB3 of Port-B**

## 3.11 OVERVIEW OF TIMER MODULES

PIC 16C74A has three modules, viz., Timer-0, Timer-1 and Timer-2. Timer-0 and Timer-2 are 8-bit timers. Timer-1 is a 16-bit timer. Each timer module can generate an interrupt on timer overflow.

**Timer-0 Overview:**

The timer-0 module is a simple 8-bit UP counter. The clock source can be either the internal clock ($f_{osc}/4$) or an external clock. When the clock source is external, the Timer-0 module can be programmed to increment on either the rising or falling clock edge. Timer-0 module has a programmable pre-scaler option. This pre-scaler can be assigned either to Timer-0 or the Watch dog timer, but not to both. The Timer-0 Counter sets a flag T0IF (Timer-0 Interrupt Flag) when it overflows and can cause an interrupt at that time if that interrupt source has been enabled, (T0IE = 1), i.e., timer-0 interrupt enable bit = 1.

**OPTION Register Configuration :**

Option Register (Addr: 81H) Controls the prescaler and Timer -0 clock source. The following OPTION register configuration is for clock source = $f_{osc}/4$ and no Watchdog timer.

**Timer-0 Use without Pre-scalar**

Internal clock source of $f_{osc}/4$. (External clock source, if selected, can be applied at RA4/TOCKI input at PORTA).

The following diagram shows the timer use without the prescaler.

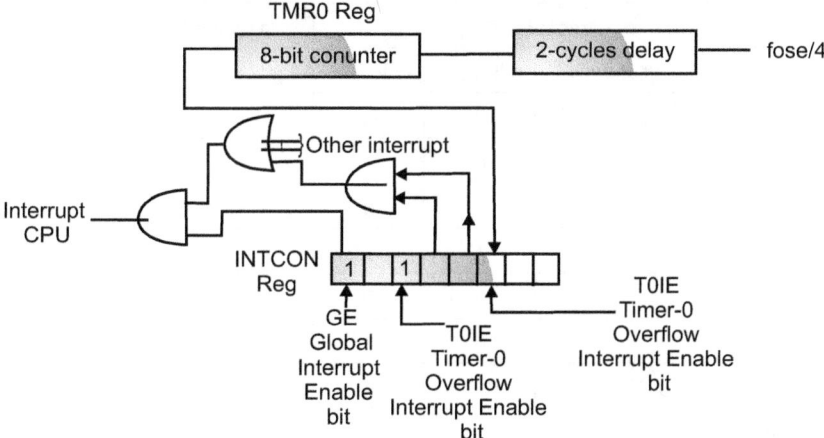

**Fig. 3.18 : Timer - 0 operation without prescaler**

**Timer-0 Use with Pre-scalar:**

The pre-scalar can be used either with the Timer-0 module or with the Watchdog timer. The pre-scalar is available for Timer-0 if the pre-scalar assignment bit PSA in the OPTION register is 0. Pre-scalar is a programmable divide by n counter that divides the available clock by a pre-specified number before applying to the Timer-0 counter.

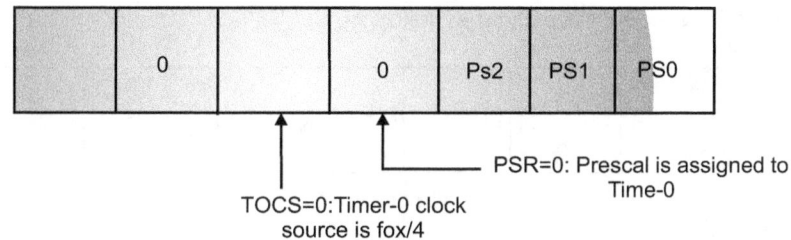

**Fig. 3.19 : Timer - 0 with prescaler**

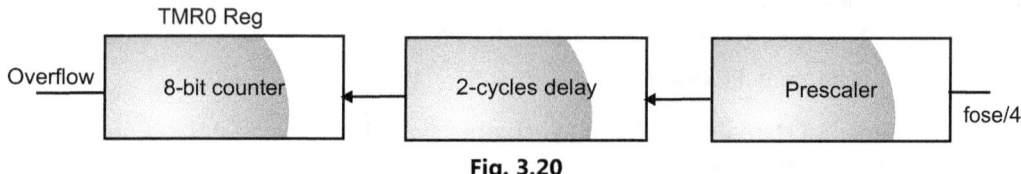

**Fig. 3.20**

| Prescaler Bits | | | Divide By |
|---|---|---|---|
| PS2 | PS1 | PS0 | N |
| 0 | 0 | 0 | 2 |
| 0 | 0 | 1 | 4 |
| 0 | 1 | 0 | 8 |
| 0 | 1 | 1 | 16 |
| 1 | 0 | 0 | 32 |
| 1 | 0 | 1 | 64 |
| 1 | 1 | 1 | 256 |

**Timer - 1 Module**

Timer 1 module is a 16-bit timer/counter consisting of two 8-bit registers (TMR1H and TMR1L) which are readable and writable. The TMR1 register pair (TMR1H:TMR1L) increments from 0000H to FFFFH and rolls over to 0000H. The TMR1 interrupt, if enabled, is generated on overflow, which sets the interrupt flag bit TMR1IF (bit-0 of PIR1 register). This interrupt can be enabled/disabled by setting/clearing TMR1 interrupt enable bit TMR1IE (bit-0 of the PIE1 register).

The operating and control modes of Timer1 are determined by the special purpose register T1CON.

Various bits of T1CON register are given as follows:-

| Bit7 | | | | | | | Bit0 |
|---|---|---|---|---|---|---|---|
| - | - | T1CKPS1 | T1CKPS0 | T1OSCEN | $\overline{\text{T1SYNC}}$ | TMR1CS | TMR1ON |

**Fig. 3.21**

TMR1 ON :  Timer1 ON bit
  0 = stops Timer 1;   1 = Enables Timer 1

TMR1CS :  Timer 1 Clock source Select Bit
  1 = External Clock (RCO/T1OSO/T1CKI)
  0 = Internal Clock ($f_{osc}/4$)

$\overline{\text{T1SYNC}}$ :  Timer 1 External Clock Input Synchronization Bit
  (Valid if TMR1CS = 1)
  1 - Do not synchronize
  0 - Synchronize

T1OSCEN:  Oscillator enable control bit

    1 = Oscillator is enabled

    0 = Oscillator is shut off

Timer 1 Input Clock Prescaler

| Select Bits | | Prescaler Value |
|---|---|---|
| T1CKPS1 | T1CKPS0 | |
| 1 | 1 | 1:8 |
| 1 | 0 | 1:4 |
| 0 | 1 | 1:2 |
| 0 | 0 | 1:1 |

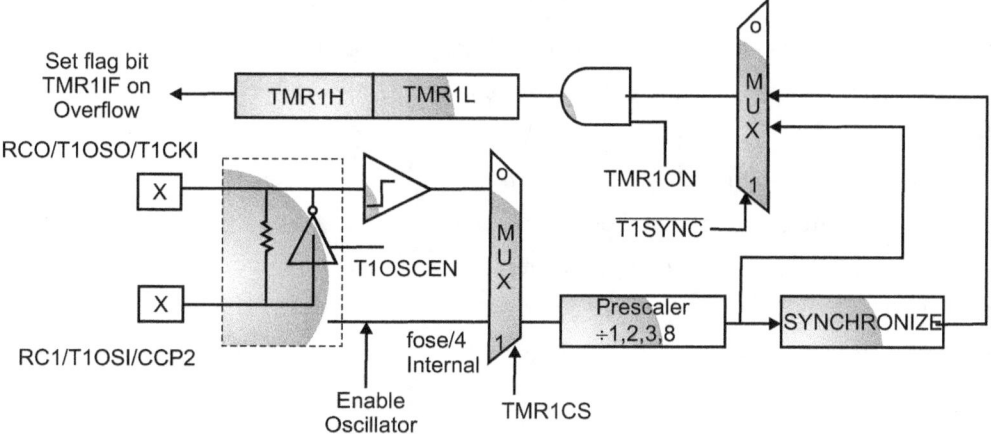

**Fig. 3.22 : Operation of Timer 1**

Timer 1 can operate in one of the two modes

- As a timer (TMR1CS = 0). In the timer mode, Timer 1 increments in every instruction cycle. The timer 1 clock source is $f_{osc}/4$. Since the internal clock is selected, the timer is always synchronized and there is no further need of synchronization.
- As a counter (TMR1CS = 1). In the counter mode, external clock input from the pin RC0/T1CKI is selected.

**Reading and writing Timer 1**

Reading TMR1H and TMR1L from Timer 1, when it is running from an external clock source, have to be done with care. Reading TMR1H or TMR1L for independent 8 - bit values does not pose any problem. When the 16-bit value of the Timer is required, the high byte (TMR1H) is read first followed by the low byte (THR1IL).

It should be ensured that TMR1L does not overflow (that is goes from FFH to 00H) since THR1H was read. This condition is verified by reading TMR1H once again and comparing with previous value of TMR1H.

**Example Program**

Reading 16bit of free running Timer 1

| movf TMR1H    | ; | read high byte                    |
| movwf TMPH    | ; | store in TMPH                     |
| movf TMR1L    | ; | read low byte                     |
| movwf TMPL    | ; | store in TMPL                     |
| movf TMR1H, W | ; | read high byte in W               |
| subwf TMPH, W | ; | subtract 1 st read with 2 nd read |
| btfsc STATUS, Z | ; | and check for equality          |

goto next

; if the high bytes differ, then there is an overflow

; read the high byte again followed by the low byte

| movf TMR1H, W | ; | read high byte |
| movwf TMPH    |   |                |
| movf TMR1L, W | ; | read low byte  |
| movwf TMPL    |   |                |

next : nop

**Timer 2 Overview :**

Timer 2 is an 8 - bit timer with a pre-scaler and a post-scaler. It can be used as the PWM time base for PWM mode of capture compare PWM (CCP) modules.

The TMR2 register is readable and writable and is cleared on device reset. The input clock ($f_{osc}/4$) has a pre-scaler option of 1:1, 1:4 or 1:16 which is selected by bit 0 and bit 1 of T2CON register respectively.

The Timer 2 module has an 8bit period register (PR2). Timer-2 increments from 00H until it is equal to PR2 and then resets to 00H on the next clock cycle. PR2 is a readable and writable register. PR2 is initailised to FFH on reset.

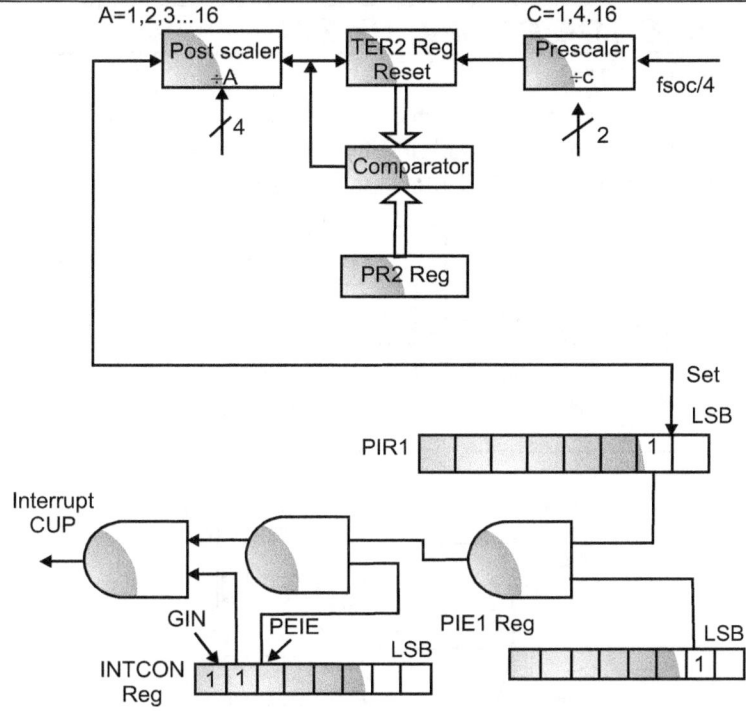

**Fig. 3.23 : Schematic diagram showing operation of Timer 2**

The output of TMR2 goes through a 4bit post-scaler (1:1, 1:2, to 1:16) to generate a TMR2 interrupt by setting TMR2IF.

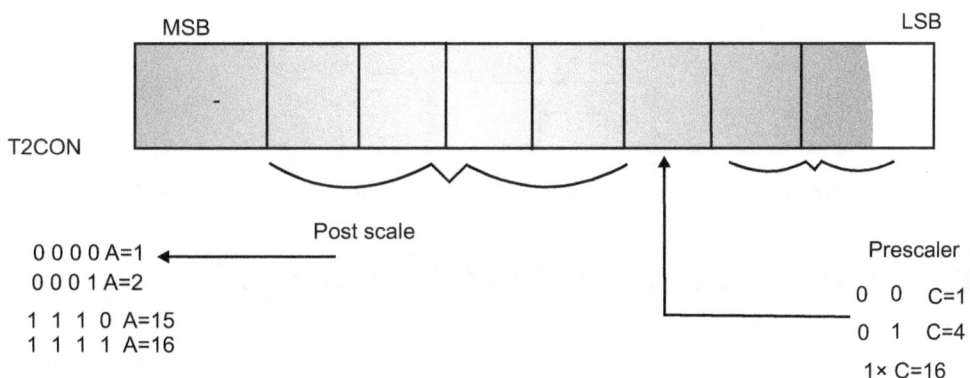

**Fig. 3.24 : The T2CON Register**

## 3.12 INTERRUPT LOGIC IN PIC 16C74A

### Interrupt Logic in PIC 16C74A

PIC 16C74A microcontroller has one vectored interrupt location (i.e., 0004H) but has 12 interrupt sources. There is no interrupt priority. Only one interrupt is served at a time. However interrupts can be masked. The interrupt logic is shown below :

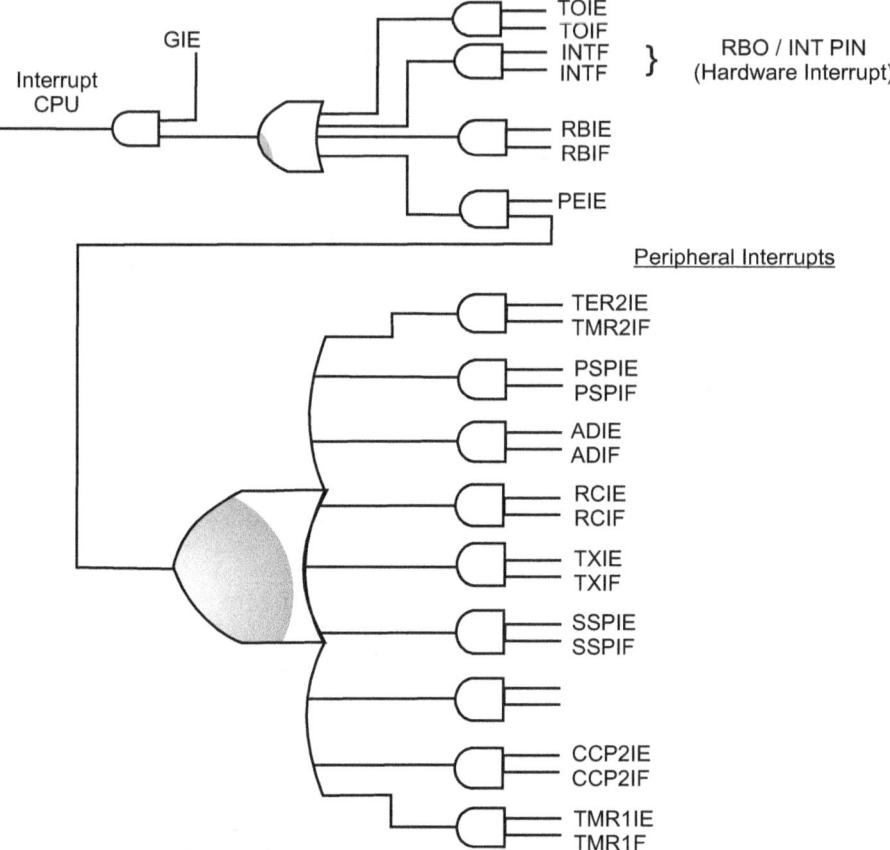

Fig. 3.25 : Schematic diagram showing the interrupt logic for PIC

## 3.13 CAPUTRE/COMPARE/PWM (CCP) MODULES

PIC16C74A has two CCP Modules. Each CCP module contains a 16 bit register (two 8-bit registers) and can operate in one of the three modes, viz., 16-bit capture, 16-bit compare, or up to 10-bit Pulse Width Modulation (PWM). The details of the two modules (CCP1 and CCp2) are given as follows.

## CCP1 Module:
CCP1 Module consists of two 8-bit registers, viz., CCPR1L (low byte) and CCPR1H (high byte). The CCP1CON register controls the operation of CCP1 Module.

## CCP2 Module:
CCP2 Module consists of two 8 bit registers, viz., CCPR2L (Low byte) and CCPR2H (high byte). The CCP1CON register controls the operation of CCP2 Module.

Both CCP1 and CCP2 modules are identical in operation with the exception of the operation of special event trigger.

The following table shows the timer resources for the CCP Mode.

| CCP Mode | Timer Used |
|----------|------------|
| Capture  | Timer 1    |
| Compare  | Timer 1    |
| PWM      | Timer 2    |

## CCP1CON Register (Address 17H )
CCP2CON Register is exactly similar to CCP1CON register. CCP2CON Register address is 1DH. CCP1CON controls CCP module1 where as CCP2CON controls CCP Module2.

Bit7                                                    Bit0

| — | — | CCP1X | CCP1Y | CCP1M3 | CCP1M2 | CCP1M1 | CCP1M0 |

**Fig. 3.26**

Bit 5-4 : CCP1X CCP1Y: PWM least significant bits. These bits are of no use in Capture mode. In PWM Mode, these bits are the two Lsbs of the PWM duty cycle. The eight Msbs are found in CCPR1L. Thus the PWM mode operates in 10-bit mode.

Bit 3-0 : CCP1M3:CCP1MO (CCP1 Mode select bits)

0000=Capture/Compare/PWM Mode off

0100=Capture mode, every falling edge

0101=Capture mode, every rising edge

0110=Capture mode, every 4 th rising edge

0111=Capture mode, every 16 th rising edge

1000=Compare mode, set output on match (CCP1IF bit is set)

1001=Compare mode, clear output on match (CCP1IF bit is set)

1010=Compare mode, generate software interrupt on match (CCP1IF bit is set, CCP1 pin unaffected)

1011=Compare mode, trigger special event (CCP1IF bit is set;CCP1 resets Tmr1; CCP2 resets TMR1 and starts A/D conversion if A/D module is Enabled)

11XX=PWM mode.

## 3.13.1 Capture Mode (CCP1)

Capture Mode captures the 16-bit value of TMR1 into CCPR1H:CCPR1L register pair in response to an event occurring on RC2/CCP1 pin. Capture Mode for CCP2 is exactly similar to that of CCP1.

An event on RC2/CCP1 pin is defined as follows:
- Every falling edge
- Every rising edge.
- Every 4 th rising edge.
- Every 16 th rising edge.

As mentioned earlier, this event is decided by bit 3-0 of CCP1CON register.

Schematic diagram for capture mode of operation

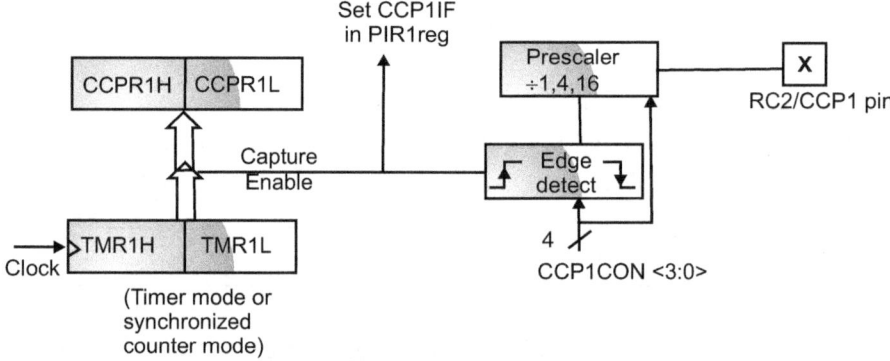

**Fig. 3.27 : Capture operation**

Required condition for capture mode:
1. RC2/CCP1 pin should be configured as an input by setting TRISC (bit 2).
2. Timer 1 should be operated from the internal clock (fosc/4), i.e., timer mode or in synchronized counter mode.

## 3.13.2 Compare Mode (CCP1)

Compare mode for CCP2 is similar to that of CCP1, except that in special event trigger mode, CCP1 resets TMR1 only, whereas CCP2 resets TMR1 and starts A/D conversion if A/D module is enabled.

In compare mode, the 16-bit CCPR1 register value is compared against TMR1 register pair (TMR1H and TMR1L) value. When a match occurs, the RC2/CCP1 pin is driven high or driven low or remains unchanged as decided by CCP1CON<3:0> bits.

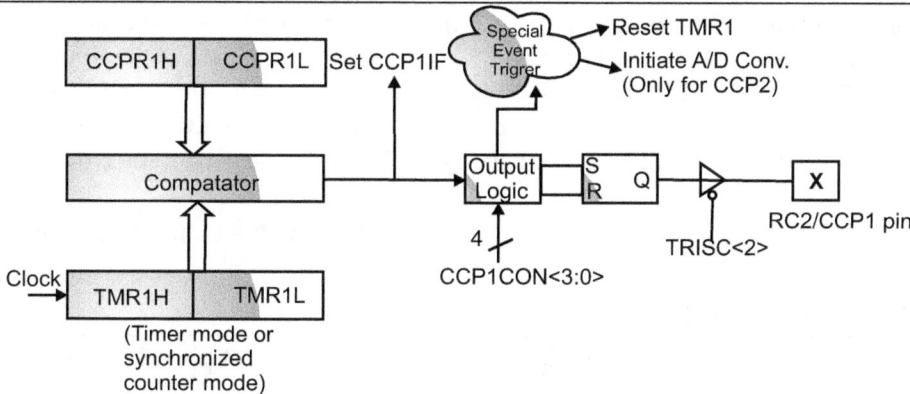

**Fig. 3.28 : Compare Operation**

Required conditions for compare mode

1. RC2/CCP1 pin must be configured as an output by clearing TRISC<2> bit.
2. Timer-1 should be operated in timer mode (i.e., internal clock source of $f_{osc}/4$) or in synchronized counter mode.

In software interrupt mode, CCP1IF bit is set but CCP1 pin in unaffected.

As shown in the figure, in special event trigger mode, both CCP1 and CCP2 intiates an A/D conversion.

## 3.13.3 PWM Mode (CCP1)

Both CCP1 and CCP2 have similar operation in PWM mode. Here we will discuss PWM with respect to CCP1. In PWM mode, the CCP1 pin produces upto a 10-bit resolution Pulse Width Modulation (PWM) output. RC2/CCP1 pin should be configured in the uotput mode by clearing TRISC<2> bit. The schematic block diagram of CCP1 module in PWM mode is shown in the figure.

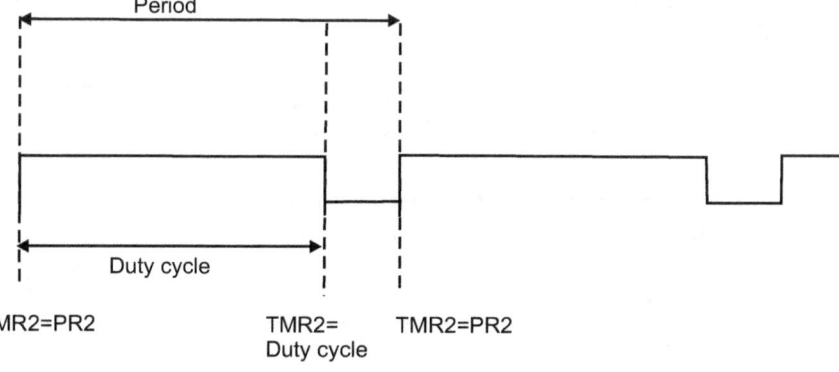

**Fig. 3.29 : PWM Operation**

It can be noted that PR2 (Period Register, 8 bit) decides the PWM period where CCPR1L (8-bits) and CCP1CON <5:4> (2-bits) decide the PWM duty cycle. When TMR2 equals PR2, the SR latch is set and RC2/CCP1 pin is pulled high. In the same time, TMR2 is cleared and the duty cycle value available in CCPR1L is latched to CCPR1H. CCPR1H, CCP1CON <5:4> decide the duty cycle and when this 10-bit ewquals the TMR2+2 prescaler or Q-bits, the SR latch is set and RC2/CCP1 pin is driven low.

A PWM output as shown has a time period. The time for which the output stays high is called duty cycle.

### 3.13.4 PWM Period

The PWM period is specified by writing to PR2 register. The PWM period can be calculated using the following formula:

PWM period = $[(PR2) + 1] \times 4 \times T_{osc} \times$ (TMR2 prescale value)  PWM frequency = 1/ PWM period

When TMR2 is equal to PR2, the following events occur on the next increment cycle.

- TMR2 is cleared
- the CCP1 pin is set (if PWM duty cycle is 0
- The PWM duty cycle is latched from CCPR1L into CCPR1H

### 3.13.5 PWM Duty Cycle

The PWM duty cycle is specified by writing to the CCPR1L register and to CCP1CON < 5 : 4 > bits. Up to 10-bit resolution is available where CCPR1L contains the eight MSBs and CCP1CON < 5 : 4 > contains the two LSB's. The 10-bit value is represented by CCPR1L : CCP1CON < 5 : 4 >.

The PWM duty cycle is given by PWM duty cycle = (CCPR1L : CCP1CON < 5 : 4 > ). $T_{osc}$. (TMR2 prescale value)

To understand the 10-bit counter configuration from Timer-2, let us first see the counting mechanism of Timer-2, as shown in Fig. 3.29.

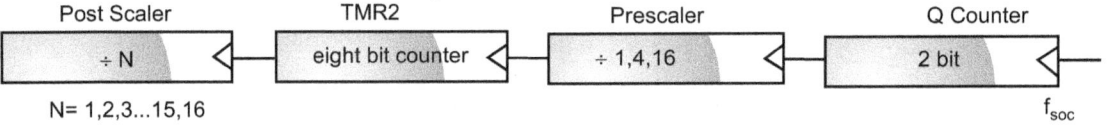

**Fig. 3.30 : Counting mechanism in Timer - 2**

If the prescaler is 1, the 10-bit counter is configured as follows

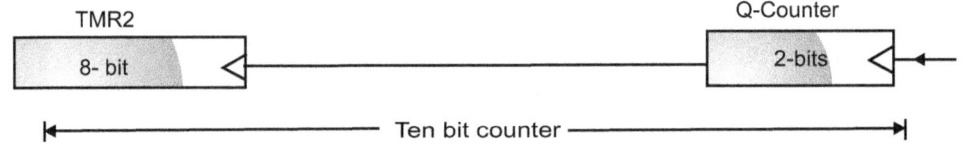

**Fig. 3.31 : Prescaler set to divide by one**

If the prescaler is 4, the 10-bit counter is configured as follows.

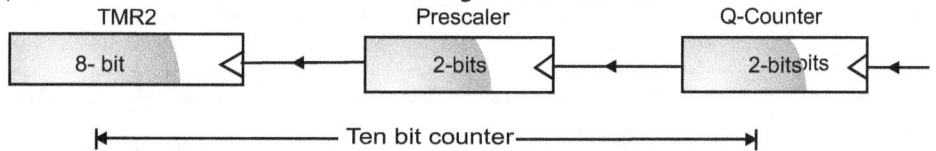

**Fig. 3.32 : Prescaler programed to divide by four**

If the prescaler is 16, the 10-bit counter is realized as follows.

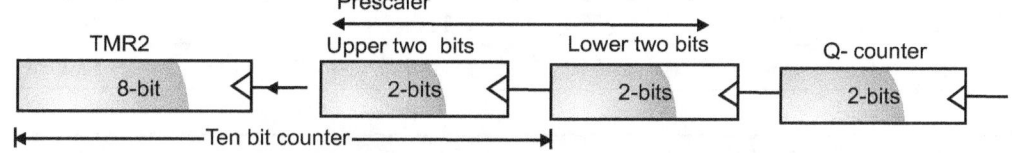

**Fig. 3.33 : Prescaler programed to divide by 16**

Although CCPR1L and CCP1CON < 5 : 4 > can be written to at anytime, the duty cycle value is not latched into CCPR1H until a match between PR2 and TMR2 occurs. In PWM mode, CCPR1H is a read-only register.

The CCPR1H register and a 2-bit internal latch are used to double buffer the PWM duty cycle. This double buffering is essential for glitchless PWM operation. When the CCPR1H and 2-bit latch match TMR2 concatenated with an internal 2-bit Q clock or 2-bits of prescaler, the CCP1 pin is cleared. Maximum PWM resolution (bits) for a given PWM frequency can be calculated as $\dfrac{\log\left(\dfrac{f_{esc}}{f_{PNM}}\right)}{\log 2}$.

If the PWM duty cycle is longer than the PWM period, then the CCP1 pin will not be cleared.

## 3.13.6 PWM Period and Duty Cycle Calculation

**Example 3.1 :**

$$\text{Desired PWM frequency} = 78.125 \text{ kHz}$$
$$f_{osc} = 20 \text{MHz}$$
$$\text{TMR2 Prescalar} = 1$$
$$\frac{1}{78.125 \times 10^3} = (PR2 + 1)\, 4 \times \frac{1}{20 \times 10^6}$$

Find the maximum resolution of duty cycle that can be used with a 78.124 kHz frequency and 20 MHz oscillator.

$$\frac{1}{78.125 \times 10^3} = 2^{PWMResolution} \frac{1}{20 \times 10^6} \cdot 1$$
$$256 = 2^{PWM\ Resolution}$$

At most, an 8-bit resolution duty cycle can be obtained from a 78.125 kHz frequency and 20 MHz oscillator i.e., 0 CCPR1L : CCP1CON <5 : 4> ≤ 255. Any value greater than 255 will result in a 100 % duty cycle. The following table gives the PWM frequency $f_{PWM}$ if $f_{osc}$ = 20MHz. **Prescaler**

| Duty Cycle Resolution | 10-Bit Counter Scale | PR2 value | Prescaler 1 | Prescaler 4 | Prescaler 16 |
|---|---|---|---|---|---|
| 10 bit | 1024 | 255 | 19.53 KHz | 4.88 kHz | 1.22 kHz |
| ≈ 10 bit | 1000 | 249 | 20 kHz | 5 kHz | 1.25 kHz |
| 8 bit | 256 | 63 | 78.125 kHz | 19.52 kHz | 4.88 kHz |
| 6 bit | 64 | 15 | 312.5 kHz | 78.125 kHz | 19.53 kHz |

## 3.14 ADC MODULE

**ADC Module**

An analog-to-digital converter (ADC) converts an analog signal into an equivalent digital number. PIC 16C74A has an inbuilt ADC with the following features -

- 8-bit conversion
- 8 analog input channels
- An analog multiplexer
- A sample and hold circuit for signal on the selected input channel
- Alternative clock sources for carrying out conversion
- Adjustable sampling rate
- Choice of an internal or external reference voltage
- Interrupt to microcontroller on end of conversion

Port A and Port E pins are used for analog inputs/reference voltage for ADC. In A/D conversion, the input analog voltage is digitized and an equivalent digital output is generated as shown in the figure.

**Port-A Pins (Alternate functions)**

RA0/AN0        -        can be used as analog input-0
RA1/AN1        -        can be used as analog input-1
RA2/AN2        -        can be used as analog input-2
RA3/AN3/$V_{ref}$ -        can be used as analog input-3 or analog reference voltage
RA4/TOCKI     -        clock input to Timer-0
RA5/ /AN4      -        can be used for analog input 4 or slave select for the synchronized serial port.

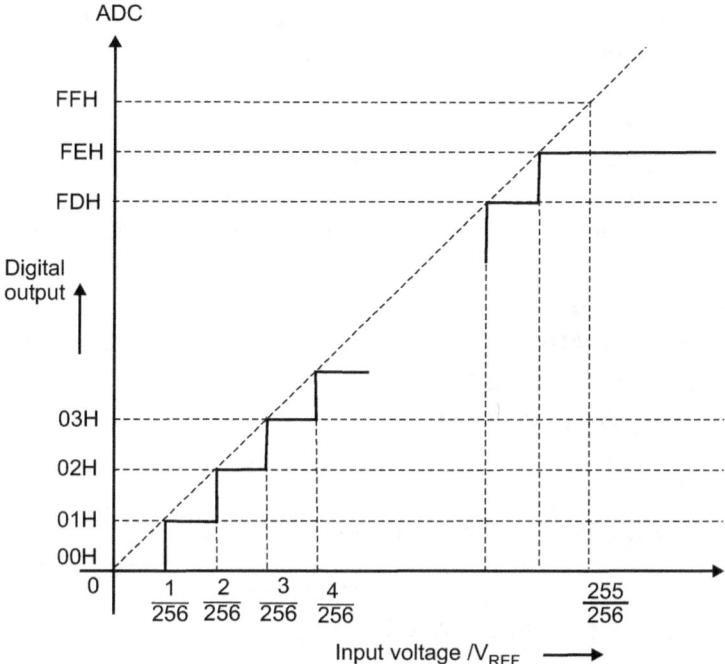

**Fig. 3.34 : Digital output versus analog input**

**Port-E pins (Alternate functions)**

RE0/ $\overline{RD}$ /AN5 - can be used as analog input-5

RE1/ $\overline{WR}$ /AN6 - can be used as analog input-6

RE2/ $\overline{CS}$ /AN7 - can be used as analog input-7

PIC microcontroller has internal sample and hold circuit. The input signal should be stable across the capacitor before the conversion is initiated.

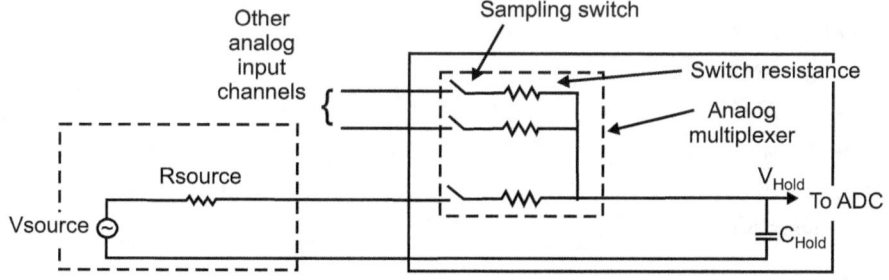

**Fig. 3.35 : Sample and Hold Circuit**

After waiting for the sampling time, a conversion can be initiated. The ADC Circuit will open the sampling switch and carry out the conversion of the input voltage as it was at the moment of opening of the switch. Upon completion of the conversion, the sampling switch is again closed and $V_{Hold}$ once again tracks $V_{Source}$.

### Using the A/D Converter

Registers ADCON1, TRISA, and TRISE must be initialized to select the reference voltage and input channels. The first step selects the ADC clock from among the four choices ($f_{osc}/2$, $f_{osc}/8$, $f_{osc}/32$, and RC). The constraint for selcting clock frequency is that the ADC clock period must be 1.6micro seconds or greater.

The A/D module has 3registers. These registers are:-

- A/D result register (ADRES)
- A/D control register 0 (ADCON 0)
- A/D control register 1 (ADCON 1)

The ADCON0 register, which is shown below, controls the operation of A/D module.

| 7 | 6 | 5 | 4 | 3 | 2 | 1 | 0 |
|---|---|---|---|---|---|---|---|
| ADCS1 | ADCS0 | CHS2 | CHS1 | CHS0 | GO/DONE | - | ADON |

**Fig. 3.36 : ADCON0 register**

Bit 7-6 - A/D Clock select bits ADCS1:ADCS0

$00 = f_{osc}/2$

$01 = f_{osc}/8$

$10 = f_{osc}/32$

$11 = f_{RC}$- clock derived from an internal RC oscillator

Bit 5-3 - A/D Channel Select

CHS2:CHS0

000 - Channel 0 - AN0

001 - Channel 1 - AN1

010 - Channel 2 - AN2

011 - Channel 3 - AN3

100 - Channel 4 - AN4

101 - Channel 5 - AN5

110 - Channel 6 - AN6

111 - Channel 7 - AN7

Bit 2 - A/D conversion status bit

GO / $\overline{DONE}$

if A/D Converter is enabled (ie. ADON = 1) then

If GO / $\overline{\text{DONE}}$ = 1, A/D conversion is in progress

(setting this bit starts A/D conversion) If GO / $\overline{\text{DONE}}$ = 0, A/D conversion is not in progress (This bit is automatically cleared by hardware when A/D conversion is complete)

Bit1 - Unimplemented

Bit 0 - ADON: A/D On bit
1. A/D Converter module is ON
2. A/D Converter module is OFF

### ADCON1 Register

This register specifies the analog inputs

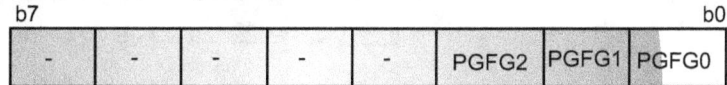

**Fig. 3.37 : ADCON1 Register**

| PCFG2:PCFG0 | RA0 | RA1 | RA2 | RA5 | RA3 | RE0 | RE1 | RE2 | $V_{REF}$ |
|---|---|---|---|---|---|---|---|---|---|
| 000 | A | A | A | A | A | A | A | A | $V_{DD}$ |
| 001 | A | A | A | A | $V_{REF}$ | A | A | A | $RA_3$ |
| 010 | A | A | A | A | A | D | D | D | $V_{DD}$ |
| 011 | A | A | A | A | $V_{REF}$ | D | D | D | $RA_3$ |
| 100 | A | A | D | D | A | D | D | D | $V_{DD}$ |
| 101 | A | A | D | D | $V_{REF}$ | D | D | D | $RA_3$ |
| 11X | D | D | D | D | D | D | D | D | - |
| A = Analog input  D = Digital I/O ||||||||||

### Steps for A/D conversion

1. Configure A/D module
    - Configure analog inputs/voltage reference and digital I/O (ADCON1)
    - Select A/D Channel (ADCON0)
    - Select A/D Conversion Clock (ADCON0)
    - Turn on A/D Module (ADCON0)
2. Configure A/D Interrupt (Optional)
    - Clear ADIF bit in PIR1 register
    - Set ADIE bit in PIE1 register
    - Set GIE bit
3. Wait for required acquisition time

4. Start Conversion - set GO/$\overline{DONE}$ bit (ADCON0)
5. Wait for A/D conversion to complete, by either polling GO/$\overline{DONE}$ bit or by waiting for the A/D interrupt
6. Read A/D result registers (ADRES). Clear ADIF if required.

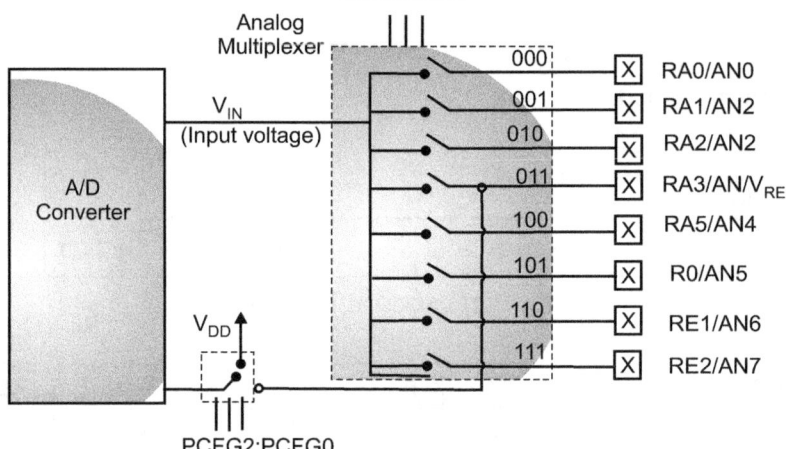

**Fig. 3.38 : Schematic diagram of A/D convertor analog inputs and reference voltage**

**Example :**

Program A/D conversion with interrupt

```
org 000H
goto Mainline
org 020H
bsf   STATUS, RP0      ;   Select Bank 1
clrf  ADCON 1          ;   Configure A/D inputs
bsf   PIE1, ADIE       ;   Enable A/D interrupt
bcf   STATUS, RP0      ;   Select Bank 0
movlw 081H             ;   Select fosc/32, channel 0, A/D on
movwf ADCON0
bcf   PIR1, ADIF
bsf   INTCON, PEIE     ;   Enable peripheral and global interrupt bits
bsf   INTCON, GIE      ;   interrupt bits
; Ensure that the required sampling time of the selected input channel has been elapsed.
; Then conversion may be started.
; bsf ADCON0, GO       ; Start A/D conversion.
```

; ADIF bit will be set and GO/$\overline{DONE}$
; bit is cleared upon completion of A/D conversion.

### Interrupt Service Routine

Org 004H Movf ADRES, W ; Result of A/D conversion in W

### Consideration of Sampling Time

When a channel is selected (writing to ADCON0), the switch 'SW' in Fig 23.8 is closed, changing $C_{HOLD}$ to $V_{Source}$. When A/D conversion is started (setting Go bit in ADCON0), SW is opened. The time from the closure of 'SW' till the voltage across $C_{HOLD}$ ($V_o$) reaches $V_{Source}$ is the minimum sampling time $T_s$. The actual sampling time can be higher than $T_s$. The graph between $T_s$ and source resistance $R_{Source}$ is shown in Fig 23.7.+

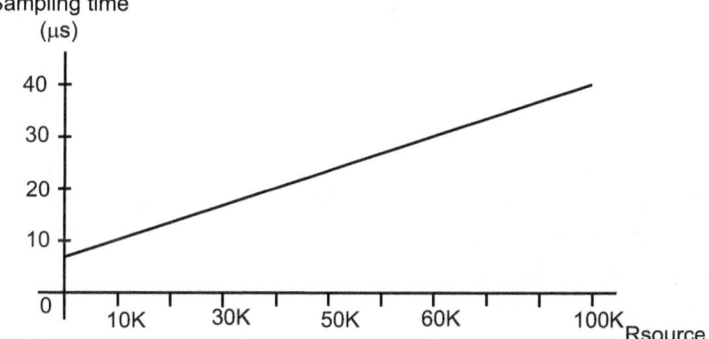

Fig. 3.39 : Relation between sampling time and source resistance

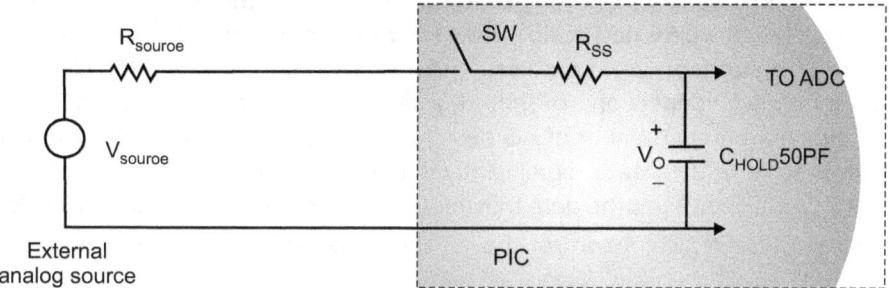

Fig. 3.40 : Sampling circuit in the PIC µC

$R_{ss}$ is the resistance of the sampling switch 'SW' and $C_{Hold}$ is the charge holding capacitance. $C_{Hold}$ is nearly 50pF. $R_{Source}$ is the impedance of the external analog source Vsource.

Once the switch 'SW' is closed, the capacitor Chold takes some time to charge up. This time it is called the sampling time ($T_s$).

This time varies linearly with $R_{Source}$ as shown. The recommended value of impedance of the external analog source, Vsource, is less than 10kΩ. The circuit in Fig. 3.38 is a first order RC circuit. When SW is closed, $V_o$ varies as shown in Fig. 3.39.

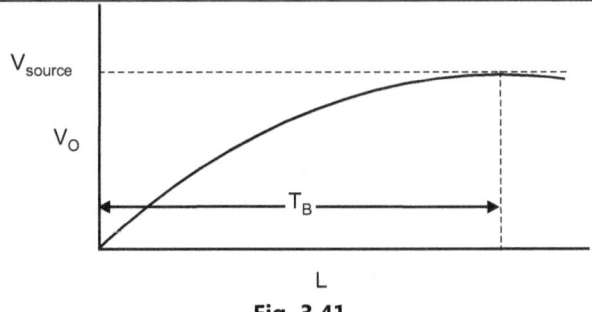

**Fig. 3.41**

From Fig. 3.39,

$T_s = 5\tau = 5(R_{source} + R_{ss})C_{HOLD}$

$= 5 R_{ss} C_{HOLD} + 5 R_{source} C_{HOLD}$

Most of mid range PIC microcontrollers include a Synchronous Serial Port (SSP) Module. The discussion in this section is relevant to PIC16C74A only. SSP Module section can be configured in either of the following two modes.

- Serial Peripheral Interface (SPI)
- Inter Integrated Circuit ($I^2C$)

Either of these modes can be used to interconnect two or more PIC chips to each other using a minimal number of wires for communication. Alternatively, either can be used to connect a PIC microcontroller to a peripheral chip. When $I^2C$ mode is selected, the peripheral chip must also have an $I^2C$ interface. On the other hand, the SPI mode provides the clock and serial data lines for direct connection to shift registers. This leads to increased I/O interface capability and an arbitrary number of I/O devices can be connected to a PIC microcontroller. SPI can also achieve data rate significantly higher than $I^2C$. Both the communication methods are synchronous, i.e., the data transfer is synchronized with an explicit clock signal.

Two special purpose registers control the synchronous serial port (SSP) operations. These registers are:

- SSPCON (Synchronous Serial Port Control Register), Address: 14H
- SSPSTAT (Synchronous Serial Port status Register), Address: 94H

## 3.15 MPLAB IDE

**MPLAB** Integrated Development Environment (IDE) is a free, integrated toolset for the development of embedded applications onMicrochip's PIC and dsPIC microcontrollers. MPLAB IDE is a Windows· -based Integrated Development Environment (IDE) for the Microchip Technology Incorporated PICmicro® microcontroller (MCU) families. MPLAB IDE allows you to write, debug, and optimize PICmicro MUC applications for firmware product designs. MPLAB IDE includes a text editor, simulator, and project manager. MPLAB IDE also supports the MPLAB-ICE and PICMASTER emulators, PICSTART® Plus and PRO MATE® II programmers, and other Microchip or third party development system tools.

**MPLAB IDE Features**

- Provides a new Call Graph for navigating complex code.
- Supports Multiple Configurations within your projects.
- Supports Multiple Versions of the same compiler.
- Support for multiple Debug Tools of the same type.
- Supports Live Parsing.
- Import existing MPLAB® 8 projects and use either IDE for the same source.
- Supports hyperlinks for fast navigation to declarations and includes.
- Supports Live Code Templates.
- Supports the ability to enter File Code Templates with license headers or template code.
- MPLAB® X can Track Changes within your own system using local history.
- Within MPLAB® X, a user can configure their own Code Format Style.

**How MPLAB IDE Helps You**

The organization of MPLAB IDE tools by function helps make pull-down menus and customizable quick keys easy to find and use. MPLAB IDE tools allow you to:

- Assemble, compile, and link source code.
- Debug the executable logic by watching program flow with the simulator, or in real time with the MPLAB-ICE emulator.
- Make timing measurements.
- View variables in watch windows.
- Program firmware with PICSTART Plus or PRO MATE II.
- Find quick answers to questions from the MPLAB IDE on-line Help and much more.

MPLAB IDE is an easy-to-learn and use Integrated Development Environment (IDE). The IDE provides firmware development engineers the flexibility to develop and debug firmware for Microchip's PICmicro MCU families. The MPLAB IDE runs under Microsoft Windows 3.1x, Windows 95/98, Windows NT, or Windows 2000. MPLAB IDE provides functions that allow you to:

- Create and Edit Source Files.
- Group Files into Projects.
- Debug Source Code.
- Debug Executable Logic Using the Simulator or Emulator(s).

The MPLAB IDE allows you to create and edit source code by providing you with a full-featured text editor. Further, you can easily debug source code with the aid of a Build Results window that displays the errors found by the compiler, assembler, and linker when generating executable files.

A Project Manager allows you to group source files, precompiled object files, libraries, and linker script files into a project format.

The MPLAB IDE also provides feature-rich simulator and emulator environments to debug the logic of executables. Some of the features are:

- A variety of windows allowing you to view the contents of all data and program memory locations
- Source Code, Program Memory, and Absolute Listing windows allowing you to view the source code and its assembly-level equivalent separately and together (Absolute Listing).
- The ability to step through execution, or apply Break, Trace, Standard, or Complex Trigger points.

## 3.16 MPLAB IDE DEVELOPMENT TOOLS

The MPLAB IDE integrates several tools to provide a complete development environment.

**MPLAB Project Manager :**

Use the Project Manager to create a project and work with the specific files related to the project. When using a project, you can rebuild sourcecode and download it to the simulator or emulator with a single mouse click.

**MPLAB Editor :**

Use the MPLAB Editor to create and edit text files such as source files, code, and linker script files.

**MPLAB C18 C Compiler**

MPLAB C18 C Compiler is a cross-compiler that runs on a PC and produces code that can be executed by the Microchip PIC18XXXX family of microcontrollers. Like an assembler, the MPLAB C18 compiler translates human-understandable statements into ones and zeros for the microcontroller to execute. Unlike an assembler, the compiler does not do a one-to-one translation of machine mnemonics into machine code.

MPLAB C18 takes standard C statements, such as "if(x==y)" and "temp=0x27", and converts them into PIC18XXXX machine code. The compiler incorporates a good deal of intelligence in this process. It can optimize code using routines that were employed on one C function to be used by other C functions. The compiler can rearrange code, eliminate code that will never be executed, share common code fragments among multiple functions, and can identify data and registers that are used inefficiently, optimizing their access.

Code is written using standard ANSI C notation. Source code is compiled into blocks of program code and data which are then "linked" with other blocks of code and data, then placed into the various memory regions of the PIC18XXXX microcontroller. This process is called a "build," and it is often executed many times in program development as code is written, tested and debugged. This process can be made more intelligent by using a "make" facility, which invokes the compiler only for those C source files in the project that have changed since the last build, resulting in faster project build times.

MPLAB C18 compiler and its associated tools, such as the linker and assembler, can be invoked from the command line to build a .HEX file that can be programmed into a PIC18XXXX device. MPLAB C18 and its other tools can also be invoked from within MPLAB IDE. The MPLAB graphical user interface serves as a single environment to write, compile and debug code for embedded applications. The MPLAB dialogs and project manager handle most of the details of the compiler, assembler and linker, allowing the task of writing and debugging the application to remain the main focus. MPLAB® C18 compiler is one of the compiling tools for programming PIC18 MCUs. It is supported by MPLAB IDE as a compiler; hence very little effort is needed by the programmer to compile the source code. There are also other C compiler tools of MPLAB for programming 16 and 32 bit PIC microcontrollers (PIC24 and PIC32). However, only the C18 compiler is considered in this tutorial as it is the primary tool for programming the most commonly used PIC18 devices in the market (PIC18F4550, PIC18F2550, PIC18F4450 etc.).

**Microchip's C18 (v2.10)**

This appears to be Microchips first compiler and it kind of shows. They implemented their compiler a bit different than most compilers, in that they have separate pointers for program and data memory. This leads to a problem as shown below:

char data[]="hello world"; //data is in data memory and is initialized at program start up printf("hello world"); //this string is stored in program memory only printf(data);

This code will not work on C18 as that the first printf is passed a pointer to program memory and the second printf is passed a pointer to data memory. Thus most all string processing functions require two versions one where the string is in program memory and one where the string is in data memory. I also crashed the C18 compiler right out of the box by not ending my source code with a newline. I have also currently have crashed the C18 again, which I am waiting on a response from tech support as to why. For those of you planning to use v2.10 there are some bugs that no one tells you about, and they do know it. For example the stdarg.h is incorrect and you can work for hours like me trying to figure out why your printf function does not work, seems like they would release a 2.11 to fix it and save us time. I also found that their conversion utility from cof to cod has a limitation such that you can not have files in paths over 62 chars in length, I was informed that this would be fixed in future versions, but that does not help with your problems today.

### Technical Support

Microchip technical support is good, once you find the right people to email your questions and comments to. Do not expect much help from their phone support as they are generic for all of Microchip's products. Like all the others Microchip has a message board, which is fairly active but it also has a bad user interface, shows you old messages at the top and forcing you to scroll to the newer ones.

### Testing

Microchip informed me that their testing was done with Plum Hall's test suite.

### Libraries

You will hate that they do not include a printf statement, but I imagine they could not figure out how to get around the example above. I did finally figure out that you could using a custom linker script force all the rom constant data to be located in memory at a location higher than the end of data memory. Thus by checking the address of a pointer you could determine if it was a pointer to data in program or data memory.

## QUESTIONS

1. Draw and explain PIC18f microcontroller
2. Compare PIC 10 AND PIC 12.
3. Compare PIC 16 and PIC 18.
4. State the features of PIC 18 microcontroller.
5. What are the different types of registers used in PIC microcontroller.
6. What is stack? Why it is required.
7. Explain power down modes in PIC18f microcontroller with bit setting.
8. What are the different Input and output ports are used for peripheral support.
9. What are the different types of instructions are used in PIC18f microcontroller.
10. Describe MPLAB IDE.
11. Explain c18 compiler.

# Unit - IV
# REAL WORLD INTERFACING PART I

## 4.1 INTRODUCTION

Peripheral Interface Controllers (PIC) is one of the advanced microcontrollers developed by microchip technologies. These microcontrollers are widely used in modern electronics applications. A PIC controller integrates all type of advanced interfacing ports and memory modules. These controllers are more advanced than normal microcontroller like INTEL 8051. The first PIC chip was announced in 1975 (PIC1650).

As like normal microcontroller, the PIC chip also combines a microprocessor unit called CPU and is integrated with various types of memory modules (RAM, ROM, EEPROM ,etc), I/O ports, timers/counters, communication ports, etc.

All PIC microcontroller family uses Harvard architecture. This architecture has the program and data accessed from separate memories so the device has a program memory bus and a data memory bus (more than 8 lines in a normal bus). This improves the bandwidth (data throughput) over traditional von Neumann architecture where program and data are fetched from the same memory (accesses over the same bus). Separating program and data memory further allows instructions to be sized differently than the 8-bit wide data word. Embedded microcontrollers are a widely used technology in nearly all modern devices. Fewer electrical devices today are controlled by analog means and opt to instead operate digitally using microcontrollers that can be programmed to perform any number of tasks.

There are number of different types of microcontrollers for many different types of applications. The most familiar to the common person are the Intel processors that run a typical desktop computer; however, this paper focuses on the much smaller scale and more single-task oriented microcontrollers that operate devices such as a microwave, a radiator fan on a car, or servo motors used to move the handles on a foosball table.

One of the more popular and easier to use line of microcontroller products for such task oriented applications are the 8-bit PIC18 microcontrollers from Microchip, whom in 2006 have been ranked first in world-wide sales of 8-bit microcontrollers.

These MCUs (Microcontroller Units) offer a great price/performance ratio and use technology that has been proven to be very reliable and easy to develop with. The PIC18 family of MCUs from Microchip are some of the fastest and most feature loaded 8-bit PIC MCUs on the market, with a maximum clock speed of 40 MHz and 128 KB of Flash memory. These microcontrollers are small enough for many embedded applications, but also powerful enough to allow a lot of complexity and freedom in the design process of an embedded system.

Microchip Technology makes it easy to begin developing with their PIC18 MCUs through their various development tools and demonstrations boards.

The MPLAB Integrated Development Environment allows for a centralized interface between the programmer and all of Microchip Technology's devices. The MPLAB ICD 2 In-Circuit Debugger is the developer's most powerful and cost-efficient tool for low-cost real-time debugging of all PIC18 MCUs.

The PIC18 MCUs are programmed using a device-specific PIC assembly language, but using the MPLAB C18 compiler allows developers also to develop applications in C. Depending on the features necessary in the embedded design, various demonstration boards are offered by Microchip Technology that allow developers to realize and test their designs in a cost-effective manner before producing the final PCB for implementation.

Advantages are Small instruction set to learn, RISC architecture, Built in oscillator with selectable speeds, Easy entry level, in-circuit programming plus in circuit debugging PIC Kit units is cheaper. Inexpensive microcontrollers, Wide range of interfaces including $I^2C$, SPI, USB, USART, A/D, programmable comparators, PWM, LIN, CAN, PSP, and Ethernet.

Availability of processors in DIL package make them easy to handle for hobby use. Limitations are Only one accumulator, Register-bank switching is required to access the entire RAM of many devices, Operations and registers are not orthogonal; some instructions can address RAM and/or immediate constants, while others can use the accumulator only,

The following stack limitations have been addressed in the PIC18 series, but still apply to earlier cores. The hardware call stack is not addressable, so preemptive task switching cannot be implemented, Software implemented stacks are not efficient, so it is difficult to generate reentrant code and support local variables.

## 4.2 ARCHITECTURE OF PIC MICROCONTROLLER

| Device | Program FLASH | Data Memory | Data EEP ROM |
|---|---|---|---|
| PIC16F874 | 4K | 192 Bytes | 128 Bytes |
| PIC16F877 | 8K | 368 Bytes | 256 Bytes |

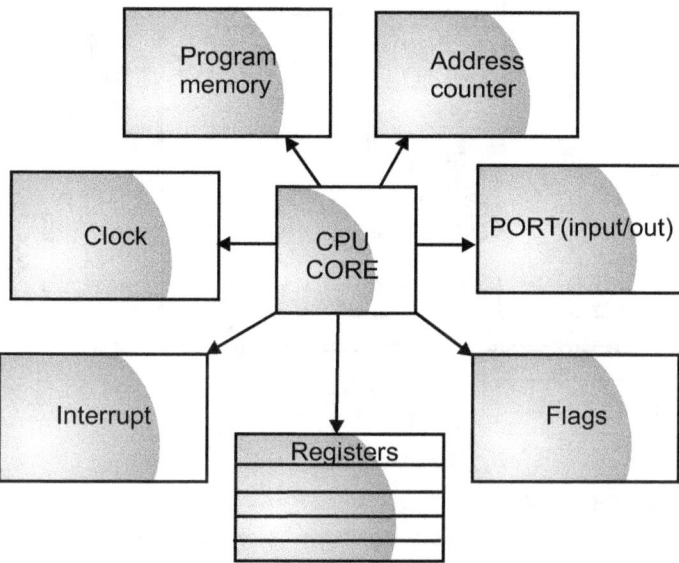

**Fig. 4.1 : Simple Architecture**

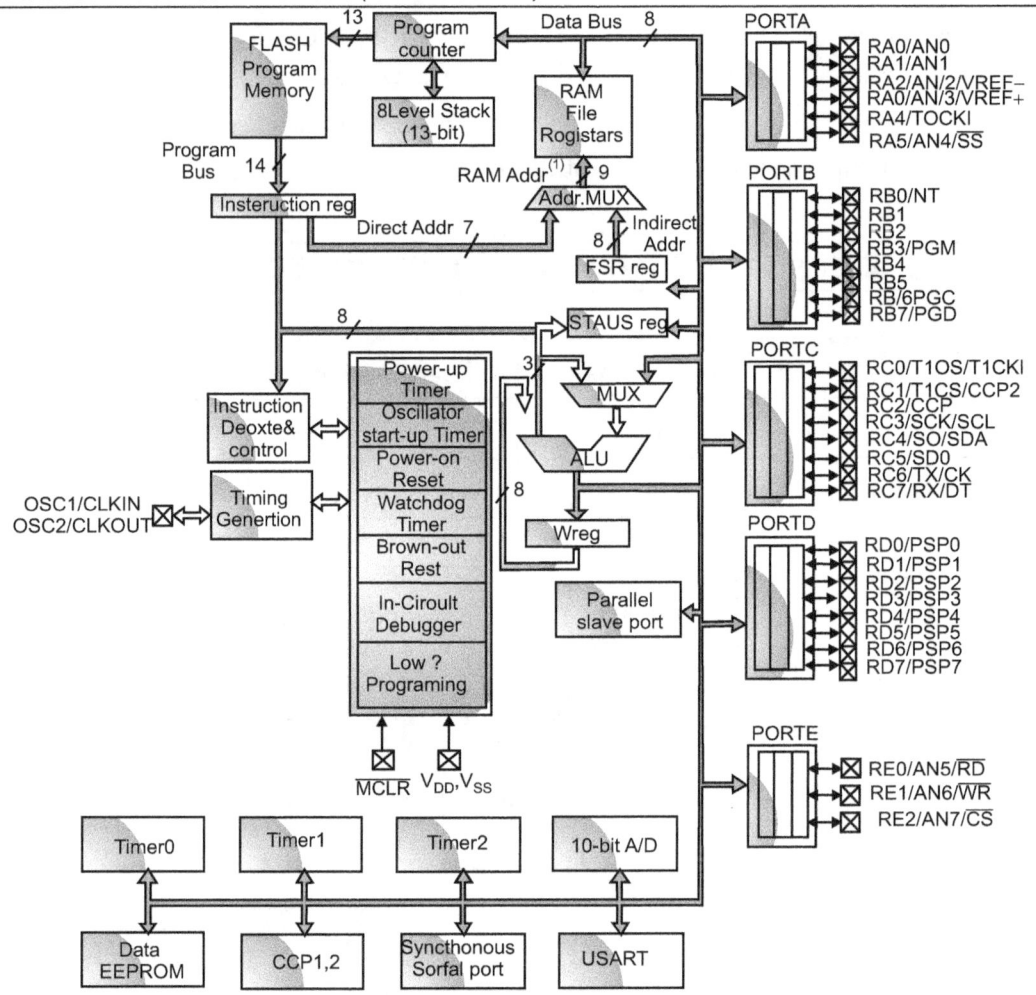

**Fig. 4.2 : Detailed Architecture**

## Central Processing Unit (CPU)

The function of CPU in PIC is same as a normal microcontroller CPU. A PIC CPU consists of several sub units such as instruction decoder, ALU, accumulator, control unit, etc. The CPU in PIC normally supports Reduced Instruction Set Computer (RISC) architecture (Reduced Instruction Set Computer (RISC), a type of microprocessor that focuses on rapid and efficient processing of a relatively small set of instructions. RISC design is based on the premise that most of the instructions a computer decodes and executes are simple. As a result, RISC architecture limits the number of instructions that are built into the microcontroller but optimizes each so it can be carried out very rapidly (usually within a single clock cycle.). These RISC structure gives the following advantages.

- The RISC structure only has 35 simple instructions as compared to others
- The execution time is same for most of the instructions (except very few numbers).
- The execution time required is very less (5 million instructions/second (approximately).

**Memory**

The memory in a PIC chip used to store the data and programs temporary or permanently. As like normal microcontrollers, the PIC chip also has certain amount of RAM, ROM, EEPROM, other flash memory, etc. ROM memory is used for permanent storage. The ROM memory also called as n program memory. A PI chip has certain amount of ROM memory. EEPROM memory is another category of ROM memory. The contents in the EEPROM changes during run time and at that time it acts like a RAM memory. But the difference is after the power goes off, the data remains in this ROM chip. This is the one of the special advantages of EEPROM. In the PIC chip the function of EPROM is to store the values created during the runtime. RAM memory is the one of the complex memory module in a PIC chip. This memory associated with various type of registers (special function registers and general purpose registers) and memory BANK modules (BANK 0, BANK 1, etc.). Once the power goes off, the contents in the RAM will be cleared. As like normal microcontrollers, the RAM memory is used to store temporary data and provide immediate results.

**Flash memory**

This is a special type of memory where READ, WRITE, and ERASE operations can be done many times. This type of memory was invented by INTEL corporation in 1980. A PIC Chip normally contains a certain amount of flash memory.

**Registers**

Information is stored in a CPU memory location called a register. Registers can be thought of as the CPU's tiny scratchpad, temporarily storing instructions or data. Registers basically classified into the following.

**(1) General Purpose Register (GPR)**

A general purpose register (or processor register) is a small storage area available on a CPU whose contents can be accessed more quickly than other storage that available on PIC. A general purpose register can store both data addresses simultaneously.

**(2) Special Function registers (SFR)**

These are also a part of RAM memory locations. As compared to GPR, their purpose is predetermined during the manufacturing time and cannot be changed by the user. It is only for special dedicated functions.

**Interrupts**

Interrupt is the temporary delay in a running program. These delays stop the current execution for a particular interval. This interval/delay is usually called as interrupt. When an interrupt request arrives into a current execution program, then it stops its regular execution. Interrupt can be performed by externally (hardware interrupt) or internally (by using software).

**Bus**

BUS is the communication or data transmission/reception path in a microcontroller unit. In a normal microcontroller chip, two types of buses are normally available.

**(1) Data bus**

Data bus is used for memory addressing. The function of data bus is interfacing all the circuitry components inside the PIC chip.

**(2) Address bus**

Address bus mostly used for memory addressing. The function of address bus is to transmit the address from the CPU to memory locations.

**USART or UART**

These ports are used for the transmission (TX) and reception (RX) of data. These transmissions possible with help of various digital data transceiver modules like RF, IR, Bluetooth, etc. This is the one of the simplest way to communicate the PIC chip with other devices.

**Oscillators**

Oscillator unit basically an oscillation/clock generating circuit which is used for providing proper clock pulses to the PIC chip. This clock pulses also helps the timing and counting applications. A PIC chip normally use various types of clock generators. According to the application and the type of PIC used, the oscillators and its frequencies may vary. RC (Resistor-Capacitor), LC (Inductor-Capacitor), RLC (Resistor-Inductor-capacitor), crystal oscillators, etc are the normal oscillators used with A PIC chip.

**STACK**

The entire PIC chip has an area for storing the return addresses. This area or unit called Stack is used in some Peripheral interface controllers. The hardware stack is not accessible by software. But for most of the controllers, it can be easily accessible.

**Input/output ports**

These ports are used for the interfacing various input/output devices and memories. According to the type of PIC, the number of ports may change.

**Advanced functioning blocks**

These sections include various advanced features of a PIC chip. According to the type of PIC, these features may change. Various advanced features in a peripheral interface controller are power up timer, oscillator start up timer, power on reset, watch dog timer, brown out reset, in circuit debugger, low voltage programming, voltage comparator, CCP modules etc.

## 4.3 LIMITATIONS OF PIC ARCHITECTURE

**Limitations of PIC Architecture**
- Peripheral Interface Controller has only one accumulator.
- Small instruction set.
- Register banking switch required to access RAM of other devices.
- Operations and registers are not orthogonal.
- Program memory is not accessible.

## 4.4 ADVANTAGES OF PIC CONTROLLED SYSTEM

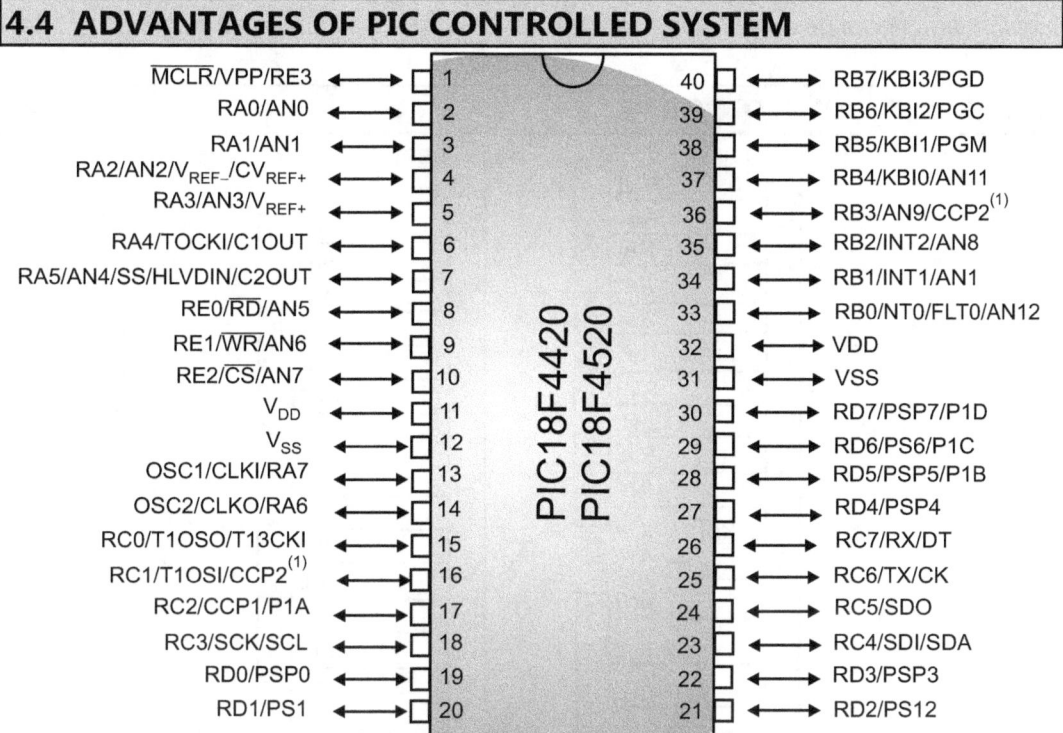

Fig. 4.3 : Pin Diagram of PIC18F

**Advantages of PIC Controlled System**

- **Reliability**

The PIC controlled system often resides machines that are expected to run continuously for many years without any error and in some cases recover by themselves if an error occurs(with help of supporting firmware).

- **Performance**

Many of the PIC based embedded system use a simple pipelined RISC processor for computation and most of them provide on-chip SRAM for data storage to improve the performance.

- **Power consumption**

A PIC controlled system operates with minimal power consumption without sacrificing performance. Power consumption can be reduced by independently and dynamically controlling multiple power platforms.

- **Memory**

Most of the PIC based systems are memory expandable and will help in easily adding more and more memory according to the usage and type of application. In small applications the inbuilt memory can be used.

## 4.5 INPUT OUTPUT PORTS

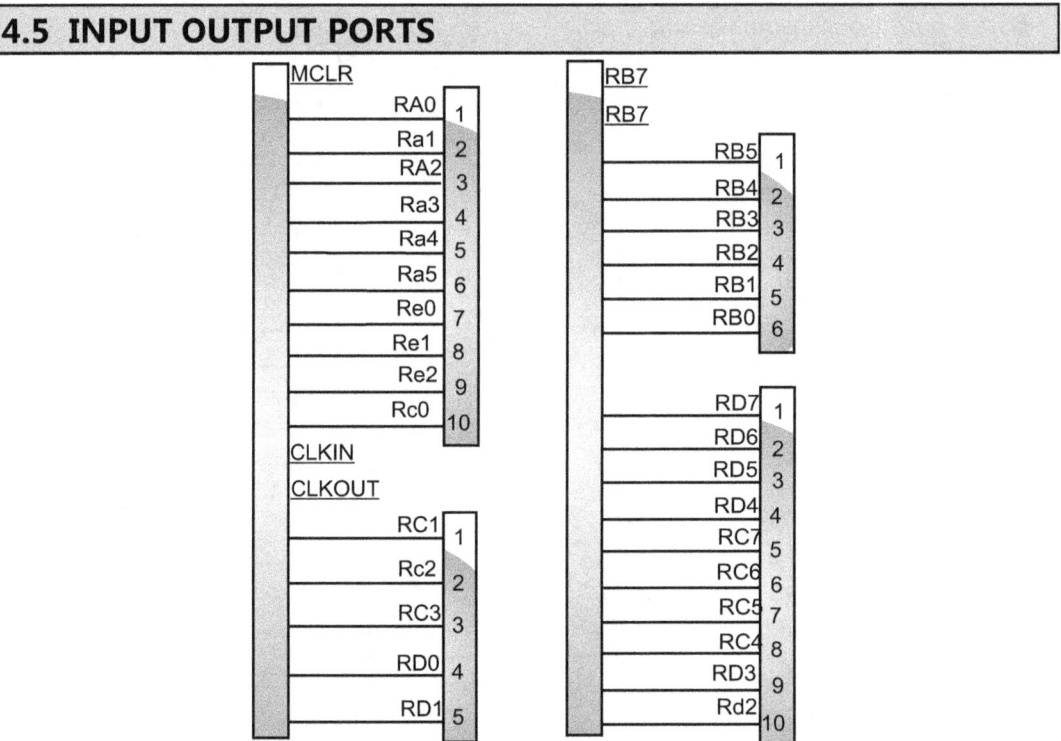

**Fig. 4.4 : I/O Ports**

One of the most important feature of the microcontroller is a number of input/output pins used for connection with peripherals. In this case, there are in total of thirty-five general purpose I/O pins available, which is quite enough for the most applications.

In order pins' operation can match internal 8-bit organization, all of them are, similar to registers, grouped into five so called ports denoted by A, B, C, D and E. They all have several features in common:

- For practical reasons, many I/O pins have two or three functions. If a pin is used as any other function, it may not be used as a general purpose input/output pin; and
- Every port has its "satellite", i.e. the corresponding TRIS register: TRISA, TRISB, TRISC etc. which determines performance, but not the contents of the port bits.

By clearing some bit of the TRIS register (bit=0), the corresponding port pin is configured as output. Similarly, by setting some bit of the TRIS register (bit=1), the corresponding port pin is configured as input. This rule is easy to remember 0 = Output, 1 = Input.

**Port A and TRISA Register**

Port A is an 8-bit wide, bidirectional port. Bits of the TRISA and ANSEL control the PORTA pins. All Port A pins act as digital inputs/outputs. Five of them can also be analog inputs (denoted as AN):

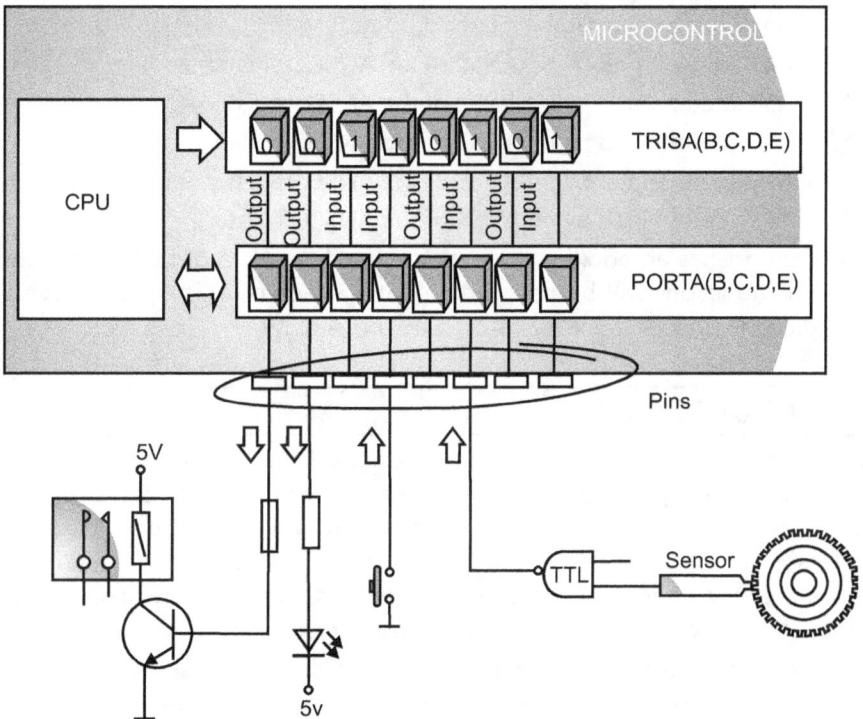

**Fig. 4.5 : Port A and TRISA Register**

| PORTA | R/W (x) RA7 bit7 | R/W (x) RA6 bit6 | R/W (x) RA5 bit5 | R/W (x) RA4 bit4 | R/W (x) RA3 bit3 | R/W (x) RA2 bit2 | R/W (x) RA1 bit1 | R/W (x) RA0 bit0 | Features Bit name |
|---|---|---|---|---|---|---|---|---|---|
| TRISA | R/W (1) TRISA7 bit7 | R/W (1) TRISA6 bit6 | R/W (1) TRISA5 bit5 | R/W (1) TRISA4 bit4 | R/W (1) TRISA3 bit3 | R/W (1) TRISA2 bit2 | R/W (1) TRISA1 bit1 | R/W (1) TRISA0 bit0 | Features Bit name |

Legend
R/W Readable/Wriable bit
(x) After reset, bit is unknown
(1) After reset, bit is set

**Fig. 4.6**

Similar to bits of the TRISA register which determine which of the pins will be configured as input and which as output, the appropriate bits of the ANSEL register determine whether the pins will act as analog inputs or digital inputs/outputs.

- RA0 = AN0 (determined by bit ANS0 of the ANSEL register);
- RA1 = AN1 (determined by bit ANS1 of the ANSEL register);
- RA2 = AN2 (determined by bit ANS2 of the ANSEL register);
- RA3 = AN3 (determined by bit ANS3 of the ANSEL register); and
- RA5 = AN4 (determined by bit ANS4 of the ANSEL register).

Each bit of this port has an additional function related to some of built-in peripheral units. These additional functions will be described in later chapters. This chapter covers only the RA0 pin's additional function since it is related to Port A only.

## 4.6 ULPWU UNIT

The microcontroller is commonly used in devices which have to operate periodically and, completely independently using a battery power supply. In such cases, minimal power consumption is one of the priorities. Typical examples of such applications are: thermometers, sensors for fire detection and similar. It is known that a reduction in clock frequency reduces the power consumption, so one of the most convenient solutions to this problem is to slow the clock down (use 32KHz quartz crystal instead of 20MHz).

Setting the microcontroller to sleep mode is another step in the same direction. However, even when both measures are applied, another problem arises. How to wake the microcontroller and set it to normal mode. It is obviously necessary to have an external signal to change logic state on some of the pins. Thus, the problem still exists. This signal must be generated by additional electronics, which causes higher power consumption of the entire device. The ideal solution would be the microcontroller wakes up periodically by itself, which is not impossible at all. The circuit which enables that is shown in figure on the right.

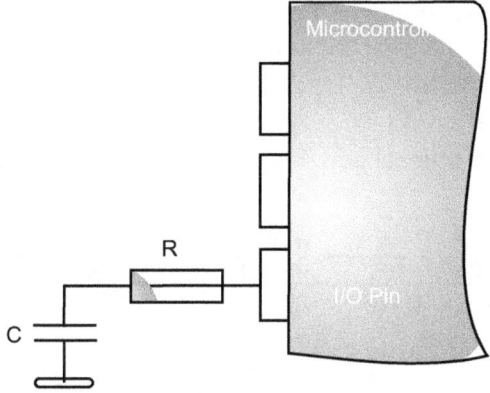

Fig. 4.7

**The principle of operation is simple:**

A pin is configured as output and logic one (1) is brought to it. That causes the capacitor to be charged. Immediately after this, the same pin is configured as an input. The change of logic state enables an interrupt and the microcontroller is set to *Sleep* mode. Afterwards, there is nothing else to be done except wait for the capacitor to discharge by the leakage current flowing out through the input pin. When it occurs, an interrupt takes place and the microcontroller continues with the program execution in normal mode. The whole sequence is repeated...

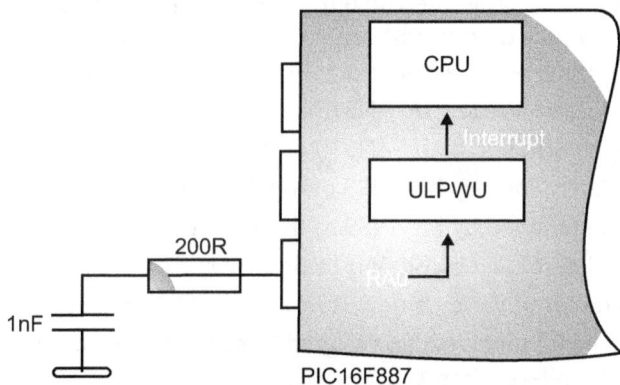

Fig. 4.8 : ULPWU Unit

Theoretically, this is a perfect solution. The problem is that all pins able to cause an interrupt in this way are digital and have relatively large leakage current when their voltage is not close to the limit values Vdd (1) or Vss (0). In this case, the capacitor is discharged for a short time since the current amounts to several hundreds of microamperes. This is why the ULPWU circuit able to register slow voltage drops with ultra low power consumption was designed. Its output generates an interrupt, while its input is connected to one of the microcontroller pins. It is the RA0 pin. Referring to Fig. 3-4 (R=200 ohms, C=1nF), discharge time is approximately 30mS, while the total consumption of the microcontroller is 1000 times lower (several hundreds of nanoamperes).

### Port B and TRISB Register

Port B is an 8-bit wide, bidirectional port. Bits of the TRISB register determine the function of its pins.

| | R/W (x) | R/W (x) | R/W (x) | R/W (x) | R/W (x) | R/W (x) | R/W (x) | R/W (x) | Features |
|---|---|---|---|---|---|---|---|---|---|
| PORTB | RB7 | RB6 | RB5 | RB4 | RB3 | RB2 | RB1 | RB0 | Bit name |
| | bit7 | bit6 | bit5 | bit4 | bit3 | bit2 | bit1 | bit0 | |

| | R/W (1) | R/W (1) | R/W (1) | R/W (1) | R/W (1) | R/W(1) | R/W (1) | R/W (1) | Features |
|---|---|---|---|---|---|---|---|---|---|
| TRISB | TRISB7 | TRISB6 | TRISB5 | TRISB4 | TRISB3 | TRISB2 | TRISB1 | TRISB0 | Bit name |
| | bit7 | bit6 | bit5 | bit4 | bit3 | bit2 | bit1 | bit0 | |

Legend
- Bit is Unimplemented
- R/W Readable/Wriable bit
- (x) After reset, bit is unknown
- (1) After reset, bit is set

**Fig. 4.9 : Sleep Mode : Port B and TRISB register**

Similar to Port A, a logic one (1) in the TRISB register configures the appropriate port pin as input and vice versa. Six pins on this port can act as analog inputs (AN). The bits of the ANSELH register determine whether these pins act as analog inputs or digital inputs/outputs:

- RB0 = AN12 (determined by bit ANS12 of the ANSELH register);
- RB1 = AN10 (determined by bit ANS10 of the ANSELH register);
- RB2 = AN8 (determined by bit ANS8 of the ANSELH register);
- RB3 = AN9 (determined by bit ANS9 of the ANSELH register);
- RB4 = AN11 (determined by bit ANS11 of the ANSELH register); and
- RB5 = AN13 (determined by bit ANS13 of the ANSELH register).

Each Port B pin has an additional function related to some of the built-in peripheral units, which will be explained in later chapters.

- All the port pins have built in *pull-up* resistor, which make them ideal for connection to push-buttons, switches and optocouplers. In order to connect these resistors to the microcontroller ports, the appropriate bit of the WPUB register should be set.*

| Features Bit name | R/W (1) | R/W (1) | R/W (1) | R/W (1) | R/W (1) | R/W(1) | R/W (1) | R/W (1) |
|---|---|---|---|---|---|---|---|---|
| WPUB | WPUB7 | WPUB6 | WPUB5 | WPUB4 | WPUB3 | WPUB2 | WPUB1 | WPUB0 |
| | bit7 | bit6 | bit5 | bit4 | bit3 | bit2 | bit1 | bit0 |

Legend
R/W Readable/Wriable bit
(1) After reset, bit is set

**Fig. 4. 10 :WPUB register**

Having a high level of resistance (several tens of kilo ohms), these "virtual" resistors do not affect pins configured as outputs, but serves as a useful complement to inputs. As such, they are connected to CMOS logic circuit inputs. Otherwise, they would act as if they are floating because of their high input resistance.

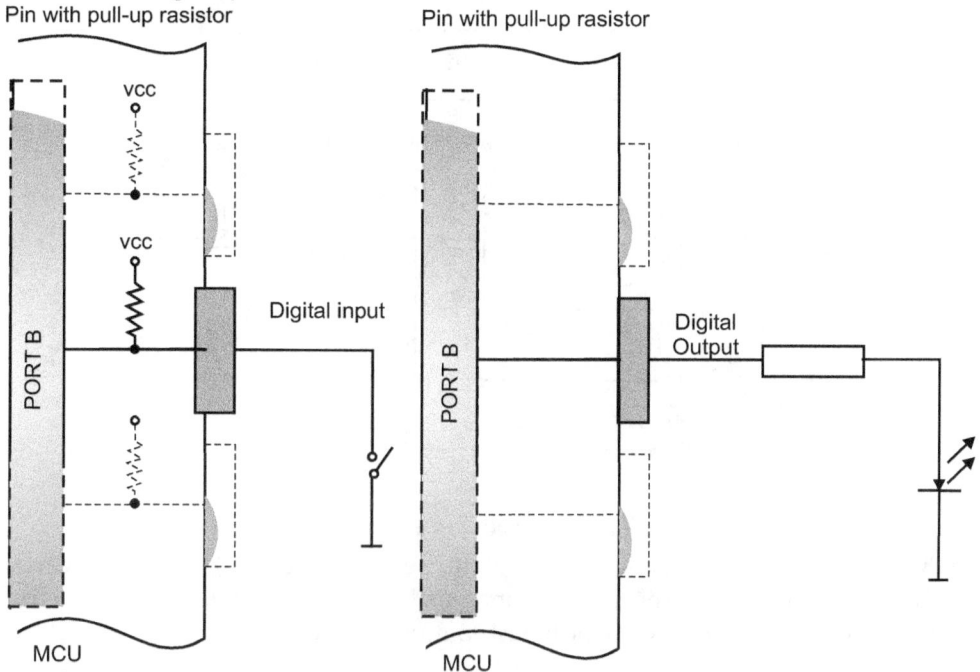

**Fig. 4.11 : Pull-up resistors**

* Apart from the bits of the WPUB register, there is another bit affecting pull-up resistors installation. It is RBPU bit of the OPTION_REG. It is a general-purpose bit because it affects installation of all Port resistors.

- If enabled, each Port B bit configured as an input may cause an interrupt by changeing its logic state. In order to enable pins to cause an interrupt, the appropriate bit of the IOCB register should be set.

| IOCB | R/W (0)<br>IOCB7<br>bit7 | R/W (0)<br>IOCB6<br>bit6 | R/W (0)<br>IOCB5<br>bit5 | R/W (0)<br>IOCB4<br>bit4 | R/W (0)<br>IOCB3<br>bit3 | R/W(0)<br>IOCB2<br>bit2 | R/W (0)<br>IOCB1<br>bit1 | R/W (0)<br>IOCB0<br>bit0 | Features<br>Bit name |
|---|---|---|---|---|---|---|---|---|---|

Legend
R/W Readable/Wriable bit
(0) After reset, bit is cleared

**Fig. 4.12 : IOCB register**

Because of these features, the port B pins are commonly used for checking push-buttons on the keyboard because they unerringly register any button press. Therefore, there is no need to "scan" these inputs all the time.

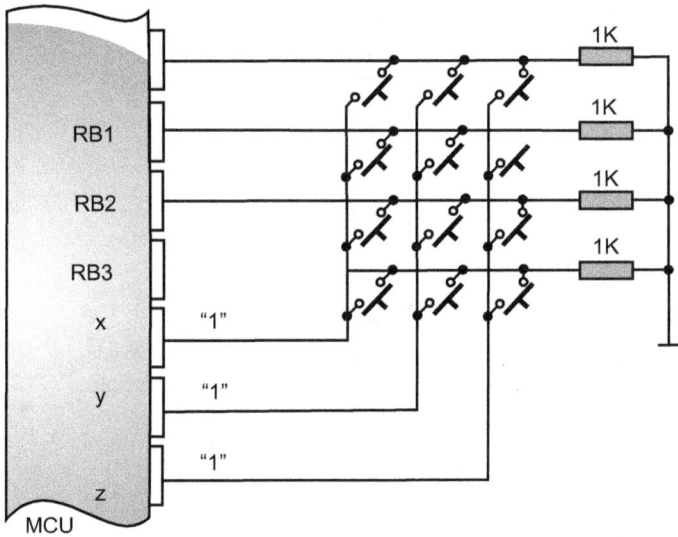

**Fig. 4.13 : Keyboard Example**

When the X, Y and Z pins are configured as outputs set to logic one (1), it is only necessary to wait for an interrupt request which arrives upon any button press. By combining zeros and units on these outputs it is checked which push-button is pressed.

### Pin RB0/INT

The RB0/INT pin is a single "true" external interrupt source. It can be configured to react to signal raising edge (zero-to-one transition) or signal falling edge (one-to-zero transition). The INTEDG bit of the OPTION_REG register selects the signal.

### RB6 and RB7 Pins

You have probably noticed that the PIC16F887 microcontroller does not have any special pins for programming (writing the program to ROM). The Ports pins available as general purpose I/O pins during normal operation are used for this purpose (Port B pins clock (RB6) and data transfer (RB7) during program loading). In addition, it is necessary to apply a power supply voltage Vdd (5V) and Vss (0V), as well as voltage for FLASH memory programming Vpp (12-14V). During programming, Vpp voltage is applied to the MCLR pin. All details concerning this process, as well as which one of these voltages is applied first, are beside the point, the programmers electronics are in charge of that. The point is that the program can be loaded to the microcontroller even when it is soldered onto the target device. Normally, the loaded program can also be changed in the same way. This function is called ICSP (In-Circuit Serial Programming). It is necessary to plan ahead when using it.

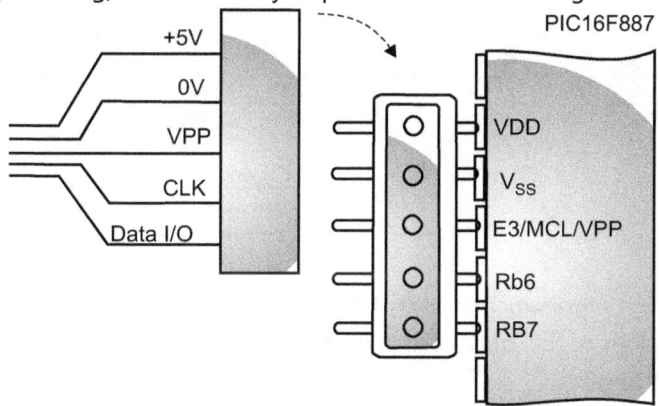

**Fig. 4.14**

It is not complicated at all! It is only necessary to install a 4-pin connector onto the target device so that the necessary programmer voltages may be applied to the microcontroller. In order that these voltages don't interfere with other device electronics, design some sort of circuit breaking into this connection (using resistors or jumpers).

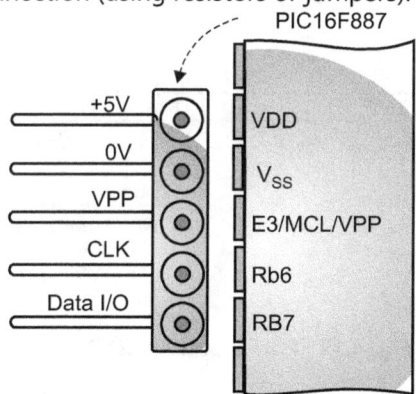

**Fig. 4.15 : 3-10 ICSP Connection**

These voltages are applied to socket pins in which the microcontroller is to be placed.

## Port C and TRISC Register

Port C is an 8-bit wide, bidirectional port. Bits of the TRISC Register determine the function of its pins. Similar to other ports, a logic one (1) in the TRISC Register configures the appropriate port pin as an input.

| | R/W (x) | R/W (x) | R/W (x) | R/W (x) | R/W (x) | R/W (x) | R/W (x) | R/W (x) | Features |
|---|---|---|---|---|---|---|---|---|---|
| PORTC | RC7 | RC6 | RC5 | RC4 | RC3 | RC2 | RC1 | RC0 | Bit name |
| | bit7 | bit6 | bit5 | bit4 | bit3 | bit2 | bit1 | bit0 | |

| | R/W (1) | R/W (1) | R/W (1) | R/W (1) | R/W (1) | R/W(1) | R/W (1) | R/W (1) | Features |
|---|---|---|---|---|---|---|---|---|---|
| TRISC | TRISC7 | TRISC6 | TRISC5 | TRISC4 | TRISC3 | TRISC2 | TRISC1 | TRISC0 | Bit name |
| | bit7 | bit6 | bit5 | bit4 | bit3 | bit2 | bit1 | bit0 | |

**Legend**
R/W Readable/Wriable bit
(x) After reset, bit is unknown
(1) After reset, bit is set

**Fig. 4.16 : Programmer On-Board Connections - Port C and TRISC Register**

All additional functions of this port's bits will be explained later.

## Port D and TRISD Register

Port D is an 8-bit wide, bidirectional port. Bits of the TRISD register determine the function of its pins. A logic one (1) in the TRISD register configures the appropriate port pin as input.

| | R/W (x) | R/W (x) | R/W (x) | R/W (x) | R/W (x) | R/W (x) | R/W (x) | R/W (x) | Features |
|---|---|---|---|---|---|---|---|---|---|
| PORTD | RD7 | RD6 | RD5 | RD4 | RD3 | RD2 | RD1 | RD0 | Bit name |
| | bit7 | bit6 | bit5 | bit4 | bit3 | bit2 | bit1 | bit0 | |

| | R/W (1) | R/W (1) | R/W (1) | R/W (1) | R/W (1) | R/W(1) | R/W (1) | R/W (1) | Features |
|---|---|---|---|---|---|---|---|---|---|
| TRISD | TRISD7 | TRISD6 | TRISD5 | TRISD4 | TRISD3 | TRISD2 | TRISD1 | TRISD0 | Bit name |
| | bit7 | bit6 | bit5 | bit4 | bit3 | bit2 | bit1 | bit0 | |

**Legend**
R/W Readable/Wriable bit
(x) After reset, bit is unknown
(1) After reset, bit is set

**Fig. 4.17 : Port D and TRISD Register**

## Port E and TRISE Register

Port E is a 4-bit wide, bidirectional port. The TRISE register's bits determine the function of its pins. Similar to other ports, a logic one (1) in the TRISE register configures the appropriate port pin as input. The exception is RE3 which is input only and its TRIS bit is always read as '1'.

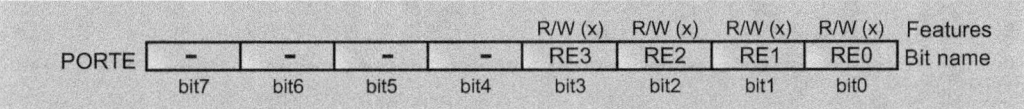

Fig. 4.18 : Port E and TRISE Register

Similar to Ports A and B, three pins can be configured as analog inputs in this case. The ANSELH register bits determine whether a pin will act as analog input (AN) or digital input/output:

- RE0 = AN5 (determined by bit ANS5 of the ANSELregister);
- RE1 = AN6 (determined by bit ANS6 of the ANSELregister); and
- RE2 = AN7 (determined by bit ANS7 of the ANSELregister).

**ANSEL and ANSELH Registers**

The ANSEL and ANSELH registers are used to configure the input mode of an I/O pin to analog or digital.

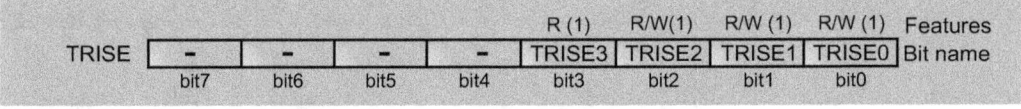

```
                            R/W (x)  R/W (x)  R/W (x)  R/W (x)  Features
PORTE  [ -  |  -  |  -  |  - | RE3  |  RE2  |  RE1  |  RE0 ]  Bit name
        bit7  bit6  bit5  bit4  bit3   bit2    bit1    bit0


                            R (1)   R/W(1)   R/W (1)  R/W (1)  Features
TRISE  [ -  |  -  |  -  |  - |TRISE3|TRISE2 | TRISE1| TRISE0]  Bit name
        bit7  bit6  bit5  bit4  bit3   bit2    bit1    bit0
```

Legend
-    Bit is Unimplemented
- R/W   Readable/Wriable bit
- (x)   After reset, bit is unknown
- (1)   After reset, bit is set

**Fig. 4.19 : ANSEL and ANSELH Registers**

The rule is: To configure a pin as an analog input, the appropriate bit of the ANSEL or ANSELH registers must be set (1). To configure pin as digital input/output, the appropriate bit must be cleared (0).

The state of the ANSEL bits has no affect on digital output functions. The result of any attempt to read some port pin configured as analog input will be 0.

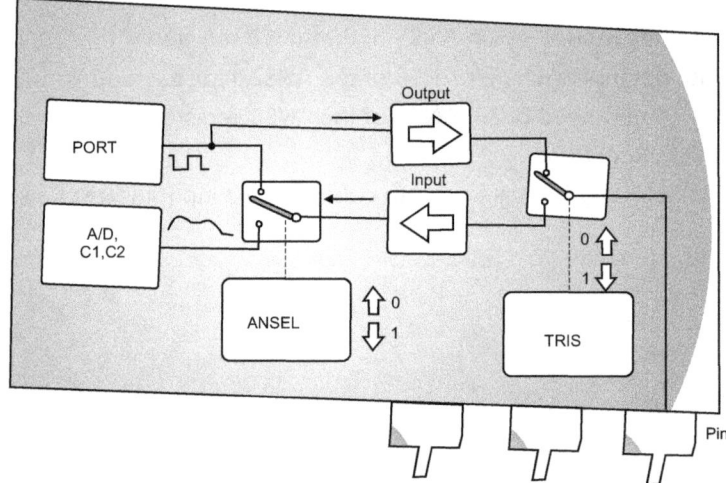

**Fig. 4.20 : ANSEL and ANSELH Configuration**

- When designing a device, select a port through which the microcontroller will communicate to the peripheral environment. If you intend using only digital inputs/outputs, select any port you want. If you intend using some of the analog inputs, select the appropriate ports supporting such pins configuration (AN0-AN13);

- Each port pin may be configured as either input or output. Bits of the TRISA, TRISB, TRISC, TRISD and TRISE registers determine how the appropriate ports pins- PORTA, PORTB, PORTC, PORTD and PORTE will act;
- If you use some of the analog inputs, set the appropriate bits of the ANSEL and ANSELH registers at the beginning of the program;
- If you use switches and push-buttons as input signal source, connect them to Port B pins because they have pull-up resistors. The use of these resistors is enabled by the RBPU bit of the OPTION_REG register, whereas the installation of individual resistors is enabled by bits of the WPUB register; and
- It is usually necessary to react as soon as input pins change their logic state. However, it is not necessary to write a program for changing pins' logic state. It is far simpler to connect such inputs to the PORTB pins and enable the interrupt on every voltage change. Bits of the registers IOCOB and INTCON are in charge of that.

## 4.7 PIC INTERRUPT STRUCTURE OF PIC18F

Interrupts are common features in almost all processor family, be it old 8051, AVR, PIC, ARM or the x86 used in desktops. So their in depth and clear knowledge is required for successful system software engineers. This guide will explain the interrupt system in general and their application using PIC18 architecture. We will also learn about handling of interrupts in HI-TECH C for PIC18.

Interrupts, as the name suggests *interrupts* the normal execution and Requests and urgent attention of CPU. Interrupts are situations that the CPU can't predict when they will happen, they can happen any time, so the CPU does not wait for them. So the CPU keeps on doing its normal job unless and interrupt occurs.

For example when the USART (Serial Communication Hardware) will receive data is unknown, it can receive data any time. So the CPU keeps on doing its normal job, which may be for example read temperature using LM35 sensor and display on LCD. The CPU keeps on doing the "normal" job, but as soon as the USART receive data it informs the CPU using an interrupt.

The CPU save its current state (so that it can resume), and jumps to the ISR (interrupt service routine) immediately. Where we can process the command or put it in a FIFO queue (to process latter). The ISR is generally kept very small and fast. As soon as the ISR ends, the CPU restores its saved state and resumes where it left. In this way CPU does not missed any data byte.

**Example of sources of Interrupts in PIC18 (also common in other MCUs)**

- **External Interrupts** : They are named INTx (like INT0, INT1 etc), they provide a means for external hardware to generate interrupts. Like if you connect a touchscreen controller to your PIC MCU. Then the touchscreens

PENINT (pen interrupt) can be connected to INT0 (or any other INTx). Then when ever the pen (or stylus) touches the screen it will interrupt the CPU. This interrupt will be explained in details in its own tutorial.

- **TIMER Interrupts :** They are also very common in MCUs. Today's MCUs comes with very sophisticated timers that can do lots of magic for you. They have they related interrupts. In most simple situation they can act like alarm clocks that can interrupt the CPU at predefined intervals. If you toggle a i/o pin in response to these alarms (interrupts), what you have is a frequency generator! For
more info on timers on PIC18, read this article.

- **Analog to Digital Converter Interrupts :** A/D Converter takes some time to complete its operation. So the CPU can either wait for it to complete or set up an AD conversion complete interrupt. In the latter case CPU can do other tasks while A/D converter converts the input. As soon as A/D converter completes its job it will inform CPU to read the value from its buffer. For more info on A/D Converter of PIC18, read this article.

- **Data Interrupts :** MCUs have many different types of data i/o engines, like USART, SPI, I2C, Parallel etc. They can also interrupt the CPU when data transmission is complete or data arrives from external source. Like an RFID reader send a packet because a user just brought his or her card near the reader. Or the GSM module detected an incoming call.

### How interrupts are managed?

In general each interrupt source have following related bits.

- **Enable Bit** – The are suffixed with IE (Interrupt Enable) example TMR0IE stands for TIMER0 Interrupt Enable. It can be used to enable/disable the related interrupt. When set to '1' it enables the interrupt.
- **Flag Bit** – It is set automatically by the related hardware when the interrupt condition occurs. It is generally suffixed with IF (Interrupt Fag). When it is set to '1' we know that interrupt has occurred. For example when TMR0IF is set by TIMER0, it indicates that TIMER0 has overflowed.
- **Priority Bit -** We can leave this for now to keep things simple. We won't be using interrupt priority feature of PIC18.

In global level their are following bits to control the interrupts globally.

- **GIE** – Global Interrupt Enable, enables/disables interrupts globally.
- **PEIE** – Enable/disable all peripheral interrupts.

## 4.8 INTERRUPT VECTOR

Address is 0008(hex). CPU jumps to this address for any interrupt. The ISR or Interrupt service routine is placed in this address. The ISR must determine the source of interrupt from the flag bit(described above).

```
1   //Main Interrupt Service Routine (ISR)
2   void interrupt ISR()
3   {
4     //Check if it is TMR0 Overflow ISR
5     if(TMR0IE && TMR0IF)
6     {
7       //TMR0 Overflow ISR
8
9       counter++;//Increment Over Flow Counter
10
11      if(counter==76)
12      {
13        //Toggle RB1 (LED)
14        if(RB1==0)
15          RB1=1;
16        else
17          RB1=0;
18
19        counter=0; //Reset Counter
20      }
21
22      //Clear Flag
23      TMR0IF=0;
24    }
25  }
```

In above code *void interrupt ISR()* is the main service routine where the CPU jumps for any interrupt (TIMER,A/D, INTx etc). As soon as we enter the ISR we check for the source of interrupt. This done using the line if(TMR0IE && TMR0IF). The above line check is the source of interrupt was TIMER0 (so it checks ifTMR0IF is set or not). It also checks TMR0IE (TIMER0 interrupt enable bit) to make sure this interrupt is enabled or not. It execute the TIMER0 ISR only of both the condition are true. One more line on interest is line 23 where we clear the flag, this is necessary otherwise the interrupt is triggered again.

You should note one more point the GIE (explained above) is cleared automatically when PIC18 enters ISR, this make sure that interrupts cannot be interrupted them self. It also automatically sets GIE on return from interrupt, which re enable interrupts.

In the above code (from line 9 to 20), you can see that for each overflow of timer (like alarm from an alarm clock) we increment a counter and as soon as this counter reaches 76 we toggle an LED. And also clear the counter (line 19). This gives us a LED that is toggled ever 1sec. So you see that LED is controlled fully by the TIMER while CPU can keep on doing other jobs but LED will always blink at its predefined rate. This example give a kind of illustration of multitasking, the LED take care of itself. You don't have to write anything on the main() function to control the LED. Your main function could go on normally, for example control a line follower robot. The TIMER will take care of the LED and toggle it every second. The LED could be used for decoration of the robot.

## 4.9 HANDLING INTERRUPT IN C

**Handling interrupt in C**

Here I will show you how we can write programs in HI-TECH C that utilizes interrupt feature of PIC MCU. The interrupt handling is very clean and straightforward in HI-TECH C (as compare to Microchip C18 Compiler). Please note that interrupt handling is not a standard feature of C language, so their is significant diffence between different compiler in handling interrupts. Please note that to simplify the situation, we are not using interrupt priority feature of PIC18(because this is a guide for first time user of interrupt). In HI-TECH C for PIC18 an ISR (interrupt service routine, that is called when interrupt condition occur) is defined like this void interrupt Function Name(void) as you can see in above code line the *"interrupt"* function qualifier is used to mark a function as ISR. The following point must be kept in mind while defining an ISR :-

1. The return type of ISR must always be *void*.
2. It must not take any parameters. That's why argument list is set to *void*.
3. The name of function can be any valid C function name. But I generally use the name ISR for ISRs.
4. Their can be at most one ISR function. (Two if using interrupt priority).

**C Program for TIMER0 Interrupt.**

The following is a simple program that demonstrate use of interrupts. The program is very simple so does not do any magic but only teaches use of interrupt. Please go through the program very carefully to check out how every feature described above are used. To understand the program you also need some knowledge of TIMER0 which is described in detail in the following article.

The program blinks a LED on RB1.

```
1   /*******************************************************************
2
3   A simple example to demonstrate the use of PIC Timers. In this
4   example the TIMER0 is configured as follows.
5
6   *8 Bit Mode
7   *Clock Source from Prescaler
8   *Prescaler = FCPU/256 (Note: FCPU= Fosc/4)
9   *Over flow INT enabled
10
11  As our FCPU=20MHz/4 (We are running from 20MHz XTAL)
12  =5MHz
13
14  Time Period = 0.2uS
15  Prescaller Period = 0.2 x 256 = 51.2uS
16  Overflow Period   = 51.2 x 256 = 13107.2 uS
17                    = 0.0131072 sec
18
19  So we need 1/0.0131072 Over Flows to count for 1 sec
20  = 76.2939 Overflows
21
22  So we keep a counter to keep track of overflows.
23
24  When an over flow occurs the PIC jumps to ISR where we
25  increment counter. And when counter becomes 76 we toggle
26  RB1 pin. This pin is connected to LED. Therefore we
27  have a LED which is ON for 1 sec and Off for 1sec.
28
29
30  Target Chip: PIC18F4520
```

```
31    Target Compiler: HI-TECH C For PIC18
32    Project: MPLAP Project File
33
34
41   NO PART OF THIS WORK CAN BE COPIED, DISTRIBUTED OR PUBLISHED WITHOUT A
42    WRITTEN PERMISSION FROM EXTREME ELECTRONICS INDIA. THE LIBRARY, NOR ANY PART
43    OF IT CAN BE USED IN COMMERCIAL APPLICATIONS. IT IS INTENDED TO BE USED FOR
44
45
46
47    **********************************************************************/
48
49    #include <htc.h>
50
51
52    //Chip Settings
53    __CONFIG(1,0x0200);
54    __CONFIG(2,0X1E1F);
55    __CONFIG(3,0X8100);
56    __CONFIG(4,0X00C1);
57    __CONFIG(5,0XC00F);
58
59    unsigned char counter=0;//Overflow counter
60
61    void main()
62    {
63      //Setup Timer0
64      T0PS0=1; //Prescaler is divide by 256
65      T0PS1=1;
66      T0PS2=1;
67
```

```
68      PSA=0;      //Timer Clock Source is from Prescaler
69
70      T0CS=0;     //Prescaler gets clock from FCPU (5MHz)
71
72      T08BIT=1;   //8 BIT MODE
73
74      TMR0IE=1;   //Enable TIMER0 Interrupt
75      PEIE=1;     //Enable Peripheral Interrupt
76      GIE=1;      //Enable INTs globally
77
78      TMR0ON=1;   //Now start the timer!
79
80      //Set RB1 as output because we have LED on it
81      TRISB&=0B11111101;
82
83      while(1);   //Sit Idle Timer will do every thing!
84    }
85
86    //Main Interrupt Service Routine (ISR)
87    void interrupt ISR()
88    {
89      //Check if it is TMR0 Overflow ISR
90      if(TMR0IE && TMR0IF)
91      {
92        //TMR0 Overflow ISR
93        counter++; //Increment Over Flow Counter
94
95        if(counter==76)
96        {
97          //Toggle RB1 (LED)
98          if(RB1==0)
99            RB1=1;
100         else
```

```
101         RB1=0;
102
103         counter=0; //Reset Counter
104     }
105     //Clear Flag
106     TMR0IF=0;
107   }
108 }
```

**Program Walk through**

- **Line 64 to 72 :** Configure the TIMER0. See tutorial on timer for more info.
- **Line 74 to 76 :** Enables Timer0 interrupt (TMR0IE=1), peripheral interrupt (PEIE=1) and finally sets GIE=1 to enable interrupts.
- **Line 83 :** The program has noting to do, so we enter an infinite loop and burn CPU cycles. Your program is free to to any tasks after interrupts are set up and enabled. We required ISR will automatically called by the hardware to service the situation. As as soon as service is complete, normal execution will be resumed.
- **Line 87 :** define the ISR.
- **Line 90 :** Checks if it is the timer interrupt (by checking the flag bit TMR0IF) and if the timer interrupts are enabled (by checking TMR0IE).
- **Line 91 to 104 :** is the service routine of TIMER0 interrupt.
- **Line 106 :** clears the timer interrupt flag, this step is very important before exiting the ISR or it will be called again!

## 4.10 INTERFACING TIMER WITH PIC18F

The timers of the PIC16F887 microcontroller can be briefly described in only one sentence. There are three completely independent timers/counters marked as TMR0, TMR1 and TMR2. But it's not as simple as that.

### 4.10.1 Timer TMR0

The timer TMR0 has a wide range of applications in practice. Very few programs don't use it in some way. It is very convenient and easy to use for writing programs or subroutines for generating pulses of arbitrary duration, time measurement or counting external pulses (events) with almost no limitations.

The timer TMR0 module is an 8-bit timer/counter with the following features:

- 8-bit timer/counter;

- 8-bit prescaler (shared with Watchdog timer);
- Programmable internal or external clock source;
- Interrupt on overflow; and
- Programmable external clock edge selection.

Figure 4-1 below represents the timer TMR0 schematic with all bits which determine its operation. These bits are stored in the OPTION_REG Register.

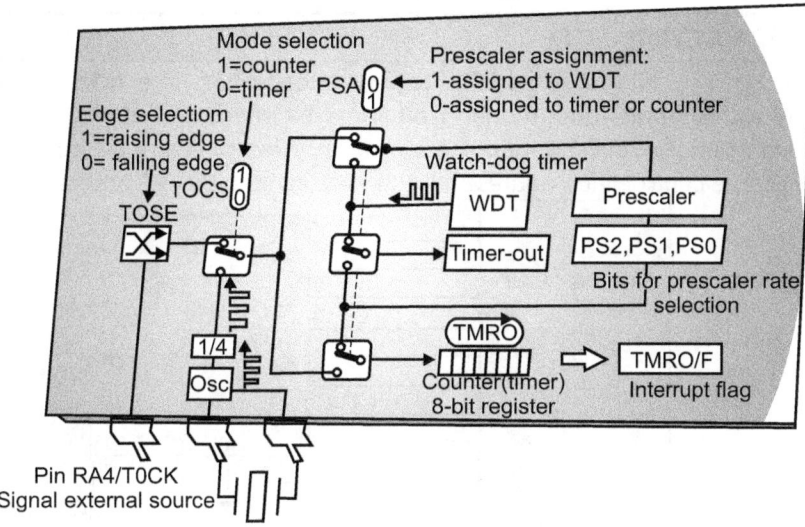

**Fig. 4.21 : Timer TMR0**

## OPTION_REG Register

- **RBPU - PORTB Pull-up enable bit**
    - 1 - PORTB pull-up resistors are disabled; and
    - 0 - PORTB pins can be connected to pull-up resistors.
- **INTEDG - Interrupt Edge Select bit**
    - 1 - Interrupt on rising edge of INT pin (0-1); and
    - 0 - Interrupt on falling edge of INT pin (1-0).
- **T0CS - TMR0 Clock Select bit**
    - 1 - Pulses are brought to TMR0 timer/counter input through the RA4 pin; and
    - 0 - Internal cycle clock (Fosc/4).
- **T0SE - TMR0 Source Edge Select bit**
    - 1 - Increment on high-to-low transition on TMR0 pin; and
    - 0 - Increment on low-to-high transition on TMR0 pin.

- **PSA - Prescaler Assignment bit**
  - 1 - Prescaler is assigned to the WDT; and
  - 0 - Prescaler is assigned to the TMR0 timer/counter.
- **PS2, PS1, PS0 - Prescaler Rate Select bit**

Prescaler rate is adjusted by combining these bits
As seen in the table 4-1, the same combination of bits gives different prescaler rate for

## 4.11 INTERFACING LCD

Fig. 1 shows how to interface the **LCD to microcontroller**. The **2x16 character LCD interface card** with supports both modes 4-bit and 8-bit interface, and also facility to adjust contrast through trim pot. In 8-bit interface 11 lines needed to create 8-bit interface; 8 data bits (D0 – D7), three control lines, address bit (RS), read/write bit (R/W) and control signal (E).

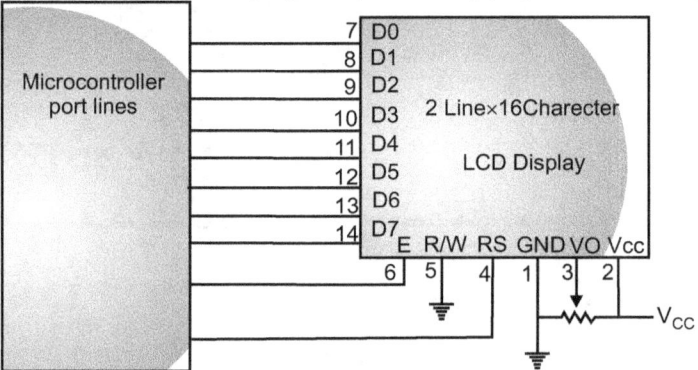

**Fig. 4.22 : Interfacing LCD to Microcontroller**

**Interfacing LCD with PIC16F877A**

We now want to display a text in **PIC16F/18F Evaluation Board** by using **LCD module**. In **PIC16F/18F Evaluation Board** contains the **LCD** connections in a single header.

The **PIC16F/18F Evaluation board** has eleven numbers of **LCD** connections, connected with I/O Port lines (PORTE.0 – PORTE.3 && PORTD.0 – PORTD.7) to make **LCD** display.

**Pin Assignment with PIC16F877A**

|  | GLCD/LCD | PIC16F/18F | LCD \| 128x64 GLCD Selection |
|---|---|---|---|
| **CONTROL L LINES** | RS | PORTE.0 | |
|  | R/W | PORTE.1 | |
|  | E | PORTE.2 | **This is a 16 line LCD Display** |
| **LCD –** | DB0 | PORTD.0 | |

MICROCONTROLLER & APPLICATION (TE E&TC SEM. – I)    REAL WORLD INTERFACING PART I

| DATA LINES | DB1 | PORTD.1 | Connections |
|---|---|---|---|
| | DB2 | PORTD.2 | Connect PORTD with JP9 (LCD) via FRC cable |
| | DB3 | PORTD.3 | |
| | DB4 | PORTD.4 | Place a Jumper on BL-SEL (J7) to Enable Backlight |
| | DB5 | PORTD.5 | |
| | DB6 | PORTD.6 | Press RESET Once. |
| | DB7 | PORTD.7 | Adjust the POT (CONTRAST) Right or Left until the letters are visible |
| Output: The Strings "PIC DEV. BOARD" and "LCD DEMO PROGRAM" will be displayed on LCD. ||||

**Circuit Diagram to Interface LCD with PIC16F877A**

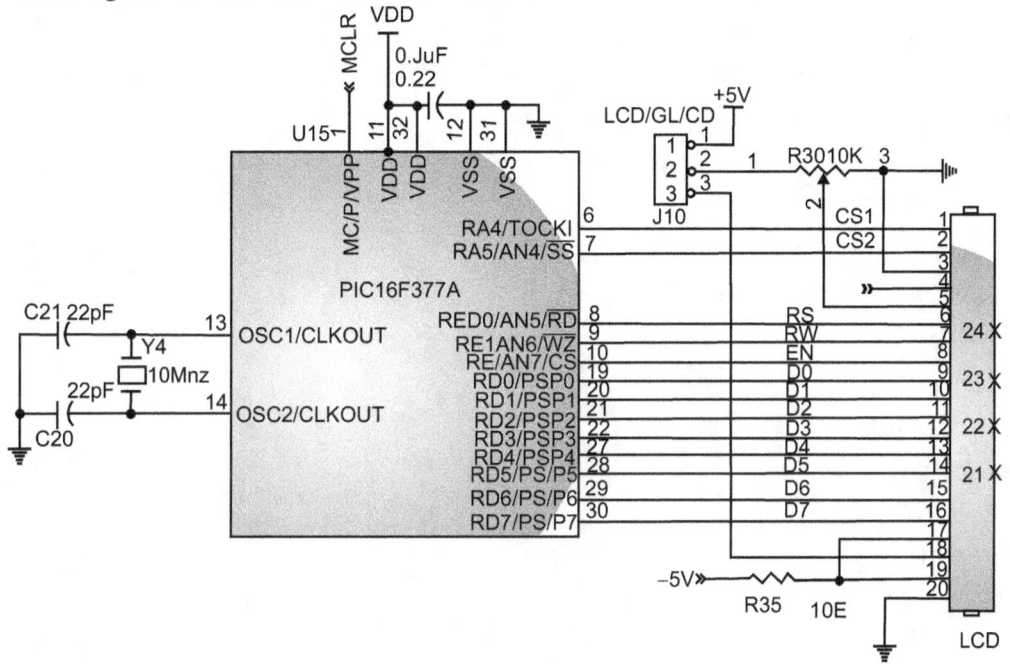

**Fig. 4.23**

**Source Code**

```c
//PROGRAM FOR LCD DISPLAY for 18f4520
//PD USED FOR DATA PINS
#include<p18f4520.h>
#pragma config OSC=HS
#pragma config PWRT=OFF
#pragma config WDT=OFF
#pragma config DEBUG=OFF, LVP=OFF
void lcdcmd(unsigned char value);
void lcddata(unsigned char value);
void msdelay(unsigned int itime);
#define ldata PORTD
#define rs PORTEbits.RE0
#define rw PORTEbits.RE1
#define en PORTEbits.RE2
void main()
{
TRISD = 0x00;
ADCON1=0X0A;
TRISE=0X00;
//en = 0;
msdelay(50);
lcdcmd(0x38);
msdelay(50);
lcdcmd(0x0E);
msdelay(15);
lcdcmd(0x01);
msdelay(15);
lcdcmd(0x06);
msdelay(15);
lcdcmd(0x81);
```

```
msdelay(50);
lcddata('L');
msdelay(50);
lcddata('O');
msdelay(50);
lcddata('G');
msdelay(50);
lcddata('S');
msdelay(50);
lcddata('U');
msdelay(50);
lcddata('N');
msdelay(50);
lcddata(0X14);
lcddata('S');
msdelay(50);
lcddata('Y');
msdelay(50);
lcddata('S');
msdelay(50);
lcddata('T');
msdelay(50);
lcddata('E');
msdelay(50);
lcddata('M');
msdelay(50);
lcddata('S');
msdelay(50);
lcdcmd(0xC1);
lcddata('P');
msdelay(50);
```

```
lcddata('I');
msdelay(50);
lcddata('C');
msdelay(50);
lcddata(0x14);
msdelay(50);
lcddata('1');
msdelay(50);
lcddata('8');
msdelay(50);
lcddata('F');
msdelay(15);
lcddata('4');
msdelay(50);
lcddata('5');
msdelay(50);
lcddata('2');
msdelay(50);
lcddata('0');
msdelay(50);

for(;;);
}


 void lcdcmd (unsigned char value)
{

ldata=value;
rs=0;
rw=0;
```

```c
en=1;

msdelay(1);
en=0;

}
void lcddata (unsigned char value)
{

ldata=value;
rs=1;
rw=0;
en=1;

msdelay(1);
en=0;

}
void msdelay (unsigned int itime)
{
int i,j;
for(i=0;i<itime;i++)
for(j=0;j<135;j++);

}
```

To compile the above C code you must need the Mplab software & Hi-Tech C Compiler. They must be properly set up and a project with correct settings must be created in order to compile the code. To compile the above code, the C file must be added to the project.

In Mplab, you want to develop or debug the project without any hardware setup. You must compile the code for generating HEX file. In debugging Mode, you want to check the port output without microcontroller Board.

The PICKIT2 software is used to download the hex file into your microcontroller through USB port.

**Testing the LCD Module with PIC16F877A**

Give +12V power supply to PIC16F/18F Evaluation Board; the LCD is connected with microcontroller PIC16f/18F Evaluation Board. When the program is downloading into PIC16F877A in Evaluation Board, the screen should show some text messages.

If you are not reading any text from **LCD**, then you just check the jumper connections and adjust the trim pot level. Otherwise you just check it with debugging mode in Mplab. If you want to see more details about debugging just see the videos in below link.

## 4.12 INTERFACING LED

**Interfacing LED**

Fig. 1 shows how to interface the LED to microcontroller. As you can see the Anode is connected through a resistor to GND & the Cathode is connected to the Microcontroller pin. So when the Port Pin is HIGH the LED is OFF & when the Port Pin is LOW the LED is turned ON.

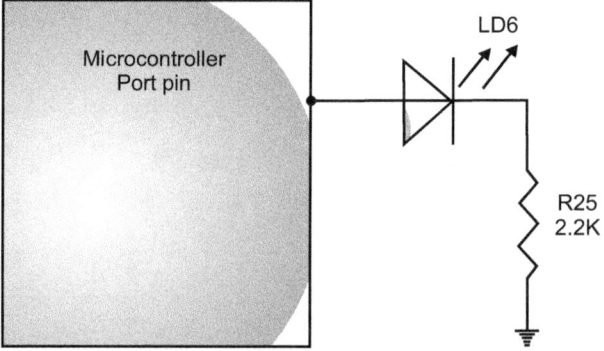

**Fig. 4.24 : Interfacing LED to Microcontroller**

**Interfacing LED with PIC16F877A**

We now want to flash a LED in PIC16F/18F Primer Board. It works by turning ON a LED & then turning it OFF & then looping back to START. However the operating speed of microcontroller is very high so the flashing frequency will also be very fast to be detected by human eye. The PIC16F/18F Primer board has eight numbers of point LEDs, connected with I/O Port lines (PORTx.0 – PORTx.7) to make port pins high.

## Circuit Diagram to Interface LED with PIC16F877A

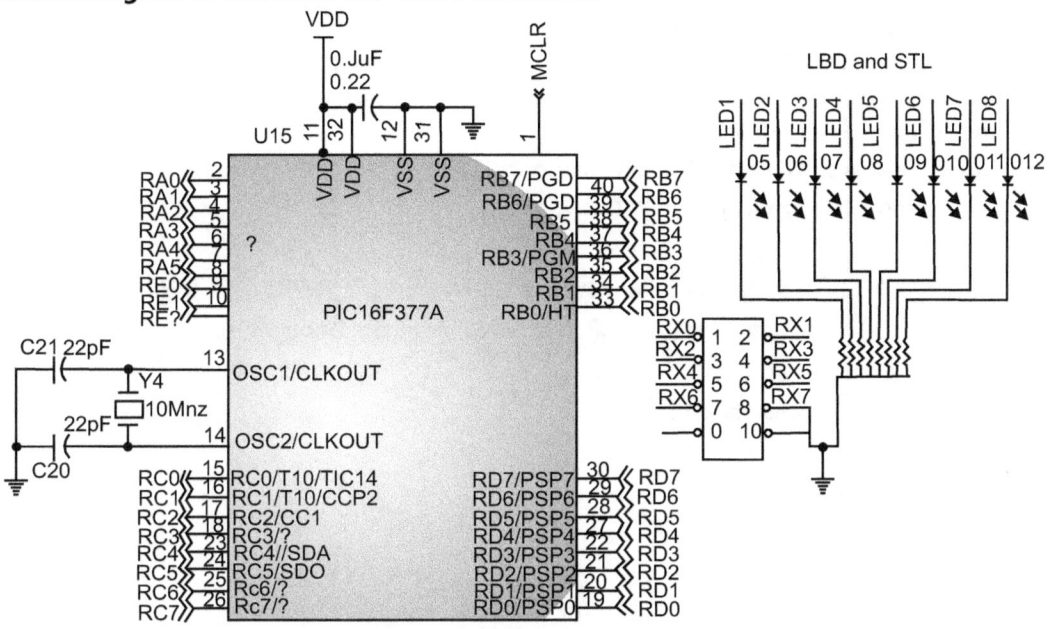

**Fig. 4.26**

## Pin Assignment with PIC16F877A

| | Point LEDs | PIC16F Lines | LED Selection | Connections |
|---|---|---|---|---|
| DIGITAL OUTPUTS | LED.0 | PORTx.0 | | |
| | LED.1 | PORTx.1 | | |
| | LED.2 | PORTx.2 | LDE Enable / LDE Disable (Fig. 4.25) | Connect Any one PORT from PORTA, PORTB, PORTC, PORTD with JP3 (LED Section) via FRC cable |
| | LED.3 | PORTx.3 | | |
| | LED.4 | PORTx.4 | | |
| | LED.5 | PORTx.5 | | |
| | LED.6 | PORTx.6 | | |
| | LED.7 | PORTx.7 | | |

**Output**: LED's will be Turned ON and OFF at 500ms interval.

## Source Code

The Interfacing LED with PIC16F877A program is very simple and straight forward, that uses a delay procedure loop based software delay. In C programs you cannot be sure of delay, because it depends on compiler how it optimizes the loops as soon as you make changes in the options the delay changes.

## C Program to switch ON and OFF LED using PIC16F

```c
#include <pic.h>  //Define PIC Registers

__CONFIG(0x3f72); //Select HS oscillator, Enable(PWRTE,BOREN),
                //Turn OFF (CPD,CP,WDTEN,In-circuit Debugger).

void DelayMs(unsigned int);

void main()
{
   ADCON1 = 7;
  //Select all the PORTA as Digital I/O pins

   TRISA = 0x00;   //PORTA Configured as O/P

   while(1)
   {
PORTA = 0xff; //Enable all the LED's connected to PORTA
DelayMs(500); //Half second Delay

PORTA = 0; //Turn OFF all the LED's connected to PORTA
DelayMs(500); //Half second Delay
   }
}

void DelayMs(unsigned int Ms)
{
  int delay_cnst;
  while(Ms>0)
```

```
{
  Ms--;
  for(delay_cnst = 0;delay_cnst <220;delay_cnst++);
}
}
```

To compile the above C code you need the Mplab software & Hi-Tech C Compiler. They must be properly set up and a project with correct settings must be created in order to compile the code. To compile the above code, the C file must be added to the project. In Mplab, you want to develop or debug the project without any hardware setup. You must compile the code for generating HEX file. In debugging Mode, you want to check the port output without PIC16F/18F Primer Board. The PICKIT2 software is used to download the hex file into your microcontroller IC PIC16F877A through USB port.

**Testing the LED with PIC16F877A**

Give +12V power supply to PIC16F/18F Primer Board; the LED is connected with PIC16F/18F Primer Board. When the program is downloading into PIC16F877A in Primer Board, the LED output is working that the LED is ON some time period and the LED is OFF some other time period.

If you are not reading any output from LED, then you just check the jumper connections & check the LED is working. Otherwise you just check it with debugging mode in Mplab. If you want to see more details about debugging just see the videos in below link.

## 4.13 PRC18F INTERFACING WITH KEYPAD

A **keypad** is a set of buttons arranged in a block or "pad" which usually bear digits, symbols and usually a complete set of alphabetical letters. If it mostly contains numbers then it can also be called a **numeric keypad.** Here we are using **4 X 4 matrix keypad**.

**Interfacing keypad**

Fig. 1 shows **how to interface the 4 X 4 matrix keypad** to two ports in microcontroller. The rows are connected to an output port and the columns are connected to an input port.

To detect a pressed key, the microcontroller grounds all rows by providing 0 to the output latch, and then it reads the columns.

If the data read from the columns is D3-D0=1111, no key has been pressed and the process continues until a key press is detected. However, if one of the column bits has a zero, this means that a key press has occurred. For example, if D3-D0=1101, this means that a key in the D1 column has been pressed. After a key press is detected, the microcontroller will go through the process of identifying the key. Starting with the top row, the microcontroller grounds it by providing a low to row D0 only; then it reads the columns.

If the data read is all 1s, no key in that row is activated and the process is moved to the next row. It grounds the next row, reads the columns, and checks for any zero. This process continues until the row is identified. After identification of the row in which the key has been pressed, the next task is to find out which column the pressed key belongs to.

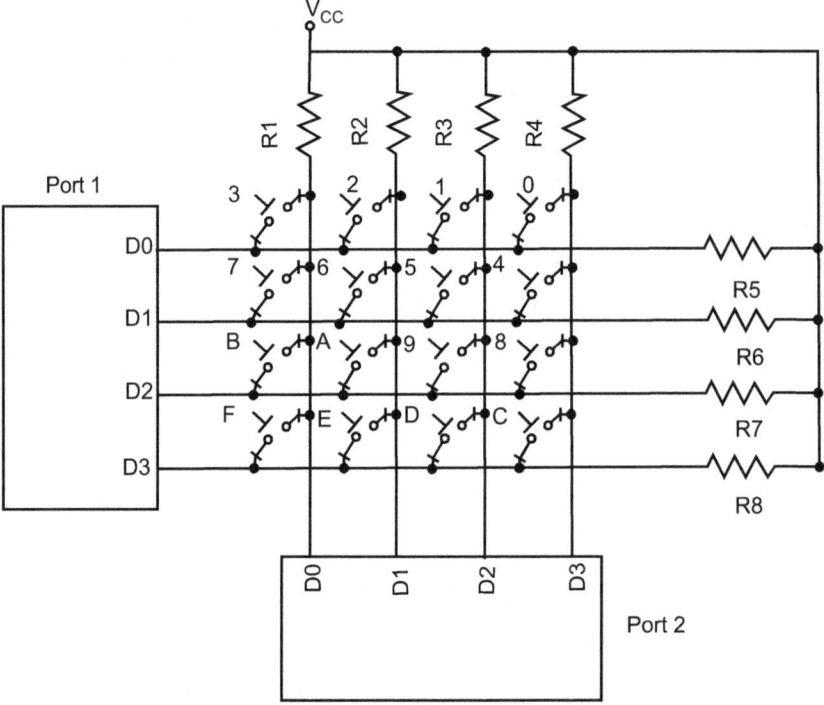

**Fig. 4.27 : Interfacing keypad to Microcontroller**

### Discoption

We now want to scan a **keypad in PIC16F/18F Slicker Board**. In case of **4X4 matrix Keypad** both the ends of switches are connected to the port pin i.e. four rows and four columns. So in all sixteen switches have been interfaced using just eight lines.

**1Keypads** arranged by matrix format, each row and column section pulled by high or low by selection J15, all row lines(PORTB.0 – PORTB.3) and column lines(PORTB.4 to PORTB.7) connected directly by the port pins.

**Pin Assignment with PIC16F877A**

| | 4x4 Matrix Lines | PIC16F Lines | 4x4 Matrix Keypad |
|---|---|---|---|
| **ROW** | ROW-0 | PORTB.0 | *Connect PORTB with JP15 (Keypad) via FRC Cable |
| | ROW-1 | PORTB.1 | |
| | ROW-2 | PORTB.2 | *Turn ON TXD and RXD Pins of CONFIG switch SW1. |
| | ROW-4 | PORTB.3 | |
| | | | *Connect Serial cable between USART Section in the Board and PC and open HyperTerminal |
| | COLUMN-0 | PORTB.4 | *Press RESET once. |
| | COLUMN-1 | PORTB.5 | **Outputs** |
| | COLUMN-2 | PORTB.6 | Press a Key and the number will be displayed in Hyper- |
| **COLUMN** | COLUMN-3 | PORTB.7 | Terminal |

**Circuit Diagram to Interface keypad with PIC16F877A**

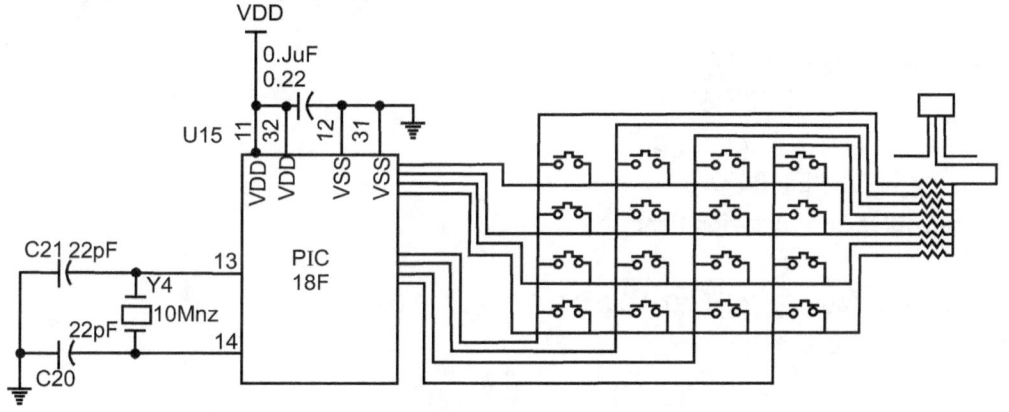

**Fig. 4.28**

**Source Code**

The **Interfacing keypad with PIC16F877A** program is very simple and straight forward, that scan a keypad rows and columns. When the rows and columns are detected then it will display in PC through UART0. The C programs are developed in Mplab software with Hi-Tech Compiler.

**Title : Program to keypad interfacing**

```c
#include <pic.h>     // Define PIC Registers
#include <stdio.h>   // Define I/O functions

__CONFIG(0x3f72);
// Select HS oscillator, Enable (PWRTE,BOREN),
// Disable (CPD,CP,WDTEN,In-circuit Debugger)

#define FOSC       10000
#define BAUD_RATE  9.6   //9600 Baudrate
#define BAUD_VAL   (char)(FOSC/ (16 * BAUD_RATE )) - 1;   //Calculation For 9600 Baudrate @10Mhz

void SerialInit(void); //Serial port Initialization Function
void ScanCol(void);    //Column Scan Function
void ScanRow(void);    //Row Scan Function
void DelayMs(unsigned int);

unsigned char KeyArray[4][4]= { '1','2','3','4',
                                '5','6','7','8',
                                '9','A','B','C',
                                'D','E','F','0'};
//Keypad value Initialization Function

unsigned char Count[4][4]={0,0,0,0,0,0,0,0,0,0,0,0,0,0,0,0};
int Col=0,Row=0,count=0,i,j;

void main()
{
  DelayMs(50);
  SerialInit();
  nRBPU=0;   //Enable PORTB Pullup values
```

```c
while(1)
{
  TRISB=0x0f; // Enable the 4 LSB as I/P & 4 MSB as O/P
  PORTB=0;
  while(PORTB==0x0f);   // Get the ROW value
  ScanRow();

  TRISB=0xf0; // Enable the 4 LSB as O/P & 4 MSB as I/P
  PORTB=0;
  while(PORTB==0xf0);   // Get the Column value
  ScanCol();

  DelayMs(150);
  Count[Row][Col]++;    // Count the Pressed key

  printf("[%c] Pressed:[%d] Times\n\r",
      KeyArray[Row][Col],Count[Row][Col]);
  DelayMs(200);
 }
}

void ScanRow()      // Row Scan Function
{

  switch(PORTB)
  {
    case 0x07:
      Row=3;    // 4th Row
    break;
    case 0x0b:
      Row=2;    // 3rd Row
    break;
```

```c
      case 0x0d:
        Row=1;    // 2nd Row
      break;
      case 0x0e:
        Row=0;    // 1st Row
      break;
  }
}

void ScanCol()   // Column Scan Function
{

  switch(PORTB)
  {
      case 0x70:
        Col=3;  // 4th Column
      break;
      case 0xb0:
        Col=2;  // 3rd Column
      break;
      case 0xd0:
        Col=1;  // 2nd Column
      break;
      case 0xe0:
        Col=0;  // 1st Column
      break;
  }
}

void SerialInit()
{
  TRISC=0xc0;      // RC7,RC6 set to usart mode(INPUT)
  TXSTA=0x24;
```

//Enable Serial Transmission, Asynchronous mode, High Speed mode

```c
  SPBRG=BAUD_VAL;  // 9600 Baud rate selection
  RCSTA=0x90;      // Enable Serial Port & Continuous Receive

  printf("Press Anyone Key:\n\r");
}

void putch(unsigned char character)
{
  while(!TXIF);    // Wait for the TXREG register to be empty
  TXREG=character; // Display the Character
}



void DelayMs(unsigned int Ms)
{
  int delay_cnst;
  while(Ms>0)
  {
    Ms--;
    for(delay_cnst = 0;delay_cnst <220;delay_cnst++);
  }
}
```

To compile the above C code you need the Mplab software & Hi-Tech Compiler. They must be properly set up and a project with correct settings must be created in order to compile the code. To compile the above code, the C file must be added to the project.

In Mplab, you want to develop or debug the project without any hardware setup. You must compile the code for generating HEX file. In debugging Mode, you want to check the port output without PIC16F/18F Slicker Board.

The PICKIT2 software is used to download the hex file into your microcontroller IC PIC16F877A through USB port.

**Testing the Keypad with PIC16F877A**

Give +12V power supply to PIC16F/18F Slicker Board; the serial cable is connected between the PIC16F/18F Slicker Board and PC.

Open the Hyper Terminal screen, select which port you are using and set the default settings. Now the screen should show some text messages & it display which key is pressed in keypad.

## 4.14 INTERFACING PWM WITH PIC18F

**Interfacing PWM with PIC18F**

PWM (Pulse Width Modulation) is the term used to describe using a digital signal to generate an analogue output signal. This is usually used to control the average power to a load in a motor speed control circuit. You can also use it to generate a contunuously variable analogue output without using any other integrated circuits by smoothing the PWM signal using a capacitor. As well as saving the costs of extra chips and interfaces the Pulse Width Modulation signal will not drift over time since it is generated from the time base of the processor i.e. a quartz crystal. Using analogue circuits to generate accurate signals that don't drift is a difficult task so PWM is very effective and cheap.

It works by changing the average voltage level and this is done by generating a constant frequency signal but one where the pulse width is changed (or modulated). For a moment if you think of the digital signal when it is at its extremes i.e. normal - it generates the maximum of 5V when the output is high and the minimum of 0V when the output is low. If you want to generate a 2.5V signal then you need to make the signal on for half of the time and off for the rest and then take the average.

Figure 1 shows four different PWM signals. One is PWM output at a 25% duty cycle. That is, the signal is on for 25% of the period and off the other 75%. Next shows PWM output at 50%, 75% and 100% duty cycles, respectively. These three PWM outputs encode three different analog signal values, at 10%, 50%, and 90% of the full strength.

**PIC16F/18F Slicker Board**

The PIC16F/18F Slicker board is specifically designed to help students to master the required skills in the area of embedded systems. The kit is designed in such way that all the possible features of the microcontroller will be easily used by the students. The kit supports in system programming (ISP) which is done through USB port. Microchip's PIC (PIC16F877A), PIC16F/18F Slicker Kit is proposed to smooth the progress of developing and debugging of various designs encompassing of High speed 8-bit Microcontrollers.

## PWM (Pulse Width Modulation)

Pulse width modulation (PWM) is a powerful technique for controlling analog circuits with a processor's digital outputs. PWM is employed in a wide variety of applications, ranging from measurement and communications to power control and conversion.

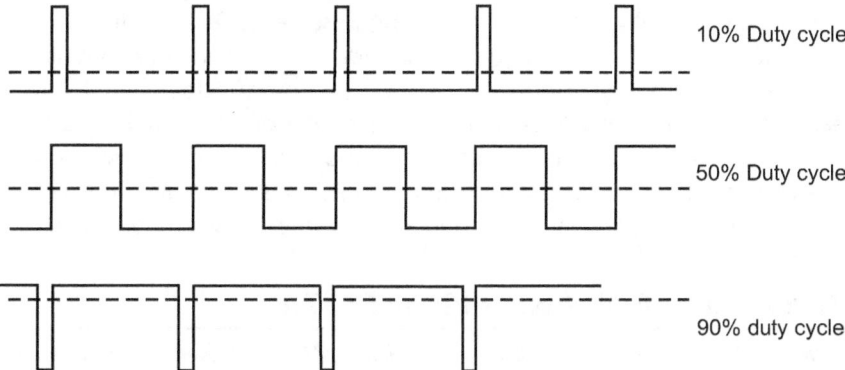

**Fig. 4.29 : PWM Outputs**

In the diagram the digital signal (solid line) is at a constant frequency while the pulse width is changed (modulated). The dotted line represents the average signal (if the digital signal is converted to an average). The duty cycle represents the amount of time that the signal is high compared to the amount of time that the signal is low.

### Duty Cycle

So the top signal is high for 10% of the period so the average is low, the middle signal is high for 50% of the period so the average is half and the bottom signal is high for 90% of the period so the average is high. For fully off you use 0% and fully on you use 100%. So the duty cycle is independent of the frequency of the PWM signal and you'll always see the same type of waveform for a specific duty cycle.

### PWM Frequency

The frequency of the PWM signal is important depending on the device you are driving. If the aim is to create a dc signal then you would want the frequency high (kHz) so a low pass filter could remove the frequency component. How high depends on how much frequency component is allowed at output and depends on how it is used i.e. what error can be tolerated.

### Averaging the PWM PIC output

To convert the PWM signal to a usable analogue signal you need to average it and you can do this by using a resistor capacitor filter (low pass). The higher the PWM frequency the less that frequency will come through the filter so you can design out the PWM frequency from the analogue output.

Note: In some cases a filter is not needed as the filtering is done by the device you are controlling e.g. a motor (is inductive anyway). Or in the case of an _RGB led_ your eye averages out the signal (persistence of vision)!

**Noise immunity of the PWM PIC signal**

Since the PWM signal is fully digital the only way noise can affect it is if the noise is strong enough to change a digital 1 to a digital 0 and vice versa. This immunity is much higher than a purely analogue signal that will be affected by any noise.

For this reason changing an analogue signal into a digital one can improve either the signal transmission distance or its immunity to spurious noise. For example you could encode an audio signal into PWM, send it over longer cables than a pure analogue signal could travel, and then remove the PWM frequency at the receiver.

## 4.14.1 Interfacing PWM with PIC16F877A

We now want to generate a **PWM in PIC16F/18F Slicker Board** at a particular frequency. **Pulse Width Modulation** is a technique for getting analog results with digital means.

Digital control is used to create a square wave, a signal switched between on and off. This on-off pattern can simulate voltages in between full on (5 Volts) and off (0 Volts) by changing the portion of the time the signal spends on versus the time that the signal spends off. The duration of "on time" is called the pulse width. To get varying analog values, you change, or modulate, that pulse width.

**Pin Assignment with PIC16F877A**

|  | PWMs | PIC16F Lines | Connections | Circuit diagram to interface PWM with PIC16F877A |
|---|---|---|---|---|
|  | PWM1 | PORTC.1 | There are no connections on the board |  |
| **Outputs** | PWM3 | Portc.2 |  |  |
| **Output :** Connect a CRO and measure the pulse width and duty cycle ||||  |

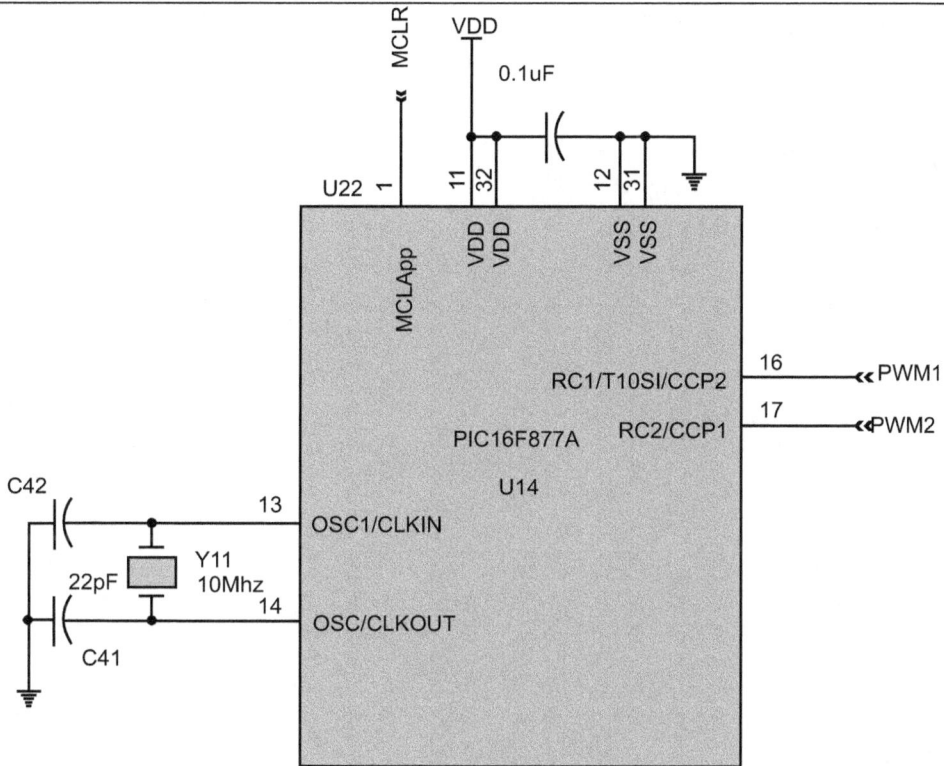

**Fig. 4.30 : Circuit Diagram**

**Source Code**

The Interfacing PWM with PIC16F877A program is very simple and straight forward, which generates a pulse pattern in a particular frequency. An ADC signal is used to varying the duty cycle of PWM signal. The C program is written in Mplab software & it executed with Hi-Tech C compiler.

**Title : Program to generate PWM**

```
#include<pic.h>   //Define PIC registers
   __CONFIG(0x3f72); //Select HS oscillator, Enable (PWRTE,BOREN),
              //Disable (CPD,CP,WDTEN,In-circuit Debugger)
#define XTAL      10000      //10Mhz=10000Khz
#define PWM_Freq  1          //1Khz PWM frequency
#define TMR2_PRE  16         //Timer2 Prescale
#define PR2_Val   ((char)((XTAL/(4*TMR2_PRE*PWM_Freq))-1))
         //Calculation for Period register PR2 (1Khz)
```

```c
#define Duty_Cyc  PR2_Val*2

unsigned int i;
void PWM_init(void);
void PWM_change(unsigned int);
void DelayMs(unsigned int);

void main(void)
{
  PWM_init();
  while(1)
  {
    i=0;
    PWM_change(i);
    DelayMs(10);

    while(i<PR2_Val)
    {
      i=i+1;
      PWM_change(i);
      DelayMs(200);
    }
  }
}

void PWM_init(void)
{
  TRISC2=0;    //PWM channel 1 and 2 configured as output
        TRISC1=0;
  PORTC = 0x00;
  CCP1CON=0x0c; //CCP1 and CCP2 are configured for PWM
  CCP2CON=0x0c;
  PR2=PR2_Val;  //Move the PR2 value
```

```c
    T2CON=0x03;    //Timer2 Prescale is 16
    TMR2=0x00;
    TMR2ON=1;    //Turn ON timer2
}

void PWM_change(unsigned int DTY) //Duty cycle change routine
{
    CCPR1L=DTY;    //Value is between 0 to 255
    CCPR2L=DTY;
}

void DelayMs(unsigned int Ms)   //Delay Routine
{
    int delay_cnst;

        while(Ms>0)
            {
        Ms--;

            for(delay_cnst = 0;delay_cnst <220;delay_cnst++);
            //delay constant for 1Ms @10Mhz
            }
}
```

To compile the above C code you need the Mplab software & Hi-Tech C Compiler. They must be properly set up and a project with correct settings must be created in order to compile the code. To compile the above code, the C file must be added to the project.

In Mplab, you want to develop or debug the project without any hardware setup. You must compile the code for generating HEX file. In debugging Mode, you want to check the port output without PIC16F/18F Slicker Board. The PICKIT2 software is used to download the hex file into your microcontroller IC PIC16F877A through USB port.

**Testing the PWM with PIC16F877A**

Give +12V power supply to PIC16F/18F Slicker Board; the PWM port line is connected in PIC16F/18F Slicker Board. When the program is downloading into PIC16F877A in Slicker Board, the PWM output is generating at a particular frequency.

## QUESTIONS

1. Explain port structure of PIC18f microcontroller.
2. Explain interrupts of PIC18f microcontroller.
3. Describe timers used in PIC18f microcontroller.
4. How switches are interfaced with PIC18F microcontroller. Explain with circuit diagram, flow chart and c-program.
5. How LEDs are interfaced with PIC18F microcontroller. Explain with circuit diagram, flow chart and c-program.
6. How LCDs are interfaced with PIC18F microcontroller. Explain with circuit diagram, flow chart and c-program.
7. How keypad is interfaced with PIC18F microcontroller. Explain with circuit diagram, flow chart and c-program.
8. How timers are interfaced with PIC18F microcontroller. Explain with circuit diagram, flow chart and c-program.
9. How PWM system is interfaced with PIC18F microcontroller. Explain with circuit diagram, flow chart and c-program.

# Unit - V

# REAL WORLD INTERFACING PART II

## 5.1 INTRODUCTION

**I2C using Master Synchronous Serial Port (MSSP) Module**

I2C are widely use for to communicate with external peripheral such as port expender, EEPROM, Real Time Clock etc. The Master Synchronous Serial Port (MSSP) module in PIC18 can be used to communicated with I2C peripheral. MSSP module can be configure to work as SPI and I2C. In this example the module will be configured as I2C to communicate with a port expender from Microchip MCP23017. The circuit below is built up on breadboard to test the MSSP function as an I2C module.

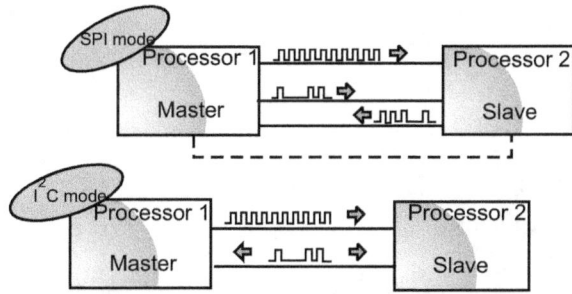

**Fig. 5.1 : Master Synchronous Serial Port**

The DIL switch on Port B is used to control the LED on Port A of the IO expender. INTB from the IC is connected to the INT2 pin of the PIC so that the PORTA output of the Port expender can be updated with the value from the DIL switch. The code function will be implemented using 2 interrupt, one at the high priority location for the External interrupt and the other for MSSP module at the low interrupt. MSSP module had to be configured as I2C master mode for this example. The code below shows the setting to initialize MSSP module.

SSPADD = 80;

SSPSTAT = 0x80;

SSPCON1 = 0x28;

SSPCON2 = 0x00;

Function for sending and receiving data for I2C is created according to the required protocol to communicate with MCP23017. The code below shows the function i2cTransmit and i2cRecieve for receiving data and the interrupt routine for the handling of transmission/reception. The 2 function is used to load the data buffer for transmission and reception. The Interrupt function will pass the data accordingly to the MSSP module according to the protocol written in the datasheet of MCP23017.

```c
unsigned char I2Cbusy = 0;
unsigned char I2CTransmitArray[20];
unsigned char I2CTransmitElement;
unsigned char I2CTransmitCurrent;
unsigned char I2CReceived;

void i2cTransmit(unsigned char *data, unsigned char Element){
int i = 0;
if(I2Cbusy == 0){
while(i < Element){
I2CTransmitArray[i] = *data;
i++;
data++;
}
I2Cbusy = 1;
I2CTransmitCurrent = 0;
I2CTransmitElement = Element;
SSPCON2bits.SEN = 1;
}
}
void i2cReceive(unsigned address, unsigned regis){
if(I2Cbusy == 0){
I2CTransmitArray[0] = address;
I2CTransmitArray[1] = regis;
I2CTransmitArray[2] = 0; // dummy
I2CTransmitArray[3] = address | 1;
I2Cbusy = 2;
I2CTransmitCurrent = 0;
I2CTransmitElement = 4;
SSPCON2bits.SEN = 1;
}
}
/*****************Low priority interrupt vector **************************/
```

```c
#pragma code low_vector=0x18
void interrupt_at_low_vector(void)
{
  _asm GOTO low_isr _endasm
}

#pragma code

/****************Low priority ISR **************************/
#pragma interruptlow low_isr
void low_isr (void)
{
 PIR1bits.SSPIF = 0;
 if(I2Cbusy ==1){
 if(I2CTransmitCurrent < I2CTransmitElement)
 SSPBUF = I2CTransmitArray[I2CTransmitCurrent];
 else if(I2CTransmitCurrent == I2CTransmitElement)
 SSPCON2bits.PEN = 1;
 else
 I2Cbusy = 0;
 }
 else{
 if(I2CTransmitCurrent == 2)
 SSPCON2bits.RSEN = 1;
 else if(I2CTransmitCurrent < I2CTransmitElement)
 SSPBUF = I2CTransmitArray[I2CTransmitCurrent];
 else if(I2CTransmitCurrent == I2CTransmitElement)
 SSPCON2bits.RCEN = 1;
 else if(I2CTransmitCurrent == I2CTransmitElement+1){
 I2CReceived = SSPBUF;
 SSPCON2bits.ACKDT = 1;
 SSPCON2bits.ACKEN = 1;
 }
```

```
else if(I2CTransmitCurrent == I2CTransmitElement+2)
SSPCON2bits.PEN = 1;
else
I2Cbusy = 0;


}
I2CTransmitCurrent++;
}
```

In the interrupt service routine, transmission and reception is differentiated based on the value in I2Cbusy; 1 for transmission and 2 for reception. The device address byte with write flag set need to be send to the module follow by the register address and the data to write. Step for writing N number of data is shown below. The steps below is initiated by the function i2cTransmit.

**Steps to write register in MCP23017:**

*Start Condition -> Device Address + Write flag -> Register Address -> Data 1 -> Data 2 .......-> Data N -> Stop Condition*

Below is the example code for the transmission of config1 in the code. The I2Cbusy check is to wait until the whole transmission of the config is done.

```
unsigned char config1[] = {0x40, 0x00, 0x00, 0xFF};
i2cTransmit(config1, 4);
while(I2Cbusy != 0);
```

Reading data from one register location is implemented in for the read function although more than one data continuously can be achieve. Since for this example only 1 read in is required, a Nack is sent to the port expender once the on data is received. Based on the data sheet the step below is used to get data from a register location.

## 5.1.1 Steps to read register in MCP23017

*Start Condition -> Device Address + Write flag -> Register Address -> Restart Condition ->...*
*Device Address + Read flag -> Data from MCP23017 -> NACK from Master ->Stop Condition*

Only 1 data at the address will be read from MCP23017. Code below show reading of data from Device with address of 0x40 and register address of 0x13. The data read in will be stored in the variable I2CReceived.

```
i2cReceive(0x40, 0x13);
while(I2Cbusy != 0);
output[2] = I2CReceived;
```

For the example data is read only when interrupt is generated by MCP23017. Connected to the INT2 data will be read when interrupt occur.

MCP23017 must be configure to generate interrupt on the change of value on the pin by setting the GPINTEN byte in the register. When interrupt occurs I2C read is called to get the data from the port expender.

```
#pragma code high_vector=0x08
void interrupt_at_high_vector(void)
{
  _asm GOTO high_isr _endasm
}

#pragma code
/*****************High priority ISR **************************/

#pragma interrupt high_isr
void high_isr (void)
{
 INTCON3bits.INT2IF = 0;
 i2cReceive(0x40, 0x13);
}
```

The function of the communication is illustrated by controlling the LED with the switches. Main code of the control is shown below. When there is changes to the input at the interrupt, the LED will be updated with the value on the input ports.

```
while(1){
if(I2Cbusy == 2){
while(I2Cbusy != 0);
output[2] = I2CReceived;
i2cTransmit(output, 3);
}
}
```

## 5.2 UART

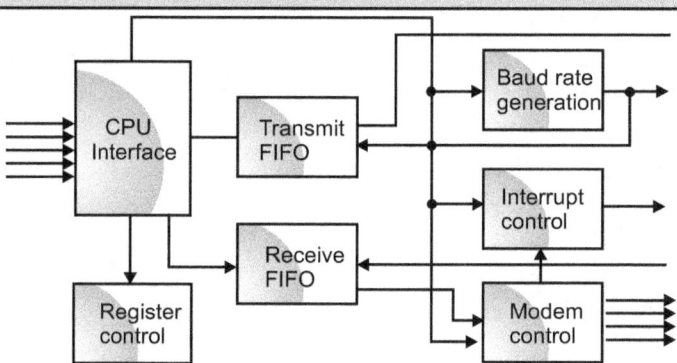

**Fig. 5.2**

### 5.2.1 Serial UART, an introduction

A UART, universal asynchronous receiver / transmitter is responsible for performing the main task in serial communications with computers. The device changes incoming parallel information to serial data which can be sent on a communication line. A second UART can be used to receive the information. The UART performs all the tasks, timing, parity checking, etc. needed for the communication. The only extra devices attached are line driver chips capable of transforming the TTL level signals to line voltages and vice versa.

To use the UART in different environments, registers are accessible to set or review the communication parameters. Setable parameters are for example the communication speed, the type of parity check, and the way incoming information is signalled to the running software.

### 5.2.2 Serial UART Types

Serial communication on PC compatibles started with the 8250 UART in the IBM XT. In the years after, new family members were introduced like the 8250A and 8250B revisions and the 16450. The last one was first implemented in the AT. The higher bus speed in this computer could not be reached by the 8250 series. The differences between these first UART series were rather minor. The most important property changed with each new release was the maximum allowed speed at the processor bus side. The 16450 was capable of handling a communication speed of 38.4 kbs without problems. The demand for higher speeds led to the development of newer series which would be able to release the main processor from some of its tasks. The main problem with the original series was the need to perform a software action for each single byte to transmit or receive. To overcome this problem, the 16550 was released which contained two on-board FIFO buffers, each capable of storing 16 bytes. One buffer for incoming, and one buffer for outgoing bytes.

A marvellous idea, but it didn't work out that way. The 16550 chip contained a firmware bug which made it impossible to use the buffers. The 16550A which appeared soon after was the first UART which was able to use its FIFO buffers. This made it possible to increase maximum reliable communication speeds to 115.2 kbs. This speed was necessary to use effectively modems with on-board compression. A further enhancment introduced with the 16550 was the ablity to use DMA, direct memory access for the data transfer. Two pins were redefined for this purpose. DMA transfer is not used with most applications. Only special serial I/O boards with a high number of ports contain sometimes the necessary extra circuitry to make this feature work. The 16550A is the most common UART at this moment. Newer versions are under development, including the 16650 which contains two 32 byte FIFO's and on board support for software flow control. Texas Instruments is developing the 16750 which contains 64 byte FIFO's.

## 5.2.3 Registers

Eight I/O bytes are used for each UART to access its registers. The following table shows, where each register can be found. The base address used in the table is the lowest I/O port number assigned. The switch bit DLAB can be found in the line control register LCR as bit 7 at I/O address base + 3.

| | UART register to port conversion table | | | |
|---|---|---|---|---|
| | **DLAB = 0** | | **DLAB = 1** | |
| **I/O port** | **Read** | **Write** | **Read** | **Write** |
| base | **RBR** receiver buffer | **THR** transmitter holding | **DLL** divisor latch LSB | |
| base + 1 | **IER** interrupt enable | **IER** interrupt enable | **DLM** divisor latch MSB | |
| base + 2 | **IIR** interrupt identification | **FCR** FIFO control | **IIR** interrupt identification | **FCR** FIFO control |
| base + 3 | **LCR** line control | | | |
| base + 4 | **MCR** modem control | | | |
| base + 5 | **LSR** line status | – factory test | **LSR** line status | – factory test |
| base + 6 | **MSR** modem status | – not used | **MSR** modem status | – not used |
| base + 7 | **SCR** scratch | | | |

RBR= receiver buffer register
THR= transmitter holding register
IER= interrupt enable register
IIR= interrupt identification register
FCR= FIFO control register
LCR= line control register
MCR= modem control register
LSR= line status register
MSR= modem status register
SCR= scratch register
DLL= divisor latch LSB
DLM= divisor latch MSB

**UART (Universal Asynchronous Receiver Transmitter)** are one of the basic interfaces which provide a cost effective simple and reliable communication between one controller to another controller or between a controller and PC.

**PIC16F/18F Primer Board**

The PIC16F/18F Primer board is specifically designed to help students to master the required skills in the area of embedded systems. The kit is designed in such way that all the possible features of the microcontrollerwill be easily used by the students. The kit supports in system programming (ISP) which is done through USB port.

Microchip's PIC (PIC16F877A), PIC16F/18F Primer Kit is proposed to smooth the progress of developing and debugging of various designs encompassing of High speed 8-bit Microcontrollers.

RS-232 Level Converter

Usually all the digital ICs work on TTL or CMOS voltage levels which cannot be used to communicate over RS-232 protocol. So a voltage or level converter is needed which can convert TTL to RS232 and RS232 to TTL voltage levels. The most commonly used RS-232 level converter is MAX232.

This IC includes charge pump which can generate RS232 voltage levels (-10V and +10V) from 5V power supply. It also includes two receiver and two transmitters and is capable of full-duplex UART/USART communication.

RS-232 communication enables point-to-point data transfer. It is commonly used in data acquisition applications, for the transfer of data between the microcontroller and a PC. The voltage levels of a microcontroller and PC are not directly compatible with those of RS-232, a level transition buffer such as MAX232 be used.

## 5.2.4 Interfacing UART

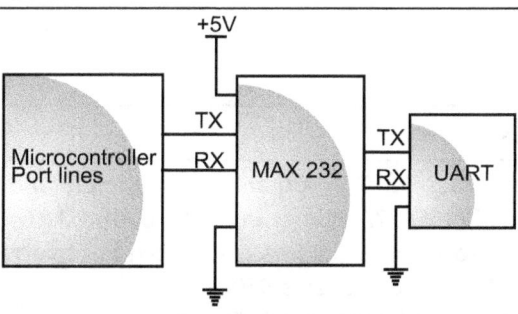

**Fig. 5.3 : Schematic diagram under SPI Mode**

Above fig shows how to interface the UART to microcontroller. To communicate over UART or USART, we just need three basic signals which are namely, RXD (receive), TXD (transmit), GND (common ground). So tointerface UART with LPC2148, we just need the basic signals.

Interfacing UART with PIC16F877A

We now want to display a text in PC from PIC16F/18F Primer Board by using UART module. In PIC16F/18F Primer Board contains a single serial interface that are UART. The Transmitter pins send the data into PC and the receiver pin receives the data from PC. The PC and microcontroller speed are denoted by using baud rate. When the baud rates of both PC and Microcontroller are same, then only the data transmit and receive correctly otherwise not. The TXD (PORTC.6) & RXD (PORTC.7) pins are used to data transmit or receive operation.

**Pin Assignment with PIC16F877A**

| | UART DB-9 Connector | PIC16F Processor Lines | Serial Port Section | Connections |
|---|---|---|---|---|
| **UART** | TXD | PORTC.6 | | * Turn ON TXD and RXD Pins of CONFIG switchSW1. * Connect Serial cable between USART Section in the Board and PC. * Open HyperTerminal * Press RESET |
| | RXD | PORTC.7 | | |
| Output: **Type a character, same character will be returned from Board.** | | | | |

## 5.2.5 Source Code

The Interfacing UART with PIC16F877A program is very simple and straight forward, which display a text in PC from PIC16F877A Primer Board through UART. Some delay is occurring when a single data is sent to PC. C programs are written in Mplab software with Hi-Tech C Compiler. The baud rate of microcontroller is 9600.

**C Program to display a text in PC from PIC16F877A**

```c
#include<pic.h>

__CONFIG(0x3f72);

#define FOSC        10000     //10Mhz==>10000Khz
#define BAUD_RATE   9.6       //9600 Baudrate
#define BAUD_VAL    ((char)(FOSC/ (16 * BAUD_RATE )) - 1)    //Calculation For 9600 Baudrate @10Mhz
void main()
  {
  unsigned char ReceiveChar;
  TRISC=0xc0;   //RC7,RC6 set to usart mode(INPUT)
  TXSTA=0x24;   //Transmit Enable
  SPBRG=BAUD_VAL; //9600 baud at 10Mhz
  RCSTA=0x90;   //Usart Enable, Continus receive enable
  TXREG='0';
  while(1)
  {
    if (RCIF==1) //char received? Send 'A' back to Terminal
      {
      ReceiveChar=RCREG;

      if(TXIF==1)
      TXREG=ReceiveChar;
    }
  }
}
```

To compile the above C code you need the Mplab software & Hi-Tech C Compiler. They must be properly set up and a project with correct settings must be created in order to compile the code. To compile the above code, the C file must be added to the project.

In Mplab, you want to develop or debug the project without any hardware setup. You must compile the code for generating HEX file. In debugging Mode, you want to check the port output without PIC16F/18F Primer Board.

The PICKIT2 software is used to download the hex file into your microcontroller IC PIC16F877A through USB port.

## 5.3 TESTING THE UART WITH PIC16F877A

Give +12V power supply to PIC16F/18F Primer Board; the serial cable is connected between the PIC16F/18F Primer Board and PC. Open the Hyper Terminal screen, select which port you are using and set the default settings. Now the screen should show some text messages.

### 5.3.1 Serial Peripheral Interface (SPI)

Port-C three pins, viz., RC5/SDO, RC4/SDI and RC3/SCK/SCL are mainly used for SPI mode. In addition, one Port-A pin, viz., RA5/$\overline{SS}$/AN4 is used for slave select. The schematic block diagram of SPI is shown in the figure.

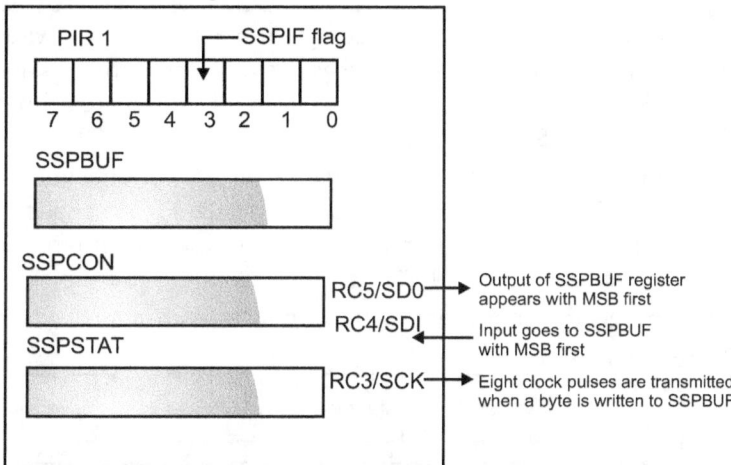

**Fig. 5.4 : SPI Master / Slave Connection**

The SPI port requires RC3/SCK pin to be an output that generates the clock signal used by the external shift registers. When SPI is configured in the slave mode, RC3/SCK pin works as the input for the clock.

When a byte is written to SSPBUF register, it is shifted out of RC5/SDO pin in synchronous with the emitted clock pulses on RC3/SCK pin. The MSB of SSPBUF is the first bit to appear on RC5/SDO pin.

Simultaneously, the same write to SSPBUF also initiates the 8 bit data reception into SSPBUF of whatever appears on RC4/SDI pin at the time of rising edges of the clock on SCK pin. Hence shifting-in and shifting-out of data occur simultaneously.

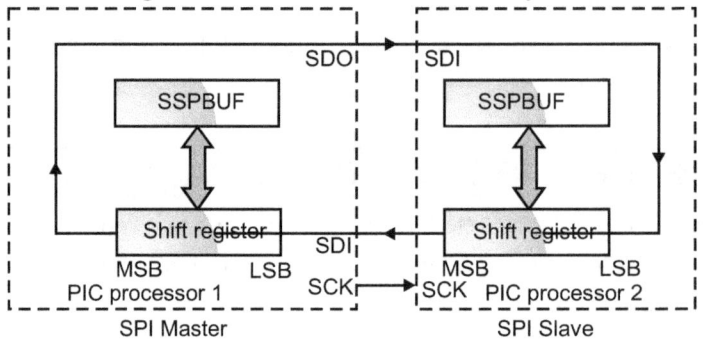

(i) Timing diagram for CKP=1   (ii) Timing diagram for CKP=0

**Fig. 5.5 : Timing Diagram under SPI mode**

The schematic diagram of SPI Master/Slave connection is shown in the figure.

## 5.3.2 I²C Communication in PIC Microcontroller

I²C stands for Inter-Integrated circuit. I²C communication is a two wire bi-directional interface for connecting one or more master processors with one or more slave devices, such as an EEPROM, ADC, RAM, LCD display, DAC, etc. I²C interface requires two open drain I/O pins, viz. SDA (Serial Data) and SCL (Serial Clock).

The reason for open drain connection is that the data transfer is bi-directional and any of the devices connected to the I²C bus can drive the data line (SDA). The serial clock line (SCL) is usually driven by the master. Since SDA and SCL pins are open drain pins, external pull-up resistances are required for operation of I²C bus.

A typical I²C bus showing the connection of multi-master and multi-slave configuration is shown in the following figure.

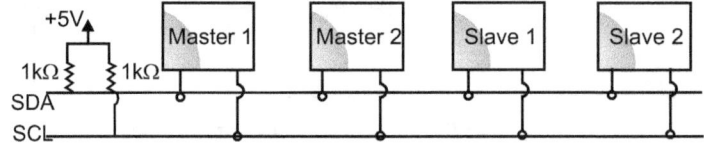

**Fig. 5.6 : Timing diagram for data transfer**

Some conventions are followed in I²C communication. Let us assume that there is one master and one slave and 8-data bits are sent. We will initially assume that the master is the transmitter and the slave is the receiver. The clock is driven by the master. On receiving 8-bits, an acknowledgement bit is driven by the receiver on SDA line. The acknowledgement bit is usually Low (0). The following diagram shows the data communication pattern having 8 data bits and one acknowledgement bit.

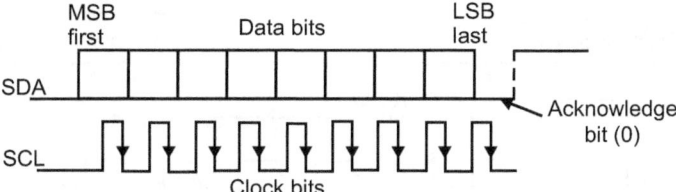

**Fig. 5.7 : Timing diagram for START and STOP Conditions**

The following features are to be noted -
1. SDA line transmits/ receives data bits. MSB is sent first.
2. Data in SDA line is stable during clock (SCL) high. A new bit is initiated at the negative clock transition after a specified hold time.
3. Serial clock (SCL) is driven by the master.
4. An acknowledgement bit (0) is driven by the receiver after the end of reception. If the receiver does not acknowledge, SDA line remains high (1).

$I^2C$ bus transfer consists of a number of byte transfers within a START condition and either another START condition or a STOP condition. During the idle state when no data transfer is taking place, both SDA and SCL lines are released by all the devices and remains high. When a master wants to initiate a data transfer, it pulls SDA low followed by SCL being pulled low. This is called START condition. Similarly, when the processor wants to terminate the data transfer it first releases SCL (SCL becomes high) and then SDA. This is called a STOP condition. START and STOP conditions are shown in the diagram as follows.

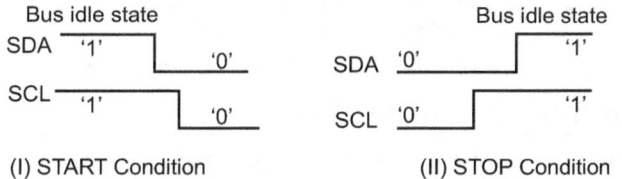

**Fig. 5.8 : Data transfer protocol for writing to a slave device**

START and STOP conditions are unique and they never happen within a data transfer.

## 5.3.3 Timing Diagram For Data Transfer In 'Master Mode'

SSPIF interrupt flag is cleared by the user software if already in the set mode. The interrupt is enabled. Any write to SSPBUF initiates the data transfer, i.e., transmission and reception. The clock pulses (8 clock pulses) are output through SCK pin. The data is received through SDI. When CKP=1 (SSPCON<4>), data changes at SDO at negative clock transition and is read through SDI at positive clock transition. The idle state of clock is high. If CKP=0, data appears at SDO at positive clock transition and is read through SDI at negative clock transition. The idle state of the clock is low. These are shown in the following diagrams.

Hence sampling time $T_s$ varies linearly with $R_{Source}$ as shown in Fig 23.7.

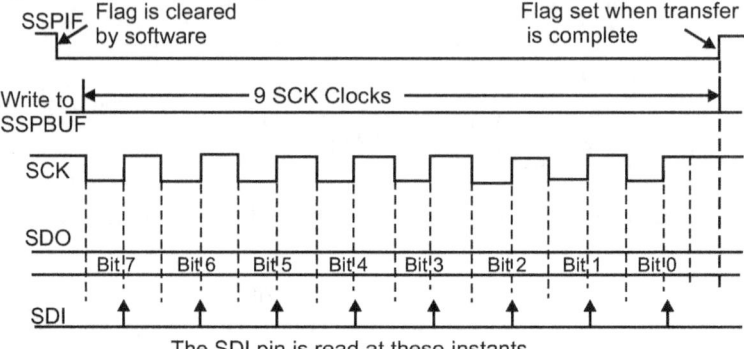

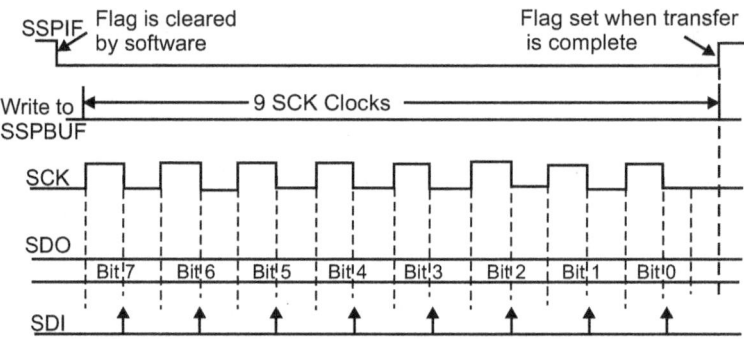

**Fig. 5.9 : Multimaster Multislave Connection**

## 5.3.4 Data Communication Protocol

In $I^2C$ communication both 7-bit and 10-bit slave addressing are possible. In 7-bit addressing mode 128 slaves can be interfaced with a single master. Similarly, in 10-bit addressing mode, 1024 slaves can be interfaced with the master. We will discuss here 7-bit addressing mode only. 10-bit addressing mode is similar to 7-bit addressing except from the fact that the number of address bits is more.

Following a 'start' condition, the master sends a 7-bit address of the slave on SDA line. The MSB is sent first. After sending 7-bit address of the slave peripheral, a $R/\overline{W}$ ($8^{th}$ bit) bit is sent by the master. If $R/\overline{W}$ bit is '0', the following byte (after the acknowledgement bit) is written by the master to the addressed slave peripheral. If R/$\overline{W}$ =1, the following byte (after the acknowledgement bit) has to be read from the slave by the master.

After sending the 7-bit address of the slave, the master sends the address (usually 8 bit) of the internal register of the slave wherefrom the data has to be read or written to. The subsequent access is automatically directed to the next address of the internal register.

The following diagrams give the general format to write and read from several peripheral internal registers.

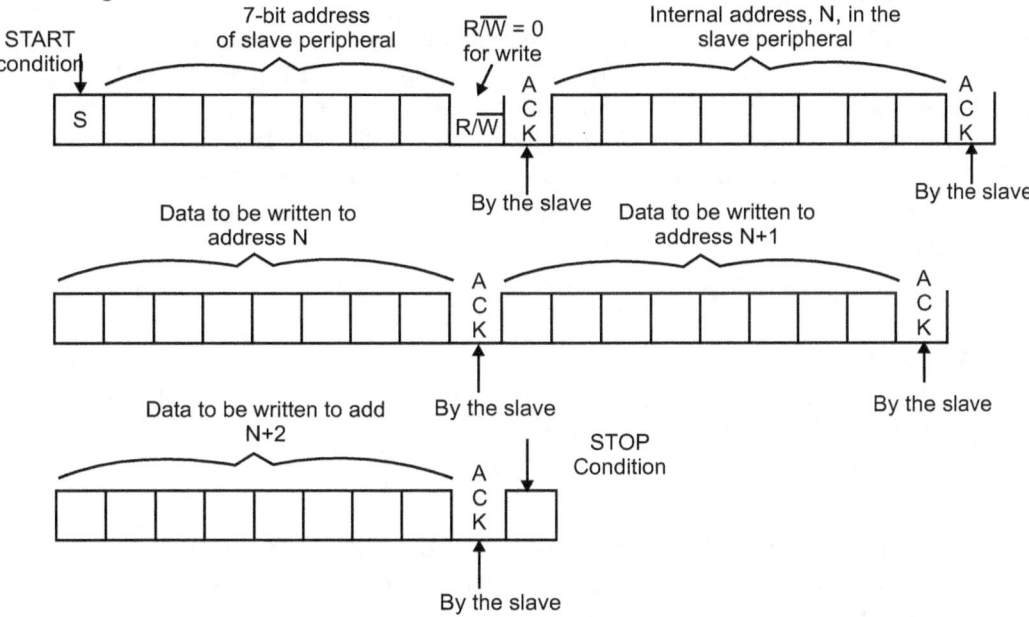

Fig. 5.10 : I²C Interface for DAC

R/$\overline{W}$ (Read / Write) bit indicates whether the data is to be written by the master or read by the master. If R/$\overline{W}$ is 1, the subsequent data are to be read by the master. If R/$\overline{W}$ = 0, the subsequent data are to be written by the master to the addressed slave. It has to be noted that the slave address is sent first, following a 'start' condition. The addressed slave responds by acknowledging and gets ready for data transfer.

If data has to be read from a specific address of the slave device, the master sends the 7-bit address of the slave first following a 'start' condition. R/$\overline{W}$ bit is sent as 'low'. The addressed slave acknowledges by pulling the ACK line low. The master then sends the 8-bit internal address of the slave from which data has to be read. The slave acknowledges. Since R/$\overline{W}$ bit was initially 0, the master is in the write mode. To change this to read mode, the 'start' condition is again generated followed by 7-bit address of the slave with R/$\overline{W}$ = 1. The slave acknowledges. The slave then sends data from previously specified internal address to the master. The master acknowledges by pulling ACK bit low. The data transfer stops when the master does not acknowledge the data reception and a 'stop' condition is generated.

## 5.3.5 Software for $I^2C$ Communication

The data transfer in $I^2C$ mode is not automatically controlled by hardware unlike UART. The Master has to be programmmed by suitable software to generate 'Start' / 'Stop' conditions, various data bits from sending / receving , acknowledgement bit and clock signal. Here, we will discuss some examples of $I^2C$ software.

Since SDA (RC4) and SCL (RC3) are both open drain pins, they can be configured either as an output or as an input. When a PIC Processor is configured is $I^2C$ master, the SCL pin will function as open drain output while the SDA pin can be either an input or an open drain output. Hence, the software $I^2C$ will repeatedly access TRISC, the data direction register for PORT C. However, TRISC is located in bank-1 at an address 87H, which cannot be accessed by direct addressing without changing RP0 bit to 1 as given in the following instruction.

bsf STATUS, RP0

Then required bit of TRISC can be changed followed by clearing RP0 and reverting back to Bank-0.

bcf STATUS, RP0

Alternately, the indirect pointer FSR can have the address of TRISC and the required bit setting and bit clearing can be done indirectly.

Consider the following definitions.

SCL equ 3 SDA equ 4

The instruction bsf INDF, SDA will release the SDA line(as RC4/SDA pin is configured as an input, hence tristated), letting the external pullup resister pull it high or some $I^2C$ Slave device/Chip pull it low.

When FSR is used for indirect addressing, care should be taken to restore FSR value when subroutine is completed and the program returns to the main line program.

## 5.3.6 $I^2C$ Subroutine

SDA equ 4
SCL equ 3

The following subroutine DATA_OUT transfers out three bytes, i.e., ADDRDEV, ADDR8, and DATAWRTE

DATA_OUT:        call START           ; Generate start condition

                 movf ADDRDEV, W      ; Sends 7-bit peripheral address with R/$\overline{W}$
=0
                 call TRBYTE          ; Transmit
                 movf ADDR8, W        ; Send 8-bit internal address

```
                        call TRBYTE
                        movf DATAWRTE, W  ; Send data to be written
                        call TRBYTE
                        call STOP         ; Generate Stop condition
                        return
```

The DATA_IN subroutine, which is given below transfers out ADDRDEV (with R/$\overline{W}$=0) and ADDR8, restarts and transfers out ADDRDEV (with R/$\overline{W}$=1) and read one byte back into RAM variable DATARD.

```
DATA_IN:                call START
                        movf ADDRDEV, W   ; Send 7-bit peripheral address R/$\overline{W}$=0
                        call TRBYTE
                        movf ADDR8, W     ; Send int. address
                        call TRBYTE
                        call START1       ; Restart
                        movf ADDRDEV, W   ; Send 7-bit peripheral address R/$\overline{W}$=1
                        iorlwl 01H
                        call TRBYTE
                        bsf TRBUF, 7      ; Generate NO ACK
                        call RCVBYTE
                        movwf DATARD
                        call STOP
                        return
```

The 'START' subroutine initializes I$^2$C bus and then generates START condition on the I$^2$C bus. START1 bypasses the initialization of I$^2$C.

```
START:                  movlw 3BH         ;enables I$^2$C master mode by programming SSPCON
                        movwf SSPCON
                        bcf PORTC, SDA    ; drive SDA low when it is an o/p
                        movlw TRISC       ;set indirect pointer to TRISC
                        movwf FSR
START1:
                        bsf INDF, SDA     ; SDA=1
                        bsf INDF, SCL     ; SCL=1
                        call DELAY        ; Generates a suitable delay
                        bcf INDF, SDA     ; SDA=0
                        call DELAY        ; Generate a suitable delay
                        bcf INDF, SCL     ;SCL=0
                        return
```

STOP:

|        | bcf INDF, SDA | ;SDA=0                    |
|        | bsf INDF, SCL | ; SCL=1                   |
|        | call DELAY    | ; Generate a suitable delay |
|        | bsf INDF, SDA | ;SDA=1                    |
|        | return        |                           |

The subroutine 'TRBYTE' send out the byte available in w. It returns with Z=1 if ACK occurs. It returns with Z=0 if NOACK occurs. TRBUF is an 8-bit RAM variable used for temporary storage. The bits are shifted to carry flag (C) and the carry bit transmitted successively. Data transfer is complete when all 8-bits are transmitted. Setting C = 1 initially sets an index for 8-bits to be transferred. C is rotated through TRBUF. After transmitting C, C-bit is cleared. When TRBUF is completely cleared, all 8-bis are transmitted.

TRBYTE:

movwf   TRBUF
bsf     STATUS,C

TR_1:

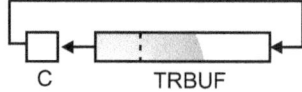

**Fig. 5.11 : Interfacing a PIC-microcontroller with a PC using Parallel Slave Port**

rlf     TRBUF, F
movf    RBUF,F
btfss   STATUS, Z
call    out_bit        ; Send a bit available in C
btfss   STATUS, Z
goto    TR_1
call    in_bit         ; Get the ACK bit in RCBUF<0>
movlw   01H            ;
andwf   RCBUF, W       ; Store the complement of ACK bit in Z flag
return

The RCVBYTE subroutine receives a byte from $I^2$ C into W using a RAM variable RCBUF buffer.

Call RCVBYTE with bit 7 of TRBUF clear for ACK

Call RCVBYTE with bit 7 of TRBUF set for NOACK

RCBUF is an 8-bit RAM variable used for recieving the data. the bit is recieved in the RCBUF<0> and is rotated successively through RCBUF as shown. The reception ends when all 8-bits are recieved.

RCVBYTE:

```
movlw   01H
movwf   RCBUF       ; Keep an index for 8-bits to be recieved.
RCV_1:
rlf     RCBUF, F
call    In_bit
btfss   STATUS, C
goto    RCV_1
rlf     TRBUF, F
call    Out_bit
movf    RCBUF,w
```

**Fig. 5.12**

```
return
```

The out_bit subroutine transmits carry bit, then clears the carry bit.

```
Out_bit:
bcf     INDF, SDA
btfsc   STATUS, C
bsf     INDF, SDA       ; Send carry bit
bsf     INDF, SCL
call    DELAY
bcf     INDF, SCL
bcf     STATUS,C        ; Clear carry bit
return
```

The in_bit subroutine receives one bit into bit-0 of RCBUF.

```
In_bit:
bsf     INDF,SDA
bsf     INDF, SCL
bcf     RCBUF, 0
btfsc   PORTC, SDA      ; Check SDA line for data bit
bsf     RCBUF, 0
bcf     INDF, SCL
return
```

## 5.3.7 Example of $I^2C$ interfacing

### DAC interfacing on $I^2C$ bus:

MAX518 is a dual 8-bit Digital to Analog Converter (DAC) with $I^2C$ interface. The address of the device is selectable through two pins $AD_1$ and $AD_0$. This device works in $I^2C$ slave mode. The connection diagram is shown as follows:

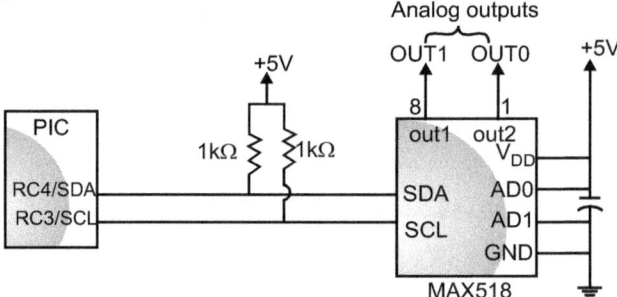

**Fig. 5.13**

The 7-bit device address is given as:

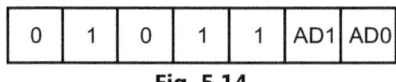

**Fig. 5.14**

For the present connection $AD_1 = 0$ and $AD_0 = 1$

The device address is 010 1101

Three bytes are sent to output an analog voltage.

First byte (Address of the DAC and $R/\overline{W}$ bit)

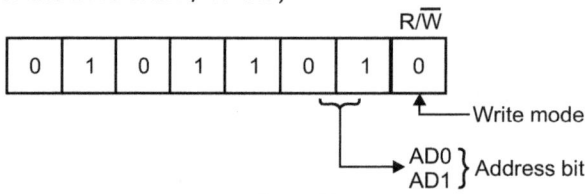

**Fig. 5.15**

Second byte (DAC Configuration)

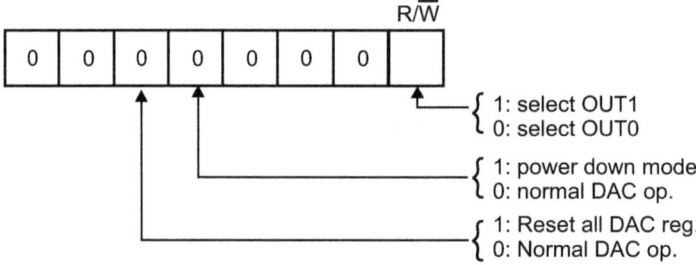

**Fig. 5.16**

Third byte (The 8-bit digital data(B) to be converted to analog voltage)
B

Analog output voltage = $V_{DD} \times B/256$

## 5.4 PARALLEL SLAVE PORT (PSP)

### Parallel slave port (PSP)

PIC Microcontroller offers a mechanism by which an 8-bit parallel bidirectional data transfer can be achieved between a PIC Microcontroller and a PC. PIC Microcontroller's Port-D and Port-E are used in this data transfer. For this data transfer, Port-D of PIC Microcontroller is configured as a Parallel slave Port (PSP) by setting bit-4 of TRISE Register. The pins of Port-E function as control pins ($\overline{RD}$, $\overline{WR}$ and $\overline{CS}$) for data transfer. The connection diagram between PC and the PIC Microcontroller in PSP Mode is shown below.

### Registers used for PSP Mode

ADCON1:

Three low significant bits (PCFG2-PCFG0) are set to enable Port-E pins for digital I/O
ADCON1, ADD: 9F H

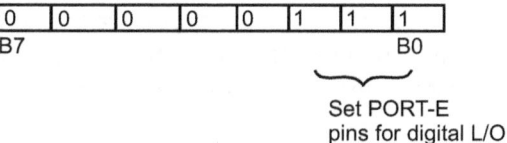

Fig. 5.17

### TRISE:

This register plays a crucial role in PSP configuration and control. The lower three bits control the data direction of PortE. the upper four bits are used in conjunction with parallel slave port as shown here.

### TRISE, ADD: 89 H

As explained, PSP Mode facilitates bidirectional 8-bit parallel data transfer. After ADCON1<b2-b0> and TRISE<b4, b2-b0> bits are set by the user program, PORTD and PORTE are configured for PSP. When PC wants to write an 8-bit data to PIC, it addresses the PIC microcontroller and the I/O address decoding circuit makes $\overline{CS}$ go low selecting the PIC chip. PC also makes $\overline{IOW}$ (I/O write) pin low and floats the data through its data bus (b7-b0). The data is written to PORTD and IBF flag in TRISE Register is set indicating that a byte is waiting at PORTD input buffer to be read by the PIC. Simultaneously PSPIF flag bit of PIR1 register is set and an interrupt is generated if PSPIE, PEIE and GIE bits have been set (i.e., the peripheral PSP interrupt is enabled.). After the data is read from PORTD, IBF bit automatically becomes zero; however PSPIF bit has to be cleared by software. If a second byte is written by the PC before the first byte is read, the second byte is lost and the IBOV flag in TRISE register is set indicating this loss.

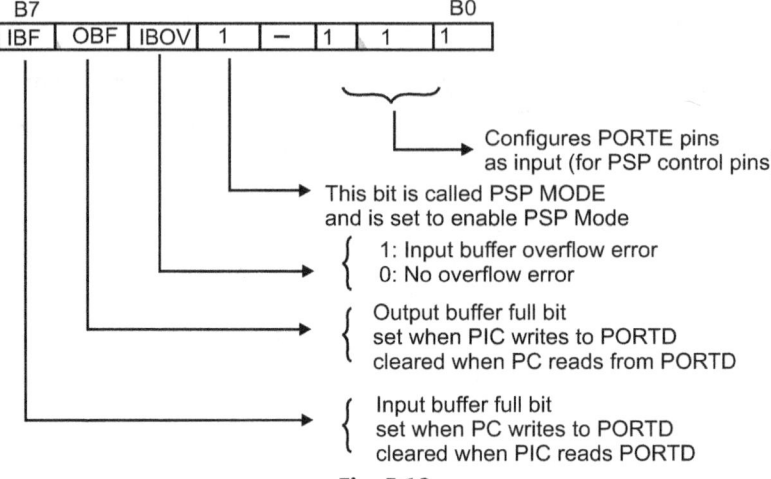

**Fig. 5.18**

Similarly a byte can also be read by the PC from the PIC microcontroller. When PIC writes a byte to PORTD, OBF flag is set indicating that the byte is waiting to be read by the PC. When the PC reads this bytes, OBF flag in TRISE Register is automatically cleared and the interrupt flag bit PSPIF is set indicating that the byte has been read by the PC from PIC microcontroller.

## 5.4.1 Serial Peripheral Interface (SPI) with Microchip PIC18 Families Microcontroller

The Serial Peripheral Interface (SPI) is one of the popular embedded serial communications widely supported by many of today's chip manufacture and it considered as one of the fastest serial data transfer interface for the embedded system. Because of its special in/out register configuration, the SPI master device could transfer its data and at the same time it receive a data from the SPI slave device with the clock speed as high as 10 MHz. Beside its superior data transfer speed; SPI also use a very simple data transfer protocol compared to the other serial data transfer methods. When the SPI master device want to send the data to the SPI slave device then the SPI master will just simply shifting its own data through a special 8-bits register and at the same time the SPI master will receive the data from the SPI slave into the same register as shown on this following picture:

With this circular shift register connection between the SPI master and the SPI slave devices, the complete data transfer from both devices will be accomplished in just 8 clock cycles. This means the SPI devices only need about 0.8 us to complete transfer the 8-bit data if we use 10 MHz clock. One of the drawbacks using the SPI especially when we use multiple SPI slave device is the SPI slave could not initiate sending its own data to the SPI master device, all the data transfer initiation is always come from the SPI master. The SPI master device has to poll each of the SPI slave devices to know whether the SPI slave device has a data to be sent to the SPI master device or not.

Polling the entire SPI slave devices will eventually consumed the SPI master resources when the SPI slave devices to be polled increase, therefore some of the SPI slave device is equipped with the interrupt pin to notify the SPI master device that it has a data to be read. You could read more about how SPI work in my previous posted blog Using Serial Peripheral Interface (SPI) Master and Slave with Atmel AVR Microcontroller.

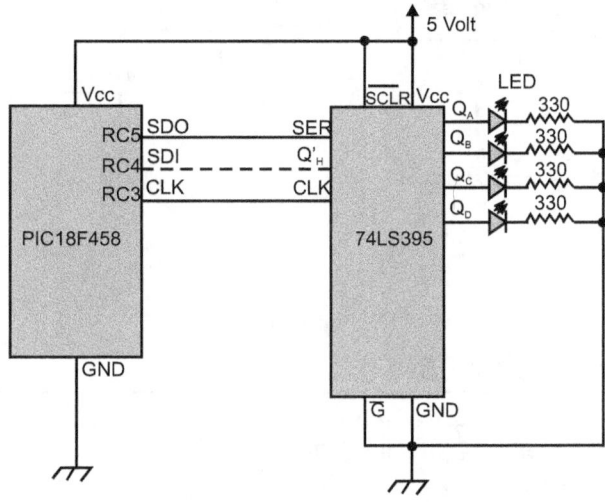

**Fig. 5.19**

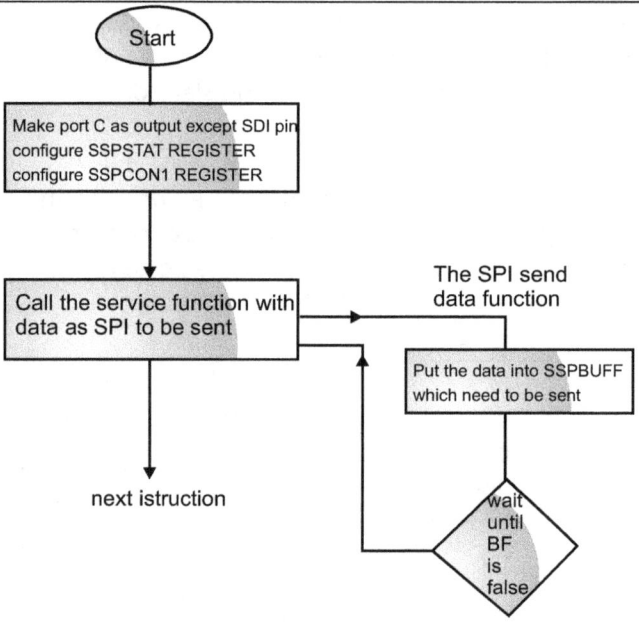

**Fig. 5.20**

## 5.4.2 Implementation of SPI

```
#pragma config OSC = HS, OSCS = OFF
#pragma config PWRT= OFF , BOR=ON, BORV = 45
#pragma config WDT = OFF
#pragma config DEBUG = OFF ,LVP =OFF , STVR =OFF        // CONFIGURATION BIT SETTING

#include <p18f458.h>

void spi(unsigned char);        //SPI Function To send the data

void delayMs(int x);            // to generate some delay

void main()                     // main program starts here
{
        SSPSTAT =0x40;          // Configure SSPSTAT for transmission occur from idle to active clock and Buffer flag =0
```

```
        SSPCON1=0x22;           //Configure  SSPCON1 for ENABLE SERIAL PORT
                                // and disable general I/O pin ,, SPI master clock= Fosc/64

        TRISC=0;                //Configure PORT C as output ,,
                                // we are only sending the data so we do't need to set SPI pin as input

        while(1)                // loop for ever so that led keep repeating that pattern
        {
            spi(0x01);          // send 01 hex to the SPI port it will glow the first led

            delayMs(1000);      // wait for approximate 1sec ,
                                //if we do't give the delay then led will flash too fast that
                                // we can't even know when it glow and when it off

            spi(0x02);          //send 02 hex to the SPI port it will glow the send led ,
                                //if you want to glow both led same time send 03 hex and so on

            delayMs(1000);      // wait for 1 sec
        }
}

void spi(unsigned char myData)
{
SSPBUF = myData;            // put the data in the SSPBUF register which going to be send

while(!SSPSTATbits.BF);     // wait until the all bits sended
}
```

```
void delayMs(int x)        // a general delay function
{
int i;
        for (x ;x>0;x--)
        {
        for (i=0;i<=110;i++);
        }
}
```

## 5.4.3 The PIC18F14K22 Microcontroller

On this tutorial I will use the Microchip PIC18F14K22 microcontroller, this microcontroller is one of my favorite 8-bit 20-pins PIC18 microcontroller families members as it is equipped with sophisticated advanced peripheral inside such as ADC, USART, ECCP (Enhanced Capture/Compare/PWM), SPI, I2C and the SR Latch (555 Timer) module for capacitive sensing. With 16K bytes flash ram and equipped with the build in circuit debug, this 8-bit 20-pins microcontroller is a perfect choice for serious embedded application or just for hobbyist's project.

| Inputs | | | | Parallel | Outputs | | Output |
|---|---|---|---|---|---|---|---|
| $\overline{CLR}$ | $\overline{SH/LD}$ | CLK | SER | A....H | $Q_A$ | $Q_B$ | $Q_H$ |
| L | X | X | X | X | L | L | L |
| H | X | L | X | X | $Q_{A0}$ | $Q_{B0}$ | $Q_{H0}$ |
| H | L | ↑ | X | a.....h | A | B | H |
| H | H | ↑ | H | X | H | $Q_{An}$ | $Q_{Gn}$ |
| H | H | ↑ | L | X | L | $Q_{An}$ | $Q_{Gn}$ |
| H | X | ↑ | X | X | $Q_{A0}$ | $Q_{B0}$ | $Q_{H0}$ |

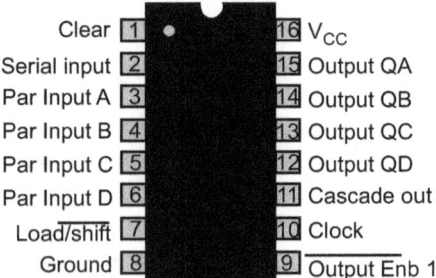

**Fig. 5.21**

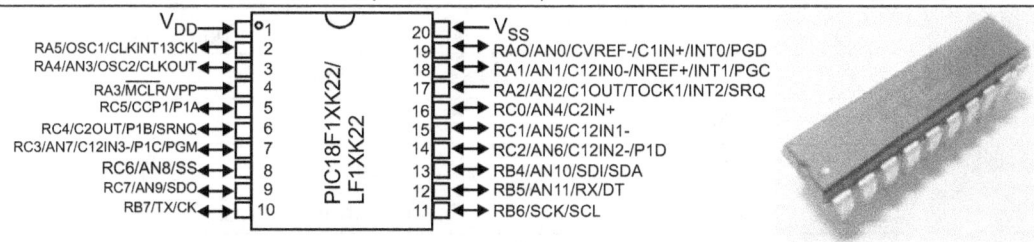

**Fig. 5.22**

The PIC18F14K22 microcontroller SPI peripheral support both master and slave mode but on this tutorial we will only exposing the PIC18F14K22 SPI master mode where on the first part we will expand the PIC18F14K22 microcontroller I/O by using the SPI I/O expansion chip and the second part we will turn the PIC18F14K22 microcontroller into a very useful SPI device testing tools that could be used to test and debug most of the SPI device chip available today. Both of these projects will give a good understanding and experience of how the PIC18F14K22 microcontroller SPI master peripheral works.

Now let's list down all the necessary hardware and software needed to accomplished these projects:

- Resistors: 330 Ohm (8) and 10K (1)
- LEDS: 3 mm Blue LED (8) and 3 mm Red LED (1)
- One momentary push button
- One Breadboard and some breadboard's jumper cables
- PICJazz 20-PIN learning board with Microchip PIC18F14K22 microcontroller from ermicro
- Microchip PICKit3 programmer (used in this project); you could also use the Microchip PICKit2 programmer.
- Microchip MPLAB IDE version 8.47 and Microchip C18 Compiler version 3.30
- Microchip Reference Document: PIC18F14K22 datasheet, MCP23S17 datasheet, and MCP42xxx datasheet

## 5.4.4 Microchip MCP23S17 SPI I/O Expander

The Microchip MCP23S17 SPI I/O expander will give you additional of 16 I/O ports where all the 2 x 8-bits general purpose I/O ports (GPIO) could be configure both as output or input. The MCP23S17 **IODIRA** and **IODIRB** I/O direction register is used to control the I/O direction for GPA and GPB respectively.

| Pin Name | Description |
|---|---|
| GPA0...7 | 8-bit General I/O Port A |
| GPB0...7 | 8-bit General I/O Port B |
| INTA | Pot A Interupt Signal |

*(Contd.)*

| Pin Name | Description |
|---|---|
| INTB | Port B Interrupt Signal |
| RESET | Reset Signal |
| A0, A1, A2 | Configuration Address |
| CS | Chip Select (Active Low) |
| CSK | Synchronous Clock |
| SI | Slave In |
| SO | Slave Out |
| $V_{DO}$ | +5 Volt |
| $V_{SS}$ | GND |

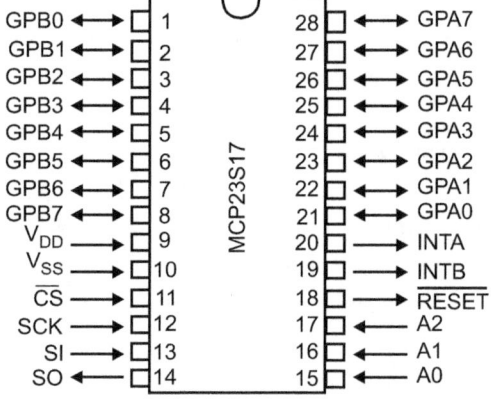

**Fig. 5.23**

One of the unique features of the Microchip MCP23S17 SPI I/O expander is in its configurable address capabilities. By setting the needed address to its address pins **A0, A1**, and **A2** we could configure up to 128 addressable SPI devices or in other world you could put up to 128 of MCP23S17 SPI I/O expander in the same SPI bus without having to have the separate **CS** (chip select) circuit logic for each of the MCP23S17 SPI I/O expander chip.

Each of the MCP23S17 general I/O pins also could be configured to generate interrupt when the ports pin changes its state (for more information please refers to Microchip MCP23S17 datasheet). For the purpose of this tutorial we will use the Microchip MCP23S17 just as the ordinary input and output expander for the PIC18F14K22 microcontroller.

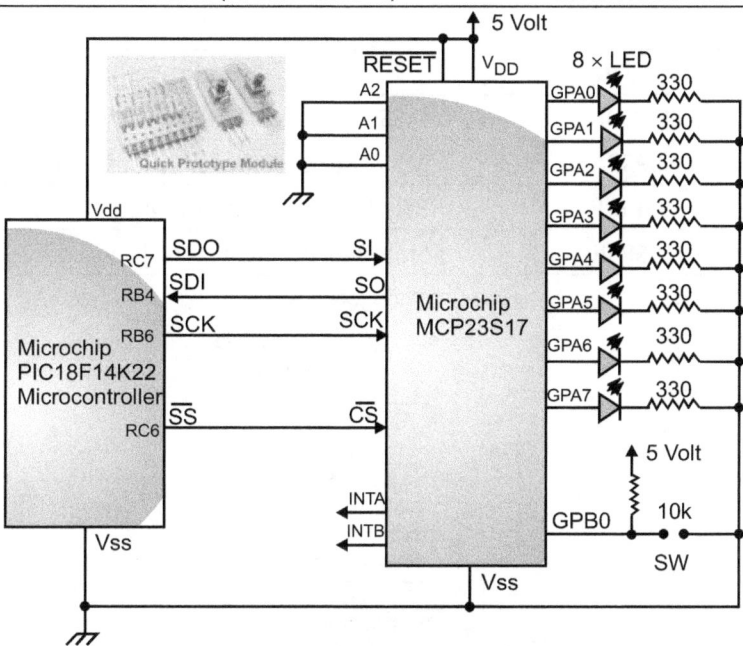

**Fig. 5.24**

For quick prototyping this project on the breadboard I used the SIL LED display and SIL push button modules which you could read more about it in my previous posted blog Single In Line (SIL) LED Display for your Microcontroller Project.

## 5.4.5 The PIC18 SPI Peripheral

The Microchip PIC18F14K22 microcontroller SPI peripheral actually is the part of Master Synchronous Serial Port (MSSP) modules inside the PIC18F14K22 microcontroller. Each module could be operated in one of the two modes: Serial Peripheral Interface (SPI) or Inter-Integrated Circuit (I2C). The SPI module could support both SPI master and SPI slave modes. For the purpose of this tutorial we will only focusing on the SPI Master mode.

| PIN | Description | Direction | I/O Port |
|---|---|---|---|
| SDO | Serial Data Out | Out | RC7 |
| SDI | Serial Data In | In | RB4 |
| SCK | Serial Clock (SPI Master Mode) | Out | RB6 |
| SS | Serial Select (SPI Slave Mode) | In | RC6 |
| SS | Serial Select (SPI Master Mode) Could be any I/O Port, currently implemented using RC6 | Out | RC6 |

| Register | Description |
|---|---|
| SSPCON1 | MSSP Control 1 Register (SPI Mode) |
| SSPSTAT | MSSP Status Register (SPI Mode) |
| SSPBUF | Serial Receive/Transmit Buffer |
| SSPSR | Shift Register (Not directly accessible) |

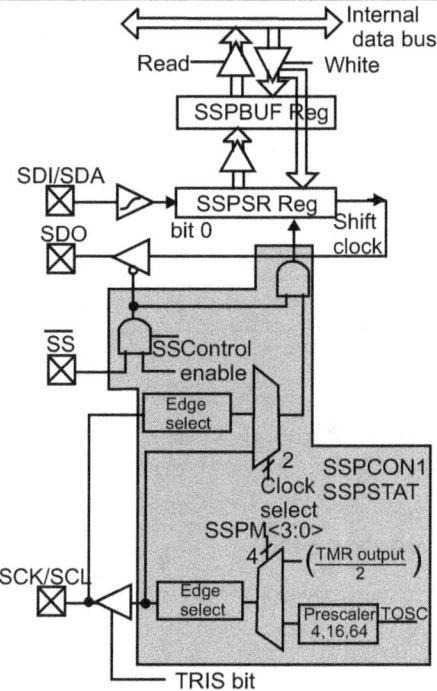

**Fig. 5.25**

To initialize the SPI peripheral inside the PIC18F14K22 microcontroller we need to enable this device for SPI master and set the master clock frequency using the MSSP control register 1 (**SSPCON1**) and the SPI status register (**SSPSTAT**), for complete information please refer to the Microchip PIC18F14K22 microcontroller datasheet.

### SSPCON1 – MSSP Control 1 Register (SPI Mode)

| R/W-0 | R/W-0 | R/W-0 | R/W-0 | R/W-0 | R/W-0 | R/W-0 | R/W-0 |
|---|---|---|---|---|---|---|---|
| WCOL | SSPOV | SSPEN | CKP | SSPM3 | SSPM2 | SSPM1 | SSPM0 |
| Bit 7 | | | | | | | Bit 0 |

| SSPM<3:0> | Description | SSPEN – Synchronous Serial Port Enable bit |
|---|---|---|
| 0011 | SPI Master mode, clock = TMR2 output/2 | 1 = Enables serial port and configures SCK, SDO, SDI and SS as serial port pins |
| 0010 | SPI Master mode, clock = FOSC/64 | 0 = Disables serial port and configures these pins as I/O port pins |
| 0001 | SPI Master Mode, Clock = FOSC/16 | CKP – Clock Polarity Select bit<br>1 = Idle state for clock is a high level |
| 0000 | SPI Master mode, clock = FOSC/4 | 0 = Idle state for clock is a low level |

| R/W-0 | R/W-0 | R-0 | R-0 | R-0 | R-0 | R-0 | R-0 |
|---|---|---|---|---|---|---|---|
| SMP | CKE | D/A | P | S | R/W | UA | BF |
| Bit 7 | | | | | | | Bit 0 |

**SMP – Sample Bit**

**SPI Master Mode :**

1 = Input data sampled at end of data output time

0 = Input data sampled at middle of data output time

SPI Slave Mode:

SMP must be cleared when SPI is used in Slave Mode.

**CKE – Clocked Select Bit**

1 = Transmit occur in transition from active to idle clock state

0 = Transmit occurs on transition from idle to active clock state

**BF – Buffer Full Status Bit (Receive mode only)**

1 = Receive complete, SSPBUF is full

0 = Receive not complete, SSPBUF is empty

The first thing before we could use the PIC18F14K22 SPI peripheral is to properly configure the PIC18F14K22 tri-state registers for the SPI master I/O operation; SDO (RC7) and SCK (RB6) as output port and SDI (RB4) as the input port, while the SS can be any port for SPI master operation but on this tutorial we will use the RC6 to select the SPI slave device. The following C code is used to set these SPI ports.

/* Initial the PIC18F14K22 SPI Peripheral */

TRISCbits.TRISC6 = 0;  // RC6/SS - Output (Chip Select)

TRISCbits.TRISC7= 0;   // RC7/SDO - Output (Serial Data Out)

TRISBbits.TRISB4= 1;   // RB4/SDI - Input (Serial Data In)

TRISBbits.TRISB6= 0;   // RB6/SCK - Output (Clock)

After initializing the I/O ports next we have to enable the PIC18F14K22 MSSP peripheral by setting theSSPEN (Synchronous Serial Port Enable) bit to logical "1" and selecting the SPI master clock frequency by setting the SSPM<3:0> (Synchronous Serial Port Mode) bits to maximum Fosc/4 (4 MHz) in theSSPCON1 register. The way the SPI data being transmitted or received is controlled by CKP (Clock Polarity) bit in the SSPCON1 register and CKE (Clock Select) bit in the SSPSTAT register. This behavior in the SPI world is known as the SPI bus mode, there are 4 SPI bus modes supported by the PIC18F14K22 MSSP module.

| SPI Bus Mode | Control Bits States | | Description |
|---|---|---|---|
| | CKP | CKE | |
| 0 | 0 | 1 | Clock Idle State = High, Transmit occurs on transition from active to Idle clock state |
| 1 | 0 | 0 | Clock Idle State = High, Transmit occurs on transition from Idle to active clock state. |
| 2 | 1 | 1 | Clock Idle State = Low, Transmit occurs on transition from active to Idle clock state |
| 3 | 1 | 0 | Clock Idle State = Low, Transmit occurs on transition from Idle to active clock state |

**The PIC18F14K22 Master Synchronous Serial Port (MSSP) SPI Bus Mode**

The following is the complete C code for initializing the PIC18F14K22 MSSP SPI mode:

SSPSTAT = 0x40;      // Set SMP=0 and CKE=1. Notes: The lower 6 bit is read only

SSPCON1 = 0x20;      // Enable SPI Master with Fosc/4

PORTCbits.RC6 = 1;   // Disable Chip Select

Last is the SMP bit in the **SSPSTAT** register, this bit is used to control how we sample the input data. Setting this bit to logical "**0**" means we sample the incoming data at the middle of data output time while setting this bit to logical "**1**" means we sample the incoming data at the end of data output time. The most commonly SPI bus mode widely supported by many SPI slave chip are mode 0 and mode 3, the different between these two mode only on the clock polarity.

Transmitting and Receiving SPI data is done in the **SSPBUF** register, therefore by placing the SPI master data on this register make the MSSP module start the SPI master transmission. After eight clock cycle then the 8-bit data in this register will be shifted out through the **SDO** pin to the SPI slave device and at the same time receive the 8-bit SPI slave data through the **SDI** pin. We could check this receive status by polling the **BF** (Buffer Full) status bit in the **SSPSTAT** register as shown on this following C code:

// Activate the SS SPI Select pin

PORTCbits.RC6 = 0;

// Start Data transmission

SSPBUF = TX_Data;

// Wait for Data Transmit/Receipt complete

```
while(!SSPSTATbits.BF);
// Get Slave Data
RX_Data = SSPBUF;
// CS pin is not active
PORTCbits.RC6 = 1;
```

Before we start the SPI master transmission to the SPI slave device, make sure we have to activate the SPI slave chip select pin and deactivate it after we finish transmitting the data. The complete SPI write and read algorithm is implemented in m the SPI_Write() and SPI_Read() functions.

**Inside The Infinite Loop**

To write and read data from and to the MCP23S17 SPI I/O expander device, first we need to send a read or write operation code followed by the MCP23S17 register address then last is the SPI master data. The first 8-bit operation code data consists of the MCP23S17 device ID (**0×40**), address (0 to 7), and read or write operation command (1 or 0).

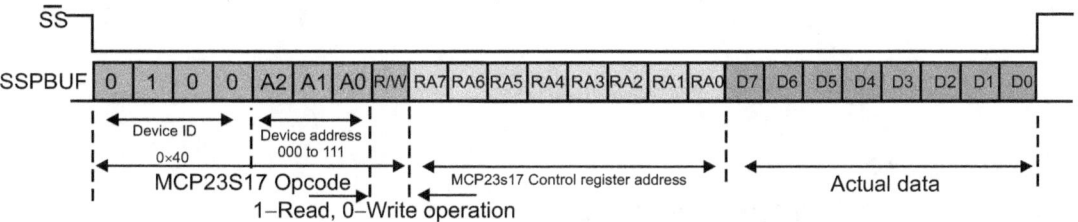

Fig. 5.26

**MCP23S17 Control Registers Address for IOCONA.BANK = 0**

| Register | Description | Address | Register | Description | Address |
|---|---|---|---|---|---|
| IODIRA | I/O Direction Register A | 0x00 | IOCONB | I/O Expander Configuration | 0x0B |
| IODIRB | I/O Direction Register B | 0x01 | GPPUA | GPIO Pull-up Resistor A | 0x0C |
| IPOLA | Input Polarity Port Register A | 0x02 | INTFA | Interrupt Flag Register B | 0x0D |
| IPOLB | Input Polarity Port Register B | 0x03 | INTFB | Interrupt Flag Register A | 0x0F |
| GPINTENA | Interrupt on Change pins A | 0x04 | INTFB | Interrupt Flag Register B | 0x0F |
| GPINTENB | Interrupt on Change Pins B | 0x05 | INTCAPA | Interrupt Capture Value A | 0x10 |
| DEFVALA | Default Value Register A | 0x06 | INTCAPB | Interrupt Capture Value B | 0x11 |
| DEFVALB | Default Value Register B | 0x07 | GPIOA | General Purpose I/O A | 0x12 |
| INTCONA | Interrupt on Change cont. A | 0x08 | GPIOB | General Purpose I/O B | 0x13 |
| INTCONB | Interrupt on Change cont. B | 0x09 | OLATA | Output Latch Register A | 0x14 |
| IOCONA | I/O Expander Configuration | 0x0A | OLATB | Output Latch Register B | 0x15 |

From the addressing diagram above you could see that at least we need to perform three SPI master writing to send or read the data to or from the MCP23S17 SPI slave I/O expander.

After configure the MCP23S17 registers, we entering the infinite loop where we simply read the MCP23S17 **GPIOB** input port and if the switch is pressed then the SPI master will start sending the LED display patterns to the MCP23S17 **GPIOA** output port.

```
// Initial the MCP23S17 SPI I/O Expander
SPI_Write(IOCONA,0x28);   // I/O Control Register: BANK=0, SEQOP=1, HAEN=1 (Enable Addressing)
SPI_Write(IODIRA,0x00);   // GPIOA As Output
SPI_Write(IODIRB,0xFF);   // GPIOB As Input
SPI_Write(GPPUB,0xFF);    // Enable Pull-up Resistor on GPIOB
SPI_Write(GPIOA,0x00);    // Reset Output on GPIOA
...
for(;;) {
  ...
  inp=SPI_Read(GPIOB);    // Read from GPIOB
  ...
  // Write to GPIOA
  SPI_Write(GPIOA,led_patern[cnt++]);
  ...
}
```

## 5.5 COMPARATORS

Analog comparator is an electronic device which compares the two voltage signals and provides TTL logic output to indicate the larger signal. The analog comparator is used in various applications where two inputs signals need to be compared. IR sensor is a very common example where analog comparator is used.

PIC18F4550 has two in-built comparators which can be used in eight different modes. These in-built comparators save the cost and connections for providing an extra IC (like LM324, LM339 etc) in the circuit. This article explains the configuration of the analog comparators of this PIC microcontroller.

PIC18F4550 consists of two analog comparators and these comparators can be used in eight different modes. The analog comparators' I/O pins are multiplexed with PortA pins (RA0 - RA5) pins of the controller. The register CMCON is configured to set the mode of the comparator in a PIC microcontroller. The bits of CMCON register are explained below.

## CMCON (Comparator Control Register)

| Bit 7 | Bit 6 | Bit 5 | Bit 4 | Bit 3 | Bit 2 | Bit 1 | Bit 0 |
|---|---|---|---|---|---|---|---|
| C2OUT | C1OUT | C2INV | C1INV | CIS | CM2 | CM1 | CM0 |

**CM2:CM0:** These bits are used to set one of the comparator modes (of 8 different modes). The comparator can be configured in following modes:

| CM2:CM0 | Mode | Description |
|---|---|---|
| 000 | Comparators Reset | The comparators remain reset and the output is read as zero |
| 001 | One Independent Comparator with Output | Comparator 1 is active with external output at RA4/C1OUT pin |
| 010 | Two Independent Comparators | Both comparators work separately with output changes at C1OUT and C2OUT bits respectively |
| 011 | Two Independent Comparators with Outputs | Both comparators work separately with external outputs at RA4/C1OUT and RA5/C2OUT pins respectively |
| 100 | Two Common Reference Comparators | The comparators works separately having common reference voltage on positive reference pins of the comparators with output changes at C1OUT and C2OUT bits respectively |
| 101 | Two Common Reference Comparators with Outputs | The comparators work separately having common reference voltage on positive reference pins of the comparators with external outputs at RA4/C1OUT and RA5/C2OUT pins respectively |
| 110 | Four Inputs Multiplexed to Two Comparators | Both comparators have multiplexed input at negative reference pin of the comparator. The common reference voltage at positive reference voltage pin comes from internal voltage reference module with output changes at C1OUT and C2OUT bits respectively |
| 111 | Comparators Off | Both comparators remain off |

**CIS:** This bit has to be configured when CM0:CM2 bit is set as 110.
    1 =     C1 VIN- connects to RA3/AN3/VREF+
    C2 VIN- connects to RA2/AN2/VREF-/CVREF
    0 =     C1 VIN- connects to RA0/AN0
               C2 VIN- connects to RA1/AN1

**C1INV:** This bit is used to invert the output bit of the comparator 1.

    1 = C1 output inverted

    0 = C1 output not inverted

**C2INV:** This bit is used to invert the output bit of the comparator 2.

    1 = C2 output inverted

    0 = C2 output not inverted

**C1OUT:** The output of the comparator 1 is stored here.

    When C1INV = 0:

    1 = C1 VIN+ > C1 VIN-

    0 = C1 VIN+ < C1 VIN-

    When C1INV = 1:

    1 = C1 VIN+ < C1 VIN-

    0 = C1 VIN+ > C1 VIN-

**C2OUT:** The output of the comparator 2 is stored here.

    When C2INV = 0:

    1 = C2 VIN+ > C2 VIN-

    0 = C2 VIN+ < C2 VIN-

    When C2INV = 1:

    1 = C2 VIN+ < C2 VIN-

    0 = C2 VIN+ > C2 VIN-

## 5.5.1 Using PIC's Analog Comparator

**Objective :**

To design proximity sensors using IR LEDs (IR sensors) using the in-built comparators of PIC microcontroller. The two IR sensors can be designed by using PIC18F4550 microcontroller. The *Two Common Reference Comparators with Outputs* (CM2:CM0 = 101) mode is selected to design the sensors. The input pins for sensor inputs are RA0/AN0 and RA1/AN1 (pins 2 & 3) and reference voltage pin is RA3/AN3 (pin 5). The outputs of the comparators 1 and 2 are obtained at RA4/C1OUT and RA5/C2OUT pins (pins 6 & 7). The diagram for both the comparators is given below low.

The complete connection layout is shown in the circuit diagram tab.

**Programming steps:**

1. Set RA0 – RA3 pins as input by data direction register.
2. Set RA4 - RA5 pins as output pins.
3. Select the relevant comparator mode from CMCON register.

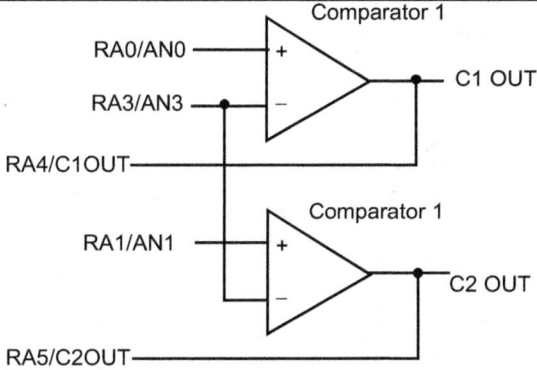

Fig. 5.27

The circuit connection for a single IR module is as follows.

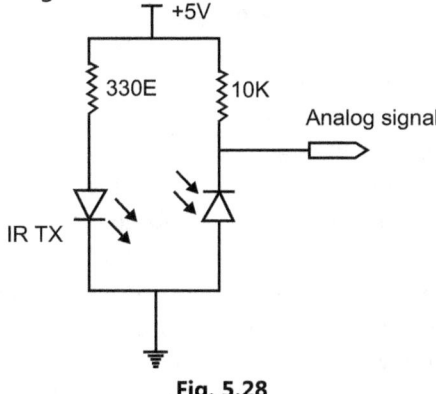

Fig. 5.28

## Comparator program

```
void main()
{
 TRISC = 0; //Configure PORTC as ouput
 TRISA.RA0=1; // Configure as input pin for negative input of Comparator 1
 TRISA.RA1=1; // Configure as input pin for negative input of Comparator 2
 TRISA.RA2=1; // Configure as input pin for positive input of Comparator 1
 TRISA.RA3=1; // Configure as input pin for positive input of Comparator 2
 TRISA.RA4=0; // Configure as output pin for output of Comparator 1
 TRISA.RA5=0; // Configure as output pin for output of Comparator 2
 CMCON=0x05; // 'Two Common Reference Comparators with Outputs' Mode
 while(1)
 {
  PORTC.F0 = CMCON.C2OUT; // Assigning output of comparator 2 to RC0
  PORTC.F1 = CMCON.C1OUT; // Assigning output of comparator 2 to RC1
  Delay_ms(100);
 }
}
```

## 5.5.2 Interfacing Serial Port

RS232 Communication with PIC Microcontroller

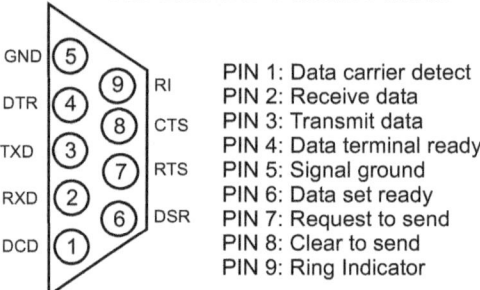

PIN 1: Data carrier detect
PIN 2: Receive data
PIN 3: Transmit data
PIN 4: Data terminal ready
PIN 5: Signal ground
PIN 6: Data set ready
PIN 7: Request to send
PIN 8: Clear to send
PIN 9: Ring Indicator

**Fig. 5.29**

This article shows how to do a simple communication via a RS232 interface with a PIC microcontroller. RS232 is a standard for a serial communication interface which allows to send and receive data via at least three wires. With the RS232 interface it is possible to setup a connection between a microcontroller and a PC (via PC's COM port) or between two microcontrollers. The RS232 interface can be used for many purposes like sending commands from a PC to a microcontroller, send debug information from a micontroller to a terminal, download new firmware to the microcontroller and many other things.

In this tutorial I will show how to link a PIC microcontroller to a standard PC. On the PC we will use a termial program to send and receive data. Data sent by the microcontroller will be shown in the terminal window and any key pressed inside the terminal will send the corresponding key code to the microcontroller. We will use this simple configuration to test and understand the RS232 communication.

Note that modern PCs don't have a serial port so you need to get a USB to serial converter. They are available at low cost.

**Block Diagram**

The following block diagram shows the whole setup:

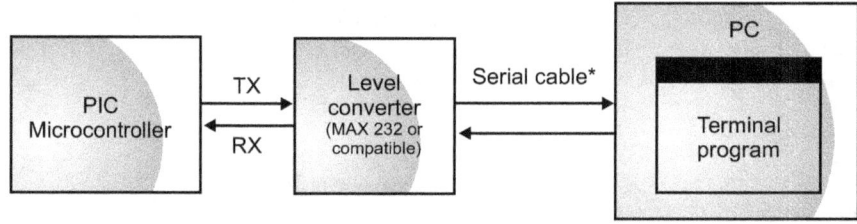

*or USB-to-Serial converter

**Fig. 5.30**

For serial communication the line used to transmit data is called TX and the line used to receive data is called RX. The level converter is required to translate the voltage level of the microntroller to RS232 voltage level. The microntroller operates at TTL level (0V = logic 0, +5V logic 1) whereas RS232 uses around +/-12V. A very famous RS232 level converter is the MAX232 chip.

### Hardware

In the schematic below a PIC microcontroller is connected to the RS232 level converter chip. A PIC18F2620 micocontroller is used, but it will also work with any other microcontroller which has a built-in UART.

### Schematic

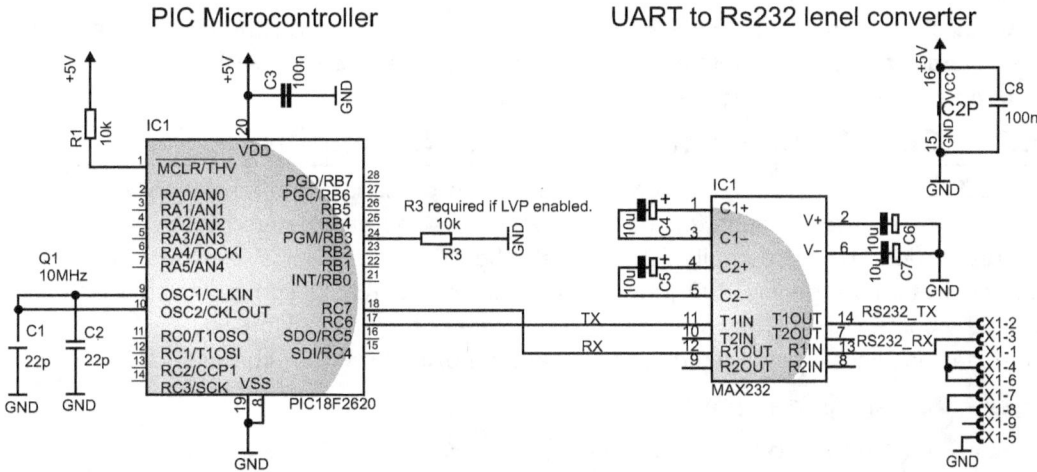

**Fig. 5.31**

The PIC is running at 10MHz. This will be important later when we configure the baudrate for the serial communication. Ther RS232 level converter uses the famous MAX232 chip, but any other MAX232 compatible chip will also work. It just requires 4 capacitors to do its job. These external capacitors are required for the charge pump inside the chip which generates the required voltage levels. The connections on the DB9 connector between pins 1,4,6 and 7,8 are required to satisfy the RS232 hardware handshake signals which we will not use here.

I have developed a RS232 module which allows direct connection to the microcontroller. It consists of a DB9 Female connector, a MAX232 compatible RS232 level converter and the capacitors. You can find the RS232 module here.

### RS232 Cable

To connect the above circuit to the PC we need a RS232 cable. The below picture shows the necessary connections.

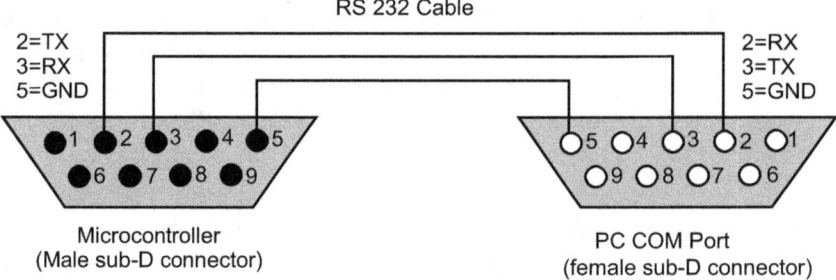

**Fig. 5.32**

**Hardware Picture**

Now since the hardware is ready we have to write the software for the PIC microcontroller. The different compiler vendors provide different ways to setup the UART in the PIC. So I will show how to use the UART for different compilers.

## 5.5.3 RS232 Communication with CCS C Compiler

The CCS C compiler provides a very simple way to do serial communication via RS232. It hides all the register settings for the user. Only the some parameters have to be provided, the rest is done by the compiler. By the way, the CCS C compiler also allows to do RS232 communication via general I/O pins, i.e. software based RS232 communication instead of using the built-in UART. That is a really great feature of the CCS C compiler.

Here the code lines which are required to setup the UART for RS232 communication.

```
#use delay(clock=40000000)
#use rs232(baud=57600,parity=N,xmit=PIN_C6,rcv=PIN_C7,bits=8)
```

As you can see, it is very simple!

The **#use delay** directive provides the compiler with the information about the clock frequency at which the PIC is running. We run the PIC at 10MHz with the 4X PLL fuse enabled, hence it is running at 40MHz, so we have to set **clock=40000000**.

The **#use rs232** directive provides the compiler the information about the RS232 parameters which shall be used for the communication. It is more or less self explaining:

**baud=57600**: specifies the baud rate for communication, we will use 57600 baud

**parity=**: specifies whether a parity bit shall be used or not, we will not use it, hence we disable it

**xmit=PIN_C6**: specifies the pin to be used for transmission, since we want to use the built-in UART we have to use pin RC6

**rcv=PIN_C7**: specifies the pin to be used for receiption, since we want to use the built-in UART we have to use pin RC7

**bits=8**: specifies the number of bits per transmitted data

To transmit data the following functions can be used:

```
int value = 1;
putc('A');                      /* transmit a character via RS232 */
puts("Test-String");            /* transmit a string via RS232 */
printf("Transmit a value: %d", value);  /* send formatted string via RS232 */
```

To receive data the following functions can be used:

```
char ch;
char string[32];
ch = getc();                    /* receives a single character via RS232 */
gets(string);                   /* receives a string via RS232, reads */
/* characters into the string until RETURN */
/* character (13) is encountered */
```

Here a simple demo program for the CCS C compiler. Project download link. To run the demo, the HEX file needs to be flashed into the PIC, e.g. with PICPgm Programmer.

```
/************************************************************************/
/* RS232 communication demo wiht CCS C compiler                         */
/************************************************************************/
#include <18F2620.h>
#device adc=16
#FUSES NOWDT            //No Watch Dog Timer
#FUSES WDT128           //Watch Dog Timer uses 1:128 Postscale
#FUSES H4               //High speed osc with HW enabled 4X PLL
#FUSES NOBROWNOUT       //No brownout reset
#FUSES LVP              //Low voltage prgming
#FUSES NOXINST          //Extended mode disabled (Legacy mode)
#use delay(clock=40000000)
#use rs232(baud=57600,parity=N,xmit=PIN_C6,rcv=PIN_C7,bits=8)
void main()
{
int value = 85;
```

```
char ch;
char string[64];
puts("***********************************");
puts(" RS232 demo with CCS C compiler ");
puts("***********************************");
/* start a new line (CR + LF) */
putc('\n');
putc('\r');
/* output variable in decimal format */
printf("Decimal variable output: %d\n\r", value);
/* output variable in hex format */
printf("Hex variable output: %x\n\r", value);
/* echo demo: PIC receives data and sends it back. */
/*       If ENTER key is received, this demo exits. */
puts("Type on the keyboard, PIC will echo back the characters:");
while (1)
{
/* read a single character */
ch = getc();
/* echo back the received character */
putc(ch);
}
}
```

## 5.5.4 Interfacing RTC with Microcontroller

Have you ever wondered how your PC and phones keep track of time even when the device is turned OFF? Well there is a Real Time Clock (RTC) that is kept powered even is the device is turned OFF. Once the device is turned ON and connected to the internet the device connects to a NTP server (Network Time Protocol) and updates the time and date. This post is intended to give a little insight over these RTCs and their interface with mid-range 8-bit microcontollers with I2C interface. It is possible to define a software I2C library if your favorite controller does not have a I2C bus, but that is beyond the scope of this post. This post will walk you through the steps involved in interfacing RTC with microcontroller.

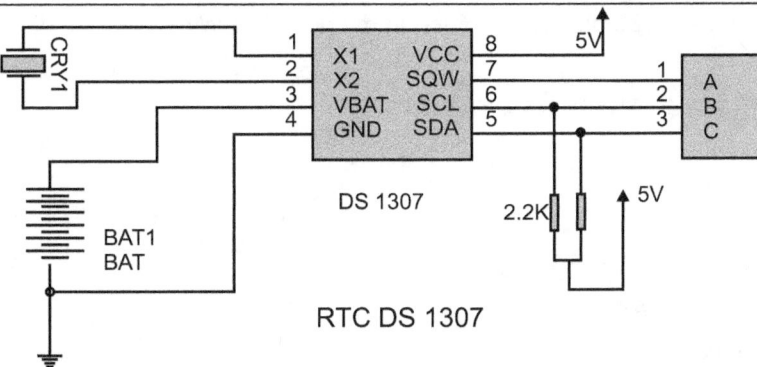

**Fig. 5.33**

This how the competed project will look like (at lest mine did) once you have gone through the entire post. The LCD display is a standard 20 character 4 line module. Asides that I have a MCU section on the right and the RTC and EEPROM breakout board with a CMOS battery on the left. You don't have to have a module to get started with you can make the circuit connection on a GP board or on a breadboard. Here is a schematic of the DS1307, as for the PIC schematic I leave it to you to make your own schematic.

I have chosen PIC18f4520 as my controller because of it availability and features. But that doesn't mean this document is restricted only to the interfacing RTC with this MCU only. If you are a PIC user then you are way off most of the code can be reused with minor modification. If you prefer using other families of controller (and good with it) you should be able to port the code to your own controller. If everything goes as intended by the end of this post you should be able to interface the RTC with any microcontroller of you choice.

The most common RTC that is available on the market is the DS1307 and its has been around for quite some time and hence there is an abundance of documentation online for its interface. The device can be interface using the I2C protocol also called as the two wire interface. This simple protocol that allows data to be read and written serially using just two line (SCL – clock and SDA – data).

I assume that readers are aware of the I2C protocol specifications if not please read my previous post here. The process of Interfacing RTC may turn out to be a little daunting if you don't fully understanding the I2C bus specification. The datasheet of the DS1307 real time clock is quiet self explanatory and little has to be explained if you have a basic idea about the interface. There are a few time keeping registers in the IC that can be read and written. Once the actual time is set the clock will keep a track of the time. For this a dedicated power supply (CMOS battery) which kicks in if the power to the system is turned OFF.

### 5.5.4.1 Programming

This function gets the time from the RTC, It takes the register address to read from as a parameter and return the content of that register one at a time. This follows the procedure to read and write data in I2C bus as explained in my post Two Wire Interface (i2c-protocol) in a nut shell.

```
1  unsigned int get_time(unsigned int address)
2  {
3      unsigned int data;
4      i2c_start();
5      i2c_write(SLAVE_DS1307|WRITE);
6      i2c_write(address);
7      i2c_restart();
8      i2c_write(SLAVE_DS1307|READ);
9      SSPCON2bits.ACKDT=1;
10     data=i2c_read();
11     i2c_stop();
12     return (data);
13 }
```

This function set the time in the RTC's time keeping register, It take the register address to read from and the data to be written as parameters. This follows the procedure to write data to I2C bus as explained in my post Two Wire Interface (i2c-protocol) in a nut shell.

```
1  void set_time(unsigned int address, unsigned int value)
2  {
3      i2c_start();
4      i2c_write(SLAVE_DS1307|WRITE);
5      i2c_write(address);
6      i2c_write(value);
7      i2c_stop();
8      return;
9  }
```

To reset the time use this function. You will have to calibrate the value for each register manually before suing this function. This may not be the most optimized means to set the time again this is the most straight forward method. This is all BCD so there is not much calculation involved if you want the hours to be 12 then just pass 0×12 to that corresponding register.

```c
1  void reset_time()
2  {
3      i2c_start();
4      i2c_write(SLAVE_DS1307|WRITE);
5      i2c_write(0x00);    // Address of the first register
6      i2c_write(0x00);    // Seconds register
7      i2c_write(0x00);    // Minutes register
8      i2c_write(0x01);    // Hours register
9      i2c_write(0x01);    // Days register
10     i2c_write(0x01);    // Date register
11     i2c_write(0x01);    // Month register
12     i2c_write(0x00);    // Year register
13     i2c_stop();
14     return;
15 }
```

This is more like a code that can be used in any controller as I have not done any MCU specific stuffs up till now. All the MCU specific stuffs are done in the subroutine calls. I strongly recommend you to write your own I2C library from scratch I will post mine just for a reference. I have tested this code and its working properly with MPLAB X and C18 compiler.

```c
1  #include "p18f4520.h"
2  void i2c_start(void)    // Initiate a Start sequence
3  {
4     TRISCbits.TRISC3=1;
5     TRISCbits.TRISC4=1;
6     PIR1bits.SSPIF=0;
7     SSPCON2bits.SEN=1;
8     while(PIR1bits.SSPIF==0);
9     return;
10 }
11 void i2c_restart(void)  // Initiate a Repeated start sequence
12 {
13    PIR1bits.SSPIF=0;
14    SSPCON2bits.RSEN=1;
```

```
15   while(PIR1bits.SSPIF==0);
16   return;
17 }
18 void i2c_write(unsigned int data)    // Write data to slave.
19 {
20   PIR1bits.SSPIF=0;
21   SSPBUF=data;
22   while(PIR1bits.SSPIF==0);
23   return;
24 }
25 void i2c_stop(void)    //Initiate a Stop sequence.
26 {
27   PIR1bits.SSPIF=0;
28   SSPCON2bits.PEN=1;
29   while(PIR1bits.SSPIF==0);
30   TRISCbits.TRISC3=0;
31   TRISCbits.TRISC4=0;
32   return;
33 }
```

## 5.6 I2C (INTER INTEGRATED CIRCUIT)

The **I2C** (Inter-IC) bus is a bi-directional two-wire serial bus that provides a communication link between integrated circuits (ICs). **I2C** is a synchronous protocol that allows a master device to initiate communication with a slave device. Data is exchanged between these devices.

**PIC16F/18F Slicker Board**

The PIC16F/18F Slicker board is specifically designed to help students to master the required skills in the area of embedded systems. The kit is designed in such way that all the possible features of the microcontroller will be easily used by the students. The kit supports in system programming (ISP) which is done through USB port.

Microchip's PIC (PIC16F877A), PIC16F/18F Slicker Kit is proposed to smooth the progress of developing and debugging of various designs encompassing of High speed 8-bit Microcontrollers.

## RTC (Real Time Clock)

The DS1307 Serial Real-Time Clock is a low-power; full binary-coded decimal (BCD) clock/calendar plus 56 bytes of NV SRAM. Address and data are transferred serially via a 2-wire, bi-directional bus. The clock/calendar provides seconds, minutes, hours, day, date, month, and year information. The end of the month date is automatically adjusted for months with fewer than 31 days, including corrections for leap year. The clock operates in either the 24-hour or 12-hour format with AM/PM indicator.

## Interfacing I2C - RTC

Fig. 1 shows how to interface the EEPROM with microcontroller through I2C. I2C is a Master-Slave protocol. I2C has a clock pulse along with the data. The master device controls the clock line, SCL. This line dictates the timing of all transfers on the I2C bus. No data will be transferred unless the clock is manipulated.

I2c bus supports many devices, each device is recognized by a unique address—whether it's a micro-controller, LCD Driver, memory or keyboard interface and can operate as transmitter or receiver based on the functioning of the device. The controller designed controls the RTC ds1307 device through I2C protocol. The I2C Controller here acts as a master device and controls RTC ds1307 which acts as a slave. The read operation is accomplished by sending a set of control signals including the address and/or data bits. The control signals must be accompanied with proper clock signals.

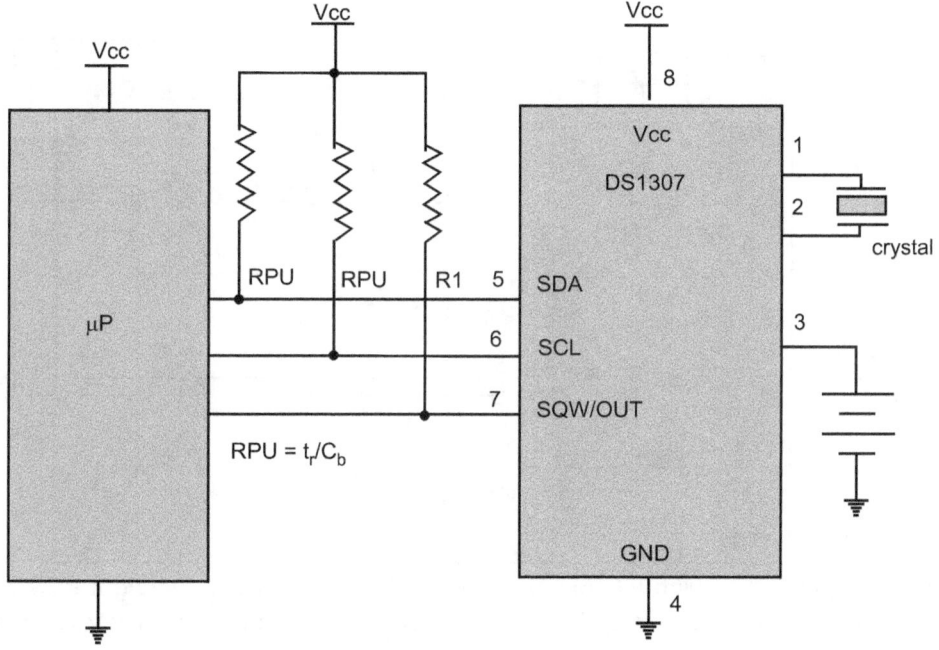

**Fig. 5.34 : Interfacing I2C - RTC to Microcontroller**

### Interfacing I2C – RTC with PIC16F877A

We now want to read date & time by using I2C - RTC in PIC16F/18F Slicker Board. Wiring up an I2C based RTC to the I2C port is relatively simple. The RTC also makes the software easier as it takes care of all calendar functions; accounting for leap years etc. The DS1307 (RTC) Real Time Clock IC (an I2C real time clock) is an 8 pin device using an I2C interface.

In PIC16F/18F Slicker Kit, 2 nos. of RTC lines are controlled by I2C Enabled drivers. I2C Lines serial clock of CLK (RC3), serial data of DATA (RC4) connected to the I2C based serial RTC ds1307 IC. The date & times are read in PIC16F/18F Slicker Kit by using these DATA & CLK I2C lines.

### Pin Assignment with PIC16F877A

| I2C RTC | | PIC16F/18F Lines | Real Time Clock |
|---|---|---|---|
| | CLK | RC3 | |
| DS1307 | DATA | RC4 | |

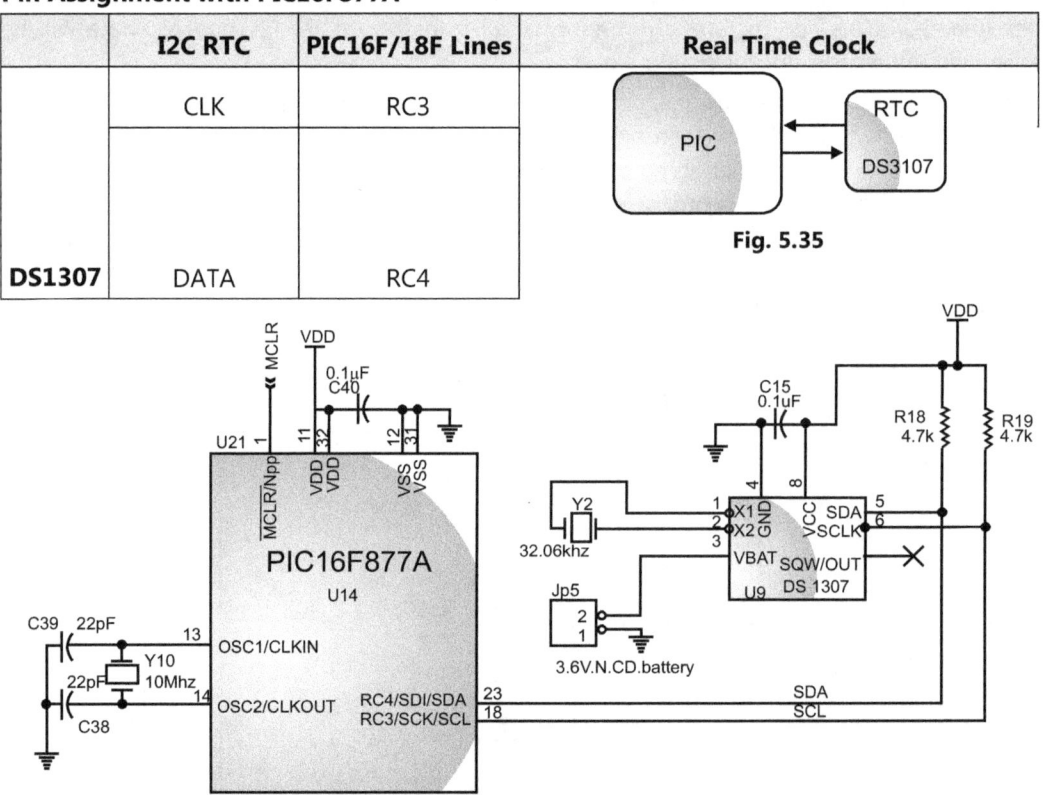

Fig. 5.35

Fig. 5.36

## 5.6.1 Source Code

The Interfacing I2C – RTC with PIC16F877A program is very simple and straight forward that read date & time in RTC by using I2C & the value is displayed in serial port. A delay is occurring in every single data read from RTC. The delay depends on compiler how it optimizes the loops as soon as you make changes in the options the delay changes.

## C Program to interface I2C – RTC with PIC16F

## Title : Program to read date & time from I2C - RTC

```c
#include<pic.h>      //Define PIC Registers
#include<stdio.h>
__CONFIG(0x3f72); //Select HS oscillator, Enable (PWRTE,BOREN),
         //Disable (CPD,CP,WDTEN,In-circuit Debugger)
#define LC01CTRLIN   0xd0
#define LC01CTRLOUT 0xd1
#define I2C_FREG   100
#define FOSC    10000
#define BAUD_RATE 9.6      // 9600 Baud rate
#define BAUD_VAL  (char)(FOSC/ (16 * BAUD_RATE )) - 1;
//Calculation For 9600 Baudrate @10Mhz

unsigned char sec,min,hour,day,date,month,year;
unsigned char data[7]={0x45,0x59,0x71,0x04,0x05,0x10,0x06};
int i;
void DS1307Write(unsigned char,unsigned char);
void WaitMSSP();
unsigned char DS1307Read(unsigned char);
void i2c_init(void);
void ds1307_init(void);
void serial_init(void);
void DelayMs(unsigned int);
void main()
{
  int count=0;
  DelayMs(20);
   ds1307_init();
   serial_init();
   for(i=0;i<7;i++)
```

```c
      DS1307Write(i,data[i]);
      printf("\033[2J");
      DelayMs(20);
       while(1)
      {
        sec=DS1307Read(0);        // Read second
        min=DS1307Read(1);        // Read minute
        hour=DS1307Read(2);       // Read hour
        day=DS1307Read(3);        // Read day
        date=DS1307Read(4);       // Read date
         month=DS1307Read(5);     // Read month
        year=DS1307Read(6);       // Read year
        printf("Time: %x : %x : %x  ",(hour&0x1f),min,sec);   //Display the Hours, Minutes, Seconds(hours is taken from 5 LSB bits
        printf("Date: %x / %x / %x   \r",date,month,year);   //Display the Date, Month, Year
        DelayMs(150);
      }
}
void DS1307Write(unsigned char addr, unsigned char data)
{
    SEN=1;     //Initiate Start condition on SDA & SCL pins
    WaitMSSP();
    SSPBUF=LC01CTRLIN;  // Slave address + Write command
    WaitMSSP();
    SSPBUF=addr;        // Write the location
    WaitMSSP();
    SSPBUF=data;        // Write the Data
    WaitMSSP();
    PEN=1;           // Enable the Stop bit
    WaitMSSP();
}
unsigned char DS1307Read(unsigned char addr)
```

```c
{
    unsigned char x;

    RSEN=1;    // Enable the repeated Start Condition
    WaitMSSP ();
    SSPBUF=LC01CTRLIN; // Slave address + Write command
    WaitMSSP ();
    SSPBUF=addr;
//Write the location (memory address of Hour, minute, etc...)
    WaitMSSP ();
    RSEN=1;    // Enable the repeated Start Condition
    WaitMSSP ();
    SSPBUF=LC01CTRLOUT; // Slave address + Read command
    WaitMSSP ();
    RCEN=1;         // Enable to receive data
    WaitMSSP ();
    ACKDT=1;   // Acknowledge the operation (Send NACK)
    ACKEN=1;   // Acknowledge sequence on SDA & SCL pins
    PEN=1;     // Enable the Stop bit
    WaitMSSP ();
    x=SSPBUF;  // Store the Receive value in a variable
    return (x);
}
 void WaitMSSP()
{
    while(!SSPIF); // SSPIF is zero while TXion is progress
    SSPIF=0;
}

void ds1307_init()
{
    TRISC3=1;    // RC3,RC4 set to I2C Mode(Input)
    TRISC4=1;
```

```c
    SSPCON=0x28;   // Enable the SDA,SCL & I2C Master Mode
    SSPADD=(FOSC / (4 * I2C_FREG)) - 1;// SSP baud rate 100Khz
    SSPSTAT=0x80;  // Disable slew Rate control
    PORTC=0x18;
    DS1307Write(0,0x00);

}


void serial_init()
{
  TRISC6=1;    // RC7, RC6 set to USART Mode
  TRISC7=1;
  TXSTA=0x24;
// Enable Transmission, Asynchronous mode, High Speed mode
  SPBRG=BAUD_VAL;   // 9600 Baud rate selection
  RCSTA=0x90;   // Enable Serial Port & Continuous Reception
  TXIF=1;      // Enable Transmission
}

void putch(unsigned char byte)//Required for printf statement
{

  while(!TXIF); // Wait for the Transmit Buffer to be empty
  TXREG = byte; // Transmit the Data
}

 void DelayMs(unsigned int Ms)
{
  int delay_cnst;
  while(Ms>0)
  {
    Ms--;
```

```
        for(delay_cnst = 0;delay_cnst <220;delay_cnst++);
    }
}
```

To compile the above C code you need the Mplab software & Hi-Tech Compiler. They must be properly set up and a project with correct settings must be created in order to compile the code. To compile the above code, the C file must be added to the project. In Mplab, you want to develop or debug the project without any hardware setup. You must compile the code for generating HEX file. In debugging Mode, you want to check the port output without PIC16F/18F Slicker Board. The PICKIT2 software is used to download the hex file into your microcontroller IC PIC16F877A through USB port.

### Testing the I2C – RTC with PIC16F/18F

Give +12V power supply to PIC16F/18F Slicker Board; the RTC Battery device is connected with the PIC16F/18F Slicker Board. First check the entire Battery device fixed properly. A serial cable is connected between the microcontroller and PC. In PC, open the Hyper Terminal for displaying the values from RTC. Now, the Hyper Terminal shows the received data from RTC Battery through I2C. If the Hyper Terminal is working but it is not reading any value from PIC16F/18F Slicker Board, then you just check the jumper connections. Change the Battery & ds1307 device.

## 5.7 EEPROM WITH PIC MICROCONTROLLER

EEPROM is an abbreviation for Electrically Erasable Programmable Read Only Memory and it is a Non-Volatile memory. It is used in computers and other electronic devices to store data that must me saved during no power supply. EEPROM is a class of ROM (Read Only Memory) which can be electrically erased in bit by bit and able to store new data. A small amount of EEPROM (usually 128/256 bytes) is available internally with PIC Microcontrollers. I have already posted about Using Internal EEPROM of PIC Microcontroller. But if the amount of data that we required to store in EEPROM is large, say in the order of Kilobytes then we have to interface external EEPROM with PIC Microcontroller. There are many types of EEPROM chips are available from a number of manufactures. 24C series are the one of the most popular serial EEPROMs. It uses I2C (Inter-Integrated Circuit) bus to interface with Microcontroller and are available up to 128KB. I2C is a multi-master serial single ended computer bus used to interface low speed devices to a cellphone, embedded system, mother board or other electronic devices. Here we are using 24C64 64K serial EEPROM. 24C64 works as a slave device on I2C bus. Register access can be obtained by implementing a START signal followed by device identification address. Then each memory locations can be accessed by using its address until a STOP condition is executed. Pin Descriptions of 24C64

EEPROM - A0, A1, A2 – Chip Address Inputs : These inputs are used for multiple device operations. The logic levels on

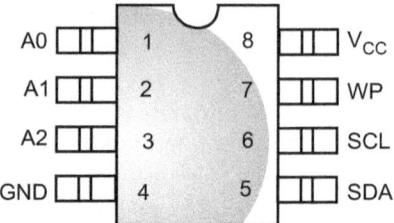

**Fig. 5.37 : 24C64 Pin Diagram**

these input pins are compared with the corresponding bits in the slave address and the chip is selected if the compare is true. Thus up to eight devices can be connected to same bus using different chip select bit combinations.

- **WP – Write Protect :** When this pin is kept LOW (grounded) normal read and write operations are possible but when it is HIGH (Vcc) write operations will be inhibited. The internal PULL DOWN resistor of this pin keep the device unprotected when it is left floating.

- **Vcc and Vss :** Vcc is the positive DC supply pin. The device is able to work with in 1.8 to 5.5V range. Vss is the ground pin (0v).

- **SDA – Serial Data :** This is bidirectional pin used to transfer data and address to and from the device.

- **SCL – Serial Clock :** This pin is used to synchronize data transfer through SDA. Device Addressing

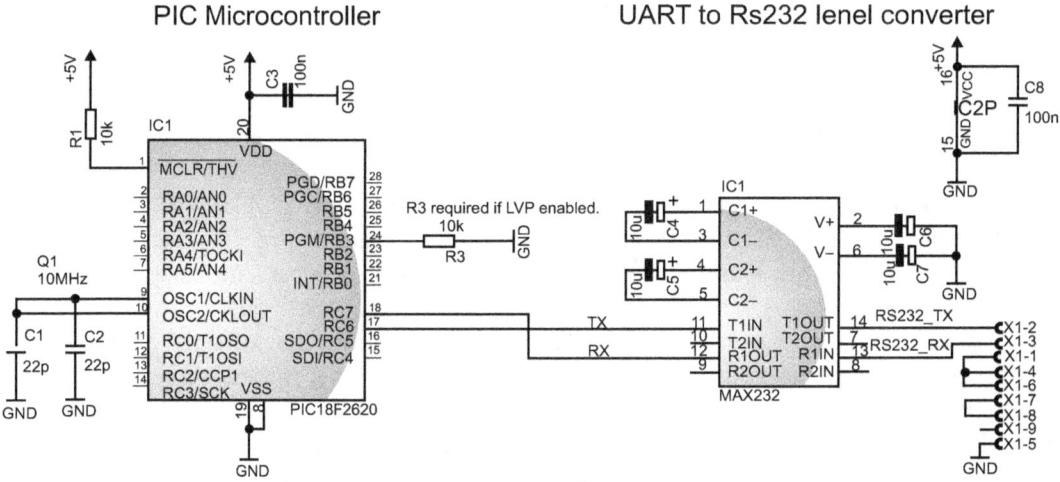

**Fig. 5.38 : 24XX64 EEPROM Device Addressing**

Control Byte is the first byte received by a slave device after receiving start signal from a master device. For 24C64 first 4 bits are control code (1010) for the device identification. Next 3 bits of the control byte are Chip Select Bits (A2, A1, A0). These bits allows us to connect up to eight 24XX64 devices on the same bus. The Chip Select Bits of control byte must be correspond to the logic levels of A2, A1, A0 of the device to be selected. The last bit of Control Byte is used to define the operation to be performed. It is set to 1 when read operation is to be performed and set to 0 when write operation is to be performed.

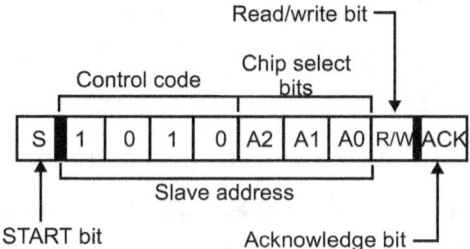

**Fig. 5.39**

Read the Next Page to read about reading and writing data from/to EEPROM. Please Jump to this page if you don't need detailed explanation.

### Writing Data to EEPROM

We can write data to 24C64 in two ways. **Byte Write** In this mode one byte is written at a time. After giving the START signal, the master send control byte, the control code (four bits), the chip select (three bits), and the R/W bit (which is a logic low) via I2C bus. This indicates the addressed device that, higher order address of memory location to be written will be follow after it has generated acknowledge signal. Thus next byte transmitted by master device will be higher order address and it will be stored in the address pointer of the 24XX64. The Least Significant Address byte will be followed after it has generated acknowledge signal. Then the master device will send data to written the address location. When the 24XX64 acknowledges, the master issues stop signal.

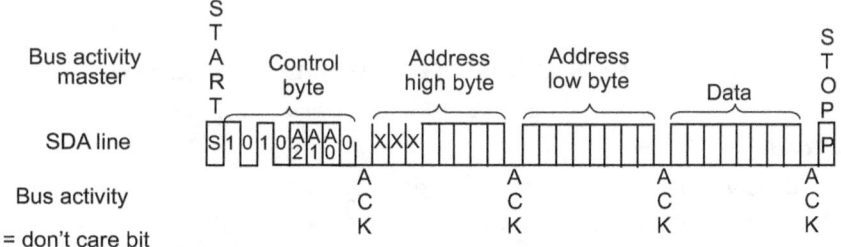

**Fig. 5.40 : 24XX64 EEPROM Byte Write**

**Note:** Some delay should be given between sequential write processes otherwise write cycle may not occur.

## Page Write

Page write is similar Byte write, instead of generating STOP signal master transmits up to 31 additional bytes. These are temporarily stored in the on-chip page buffer and will be written in to memory after the master has given STOP signal. If the master sends more than 32 bytes, previously written data will be over written

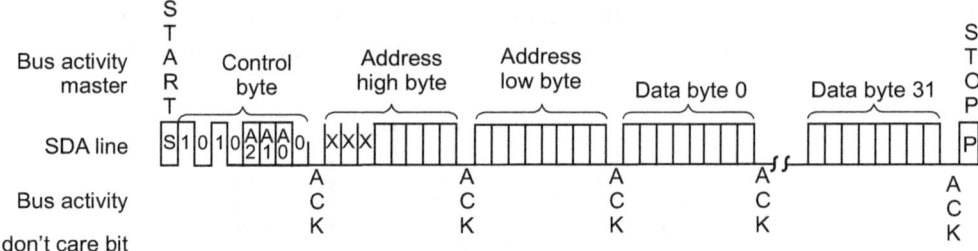

X = don't care bit

**Fig. 5.41 : 24XX64 EEPROM Page Write 4.png (16.68 KiB) Viewed 751 times**

**Note:** Some delay should be given between sequential write processes otherwise write cycle may not occur. Reading Data From EEPROM

Data can be read from 24XX64 EEPROM in 3 ways.

## Current Address Read

The 24XX64 EEPROM contains an internal counter which maintains address of last memory location accessed, incremented by one internally. Thus upon receiving control byte with read/write control bit set to 1, 24XX64 issues acknowledge signal and transmits the 8-bit data word in the next memory location.

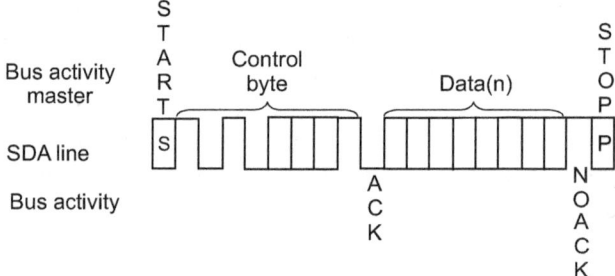

**Fig. 5.42 : 24C64 EEPROM Current Address Read**

**5.png (15.67 KiB) Viewed 751 times**

## Random Read

Random read operation allows master to access any memory location in random manner. To perform this type of operation, we want to set the address in internal address counter to the required value. This is achieved by sending address to 24XX64 EEPROM as the part of write operation.

After the acknowledge of this process, the master issues a START signal and control byte for read operation. Thus the required random memory location can be easily accessed.

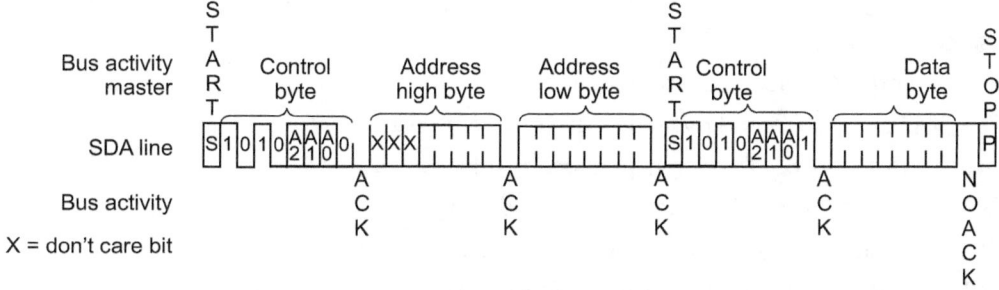

Fig. 5.43 : 24C64 EEPROM Random Read

6.png (20.2 KiB) Viewed 751 times

## Sequential Read

Sequential Reading is initiated in a similar way as Random Read, except that after the 24XX64 EEPROM transmits first data byte master issues acknowledge signal instead of STOP signal in Random Read operation. This will direct 24XX64 EEPROM to send next data byte.

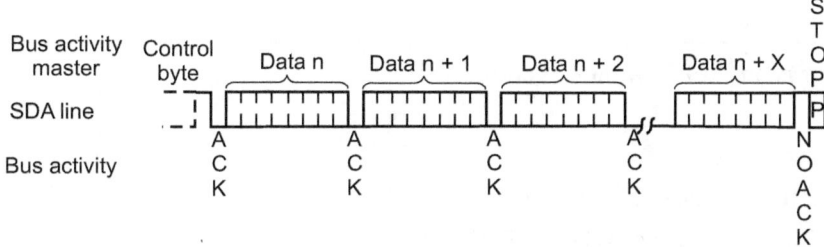

Fig. 5.44 : 24C64 EEPROM Sequential Read

7.png (14.98 KiB) Viewed 751 times

## C Programming

MikroC Pro for PIC Microcontroller provides built-in library routines to communicate with I2C devices. Here we deals only with Byte Write and Random Read operations. Using these you can easily make programs for other operations.

C Function for Write Data to EEPROM :

Code : Select All

void write_EEPROM(unsigned int address, unsigned int dat)

```c
{
    unsigned int temp;
    I2C1_Start(); // issue I2C start signal
    I2C1_Wr(0xA0); // send byte via I2C (device address + W)
    temp = address >> 8; //saving higher order address to temp
    I2C1_Wr(temp); //sending higher order address
    I2C1_Wr(address); //sending lower order address
    I2C1_Wr(dat); // send data (data to be written)
    I2C1_Stop(); // issue I2C stop signal
    Delay_ms(20);
}
```

MikroC Function to Read Data from EEPROM :

Code : Select All

```c
unsigned int read_EEPROM(unsigned int address)
{
    unsigned int temp;
    I2C1_Start(); // issue I2C start signal
    I2C1_Wr(0xA0); // send byte via I2C (device address + W)
    temp = address >> 8; //saving higher order address to temp
    I2C1_Wr(temp); //sending higher order address
    I2C1_Wr(address); //sending lower order address
    I2C1_Repeated_Start(); // issue I2C signal repeated start
    I2C1_Wr(0xA1); // send byte (device address + R)
    temp = I2C1_Rd(0u); // Read the data (NO acknowledge)
    I2C1_Stop();
    return temp;
}
```

## 5.7.1 Circuit Diagram for Demonstration :

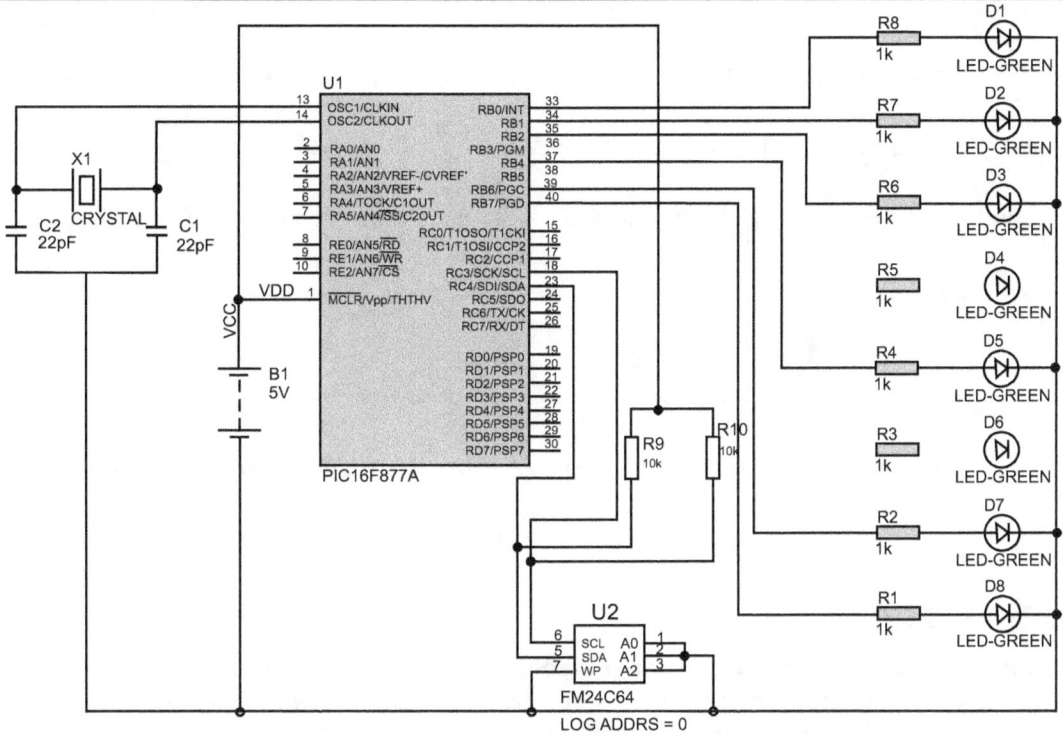

**Fig. 5.45**
**Interfacing External EEPROM with PIC Microcontroller**
8.png (215.81 KiB) Viewed 751 times

**Note:** VDD, VSS of the pic microcontroller and VDD, GND of 24C64 are not shown in the circuit diagram. Both VDD 's should be connected to +5V and VSS to GND. In this example we writes 00000001 to the first memory location, 00000010 to second, 000000100 to third etc sequentially up to 10000000. Then it is read sequentially and output through PORTB.

```
#include <16F877A.H>
#fuses XT, NOWDT, NOPROTECT, BROWNOUT, PUT, NOLVP
#use delay(clock = 8000000)
#include <2432.c>  // here is your memory device / EEPROM
#include <external_eeprom.c> // Utilities to write various data types to external eeprom

int8 sensor1_volt;  // declare global variable
```

```c
void main()
{
  // condition to read your data (volt)

  init_ext_eeprom(); // to initialize EEPROM

  sensor1_volt=read_ext_eeprom(0x0000); // to read data (volt) from EEPROM

  while(true)
  {

    // condition , while you want to write/save volt data to EEPROM

    write_ext_eeprom(0x000, sensor1_volt); // write or save data (volt) to EEPROM

  }
}
```

## 5.7.2 EEPROM

**EEPROM (electrically erasable programmable read-only memory)** is user-modifiable read-only memory (ROM) that can be erased and reprogrammed (written to) repeatedly through the application of higher than normal electrical voltage. It is a type of non-volatile memory used in computers and other electronic devices to store small amounts of data that must be saved when power is removed, e.g., calibration tables or device configuration.

**I2C (Inter Integrated Circuit)**

The I2C (Inter-IC) bus is a bi-directional two-wire serial bus that provides a communication link between integrated circuits (ICs). I2C is a synchronous protocol that allows a master device to initiate communication with a slave device. Data is exchanged between these devices.

**Interfacing I2C - EEPROM**

Fig. 1 shows how to interface the EEPROM with microcontroller through I2C. I2C is a Master-Slave protocol. I2C has a clock pulse along with the data. Normally, the master device controls the clock line, SCL. This line dictates the timing of all transfers on the I2C bus. No data will be transferred unless the clock is manipulated. All slaves are controlled by the same clock, SCL. I2c bus supports many devices, each device is recognized by a unique address—whether it's a micro-controller, LCD Driver, memory or keyboard interface and can operate as transmitter or receiver based on the functioning of the device. The controller designed controls the EEPROM device through I2C protocol. The I2C Controller here acts as a master device and controls EEPROM which acts as a slave. The read-write operations are accomplished by sending a set of control signals including the address and/or data bits. The control signals must be accompanied with proper clock signals.

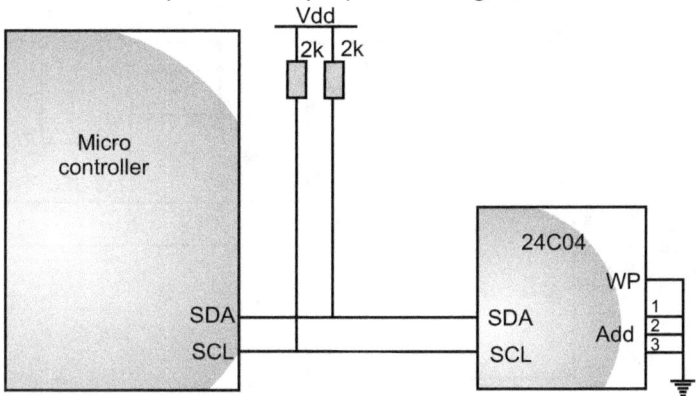

**Fig. 5.46 : Interfacing I2C - EEPROM to Microcontroller**

### Interfacing I2C – EEPROM with PIC16F877A

We now want to Read, write and Erase EEPROM by using I2C in PIC16F/18F Slicker Board. Wiring up an I2C based EEPROM to the I2C port is relatively simple. The basic operation of the I2C based EEPROM's is to send a command, such as WRITE, followed by an address and the data. In WRITE operation, the EEPROM to store the data.

In PIC16F/18F Slicker Kit, 2 nos. of EEPROM lines are controlled by I2C Enabled drivers. I2C Lines serial clock of CLK (PORTC.3), serial data of DATA (PORTC.4) connected to the I2C based serial EEPROM IC. The EEPROM read & write operations are done in PIC16F/18F Slicker Kit by using these SCK & DATA I2C lines.

### Pin Assignment with PIC16F877A

| | I2C EEPROM | PIC16F/18F Lines | Serial EEPROM | Connections |
|---|---|---|---|---|
| AT 24xx | CLK | PORTC.3 | PIC ← AT24XX EEPROM<br><br>**Fig. 5.47** | *Turn ON TXD, RXD, SCL and MISO Pins Of CONFIG switch SW1.<br>*Connect Serial cable between USART Section in the Board and PC. |
| | DATA | PORTC.4 | | |
| Output: **The string "I2C Test Program" will be displayed in Hyper- Terminal** | | | | |

## Circuit Diagram to Interface I2C–EEPROM with PIC16F

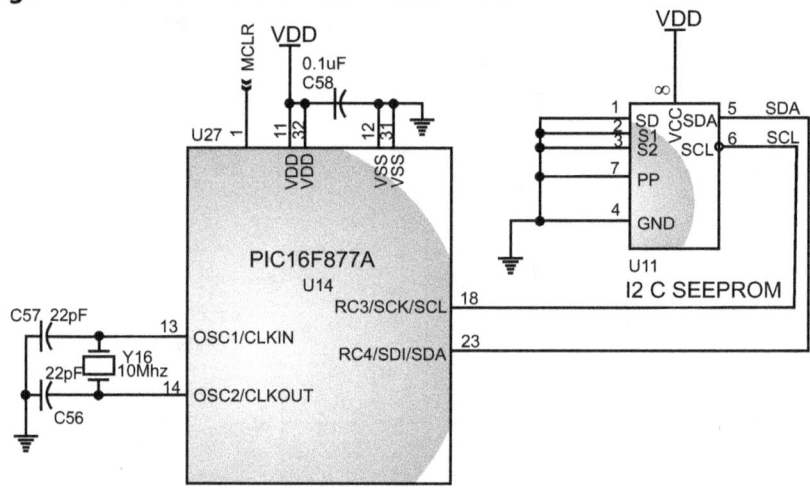

Fig. 5.48

## 5.7.3 Source Code

The **Interfacing I2C – EEPROM with PIC16F877A** program is very simple and straight forward that read, write and erase operations in **EEPROM** by using **I2C** & the value is displayed in serial port. A delay is occurring in every single data read or write in **EEPROM**. The delay depends on compiler how it optimizes the loops as soon as you make changes in the options the delay changes.

**C Program with I2C – EEPROM using PIC16F877A**

**Title : Program to read, write & erase of I2C - EEPROM**

```
#include<pic.h>
#include<stdio.h>
__CONFIG(0x3f72);
//Select HS oscillator, BODEN, PWRT and disable others


#define EEPROM_CNTRL_IN  0xa0      // EEPROM address+write
#define EEPROM_CNTRL_OUT 0xa1      // EEPROM address+read
#define I2C_FREQ    100            // 100khz at 4Mhz
#define FOSC        10000          // 10Mhz==>10000Khz
#define BAUD_RATE   9.6            // 9600 Baudrate
```

```c
#define BAUD_VAL   (char)(FOSC/ (16 * BAUD_RATE )) - 1;    //Calculation For 9600 Baudrate @10Mhz

unsigned char data[17]={"I2C Test Program"},i;
void I2CWrite(void);
void WaitMSSP(void);
void I2CRead(void);
void i2c_init(void);
void serial_init(void);
void DelayMs(unsigned int);
void main()
{
    DelayMs(100);       // Give delay for power up
    i2c_init();         // Initialize I2C
    serial_init();      // Setup serial port
    printf("\033[2J");
    DelayMs(20);
    I2CWrite();         // Sends the data to I2C EEPROM
    DelayMs(50);
    while(1)
    {
        I2CRead();      // Read back the data's
        TXREG='\n';
        while(TXIF==0);
        TXREG='\r';
        DelayMs(500);
    }
}
void I2CWrite()
{
    SEN=1;      // Send start bit
```

```c
    WaitMSSP();    // wait for the operation to be finished
    SSPBUF=EEPROM_CNTRL_IN;//Send Slave address write command
    WaitMSSP();
    SSPBUF=0x00;   // Send the starting address to write
    WaitMSSP();
    for(i=0;i<16;i++)
    {
       SSPBUF=data[i];
       // A page contains 16 locations then 16 data's are sent
       WaitMSSP();
    }
    PEN=1;        // Send stop bit
    WaitMSSP();
}
void I2CRead()
{
    int y;
    SEN=1;        //Send start bit
    WaitMSSP();   //wait for the operation to be finished
    SSPBUF=EEPROM_CNTRL_IN;//Send Slave address write command
    WaitMSSP();
    SSPBUF=0x00;   // Send the starting address to write
    WaitMSSP();
    for(y=0;y<16;y++)
    {
       RSEN=1;    // Send re-start bit
       WaitMSSP();
       SSPBUF=EEPROM_CNTRL_OUT; // Slave address read command
       WaitMSSP();
       RCEN=1;    // Enable receive
       WaitMSSP();
```

```c
    ACKDT=1;    // Acknowledge data 1: NACK, 0: ACK
    ACKEN=1;    // Enable ACK to send
    PEN=1;      // Stop condition
    WaitMSSP();
    putch(SSPBUF);  // Send the received data to PC
    DelayMs(30);
  }
  PEN=1;
  WaitMSSP();
}
void WaitMSSP()
{
  while(!SSPIF); // while SSPIF=0 stay here else exit the loop
  SSPIF=0;     // operation completed clear the flag
}
void i2c_init()
{
  TRISC3=1;    // Set up I2C lines by setting as input
  TRISC4=1;
  SSPCON=0x28;
// SSP port, Master mode, clock = FOSC / (4 * (SSPADD+1))
  SSPADD=(FOSC / (4 * I2C_FREQ)) - 1; //clock 100khz
  SSPSTAT=80;   // Slew rate control disabled
}
void serial_init()
{
  TRISC6=1;    // Enable TX and RX pin for Serial port
  TRISC7=1;
  TXSTA=0x24;   // Transmit Enable
  SPBRG=BAUD_VAL; // 9600 baud at 10 MHz
  RCSTA=0x90;   // Usart Enable, Continus receive enable
```

```
  TXIF=1;        // Make TXREG register empty
}
void putch(unsigned char Data) // transmit data
{
  while(TXIF==0);
  TXREG = Data;
}
void DelayMs(unsigned int Ms)
{
  int delay_cnst;
  while(Ms>0)
  {
    Ms--;
    for(delay_cnst = 0;delay_cnst <220;delay_cnst++);
  }
}
```

To compile the above C code you need the Mplab software & Hi-Tech Compiler. They must be properly set up and a project with correct settings must be created in order to compile the code. To compile the above code, the C file must be added to the project.

In Mplab, you want to develop or debug the project without any hardware setup. You must compile the code for generating HEX file. In debugging Mode, you want to check the port output without PIC16F/18F Slicker Board.

The PICKIT2 software is used to download the hex file into your microcontroller IC PIC16F877A through USB port.

**Testing the I2C – EEPROM with PIC16F877A**

Give +12V power supply to PIC16F/18F Slicker Board; the EEPROM device is connected with the PIC16F/18F Slicker Board. First check the entire EEPROM device fixed properly. A serial cable is connected between the microcontroller and PC. In PC, open the Hyper Terminal for displaying the values from EEPROM through I2C.

The Read & Write operations are performed in EEPROM with EEPROM address. When the EEPROM address is correct, then only you can write, read, and erase data's correctly in EEPROM.

## 5.8 RS-232 INTERFACING WITH 8085 MICROCONTROLLER

Serial communication is often used either to control or to receive data from an embedded microprocessor. Serial communication is a form of I/O in which the bits of a byte begin transferred appear one after the other in a timed sequence on a single wire. Serial communication has become the standard for intercomputer communication. Below diagram shows serial link between 8051 and PC using RS232.

8051 provides a transmit channel and a receive channel of serial communication. The transmit data pin (TXD) is specified at P3.1, and the receive data pin (RXD) is at P3.0. The serial signals provided on these pins are TTL signal levels and must be boosted and inverted through a suitable converter(Max232) to comply with RS232 standard.

All modes are controlled through SCON, the Serial CONtrol register. The SCON bits are defined as SM0, SM1, SM2, REN, TB8, RB8, TI, RI from MSB to LSB. The timers are controlled using TMOD, the Timer MODe register, and TCON, the Timer CONtrol register. RS-232 (Recommended Standard 232) is a standard for serial binary data signals connecting between a DTE (Data terminal equipment) and a DCE (Data Circuit-terminating Equipment).

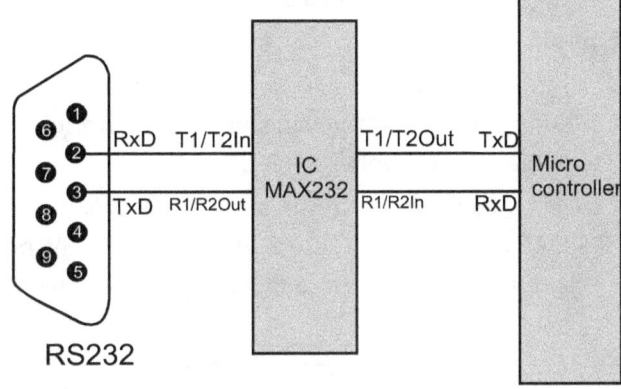

**Fig. 5.49**

**Voltage Levels:**

The RS-232 standard defines the voltage levels that correspond to logical one and logical zero levels. Valid signals are plus or minus 3 to 25 volts. The range near zero volts is not a valid RS-232 level; logic one is defined as a negative voltage, the signal condition is called marking, and has the functional significance of OFF. Logic zero is positive, the signal condition is spacing, and has the function ON. So a Logic Zero represented as +3V to +25V and Logic One represented as -3V to -25V.

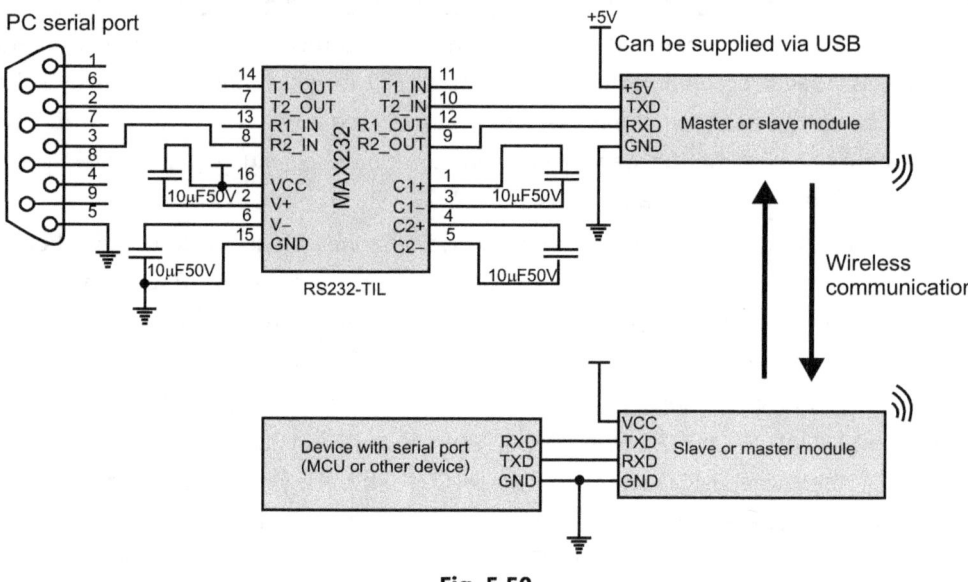

**Fig. 5.50**

### RS-232 Level Converters

Usually all the digial ICs works on TTL or CMOS voltage levels which cannot be used to communicate over RS-232 protocol. So a voltage or level converter is needed which can convert TTL to RS232 and RS232 to TTL voltage levels.

The most commonly used RS-232 level converter is MAX232. This IC includes charge pump which can generate RS232 voltage levels (-10V and +10V) from 5V power supply. It also includes two receiver and two transmitters and is capable of full-duplex UART/USART communication.

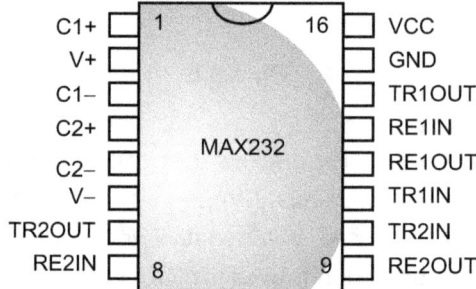

**Fig. 5.51 : A. - MAX232 Pin Description**

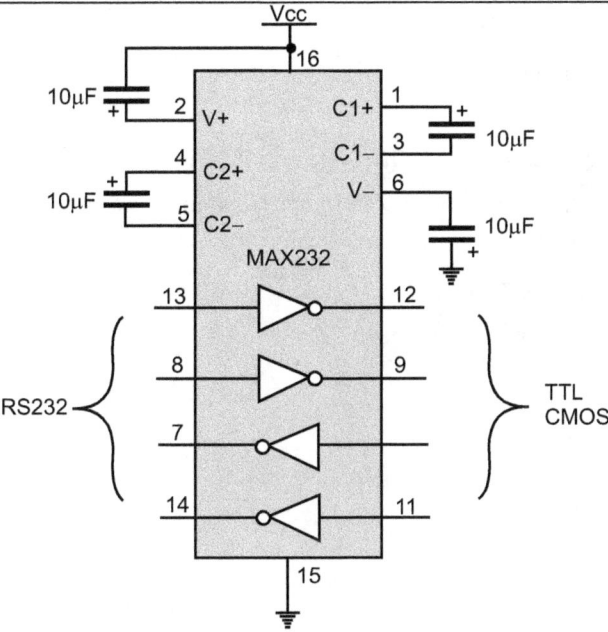

**Fig 5.52 : B. - MAX232 Typical Connection Circuit**

## MAX232 Interfacing with Microcontrollers

To communicate over UART or USART, we just need three basic signals which are namely, RXD (receive), TXD (transmit), GND (common ground). So to interface MAX232 with any microcontroller (AVR, ARM, 8051, PIC etc..) we just need the basic signals. A simple schematic diagram of connections between a microcontroller and MAX232 is shown below :

In the next part of this tutorial we will discuss programming microcontroller to communicate over UART and software implementation of half duples UART.

```
TMOD = 0x20;    /* configure timer for the correct baud rate */
TH1 = 0xe6;     /* 1200 bps for 12 MHz clock */
TCON = 0x00;    /* Set timer to not running */
SCON = 0x50;    /* Set Serial IO to receive and normal mode */
TR1 = 1;        /* start timer to Receive */
while( (SCON & 0x01) == 0 ) /* wait for receive data */;
c = SBUF;
return c;
}
```

```c
void SendSerial(unsigned char c) {

    /* initialize..set values for TMOD, TH1 and TCON */
    /* set the Tx interrupt in SCON to indicate sending data */
    /* start timer */
    /* write character to SBUF */
    /* wait for completion of sent data */
}

void main(void) {

    unsigned char c;

    while( 1 ) {

        /* Use ReceiveSerial to read in a character 'c' */
        /* Do some computation on 'c' */
        /* Send the result using SendSerial() */
    }
}
```

## RS-485 Interfacing with 8085 Microcontroller

RS-485 bus can carry up to 256 transceiver modules and over long distances. This is a circuit for connect microcontroller with Rs-485 bus. Max485 are low-power transceivers for RS-485 and RS-422 communication.

Each part contains one driver and one receiver. Line Length vs. Data Rate The RS-485/RS-422 standard covers line lengths up to 4000 feet. For line lengths greater than 4000 feet, see Typical Applications The MAX481, MAX483, MAX485, MAX487–MAX491, and MAX1487 transceivers are designed for bidirectional data communications on multipoint bus transmission lines.

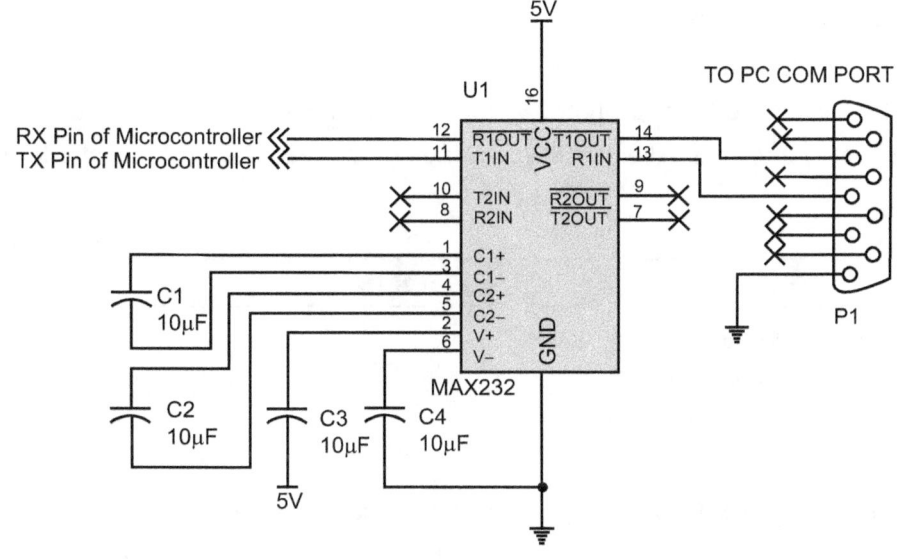

**Fig. 5.53**

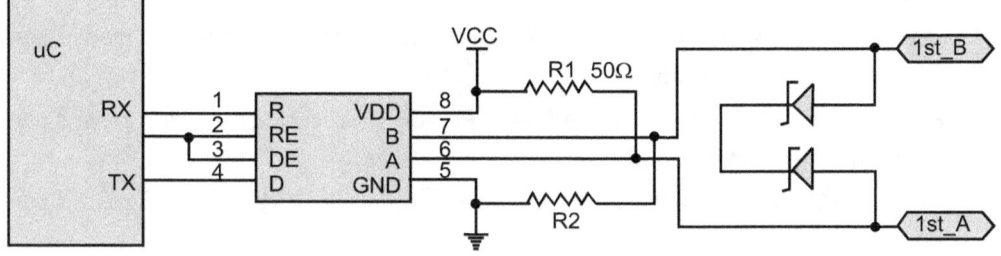

**Fig. 5.54**

**Features**

- In µMAX Package: Smallest 8-Pin SO
- Slew-Rate Limited for Error-Free Data Transmission
- 0.1µA Low-Current Shutdown Mode
- Low Quiescent Current
- -7V to +12V Common-Mode Input Voltage Range
- Three-State Outputs
- 30ns Propagation Delays, 5ns Skew

- Full-Duplex and Half-Duplex Versions Available
- Operate from a Single 5V Supply
- Allows up to 128 Transceivers on the Bus
- Current- Limiting and Thermal Shutdown for Driver Overload
- See more at: http://circuitschematicelectronics.blogspot.in/2012/03/microcontroller-to-rs-485-circuit.

## QUESTIONS

1. Draw and explain MSSP structure.
2. Draw and explain UART .
3. Draw and explain SPI .
4. Draw and explain I2C .
5. Explain how MSSP, UART, SPI and I2C are interfaced with PIC 18f microcontroller.
6. How serial port is interfaced with PIC18F microcontroller. Explain with circuit diagram, flow chart and c-program.
7. How ADC is interfaced with PIC18F microcontroller. Explain with circuit diagram, flow chart and c-program.
8. How RTC with I2C is interfaced with PIC18F microcontroller. Explain with circuit diagram, flow chart and c-program.
9. How EEPROM is interfaced with PIC18F microcontroller. Explain with circuit diagram, flow chart and c-program.

# Unit - VI

# CASE STUDIES WITH PIC

## 6.1 DATA ACQUISITION SYSTEM (DAS)

A low cost DAS has been designed using PIC12F675 having 4-channel analog input with 10-bit resolution for the monitoring of slowly varying signals. The DAS so designed is interfaced to the serial port of the PC. Firmware is written in Basic using Oshonsoft PIC IDE and burn to the microcontroller by using PICkit2 programmer. An application program is also developed using Visual Basic 6 which allows to display the waveform of the signals and simultaneously the data also can be saved into the hard disk of the computer for future use and analysis.

A low cost PC based real time data logging system can be used in the laboratories for measurement, monitoring and storage of data for slowly varying signals in science and engineering stream[1]. Data logging and recording is a very common measurement application. In its most basic form, data logging is the measurement and recording of physical or electrical parameters over a period of time. The frequency range of most of the bioelectric signals are slowly varying signals which range from 0.01 to 150 Hz but for EMG, it is from 5 to 2000 Hz. Even though there are many biomedical instruments available, still research is going on to make a better, reliable and cost effective efficient instruments. Today many biomedical signal acquisition systems are PC based because of their high efficiency. There are many biomedical instrumentation systems available in the market for detection and analysis. These systems are used for training purpose and are very expensive. NI DAQ card has a large number of functions which are not required for the present application and is also expensive. Thus, a custom novel cost effective hardware is designed, and the corresponding application software and firmware are also developed. For preventing missed data, polling technique is used that does not require a hardware interrupt. In Visual Basic, MSComm's OnComm event performs the event-driven routine which automatically jump to a routine when an event occurs. The application responds quickly and automatically to activity at the port, without having to waste time checking. This application allows the custom control, display and storing of the recorded data to the PC.

**Data Acquisition Unit :** A data acquisition system has been developed using PIC12F675 which is a mid range 8 Pin DIP microcontroller having four analog input channels and an internal crystal oscillator. Fig. the circuit diagram. It consists of a 5 volt regulated power supply, PIC12F675 microcontroller and a MAX232 driver. PIC12F675 has four channels ADC with 10 bit resolution, in which the entire operation is controlled by the firmware. Pin 2 (GP5) of PIC12F675 is used to send the serial data to the PC through the MAX232 driver. The MAX232 converts the TTL signal from the microcontroller into RS232 voltage level. Since the PIC12F675 has an internal oscillator of 4MHz, so it works without any external clock. I/O pins

GP0, GP1, GP2 and GP4 of IC2 are used as the analogue inputs. The MAX232 driver IC uses some external capacitors to enhance the voltage levels to RS232 level. A 9 Pin D Type female connector is used to connect to the COM port of the PC. The circuit is made into a PCB using ExpressPCB and the DAS is fabricated.

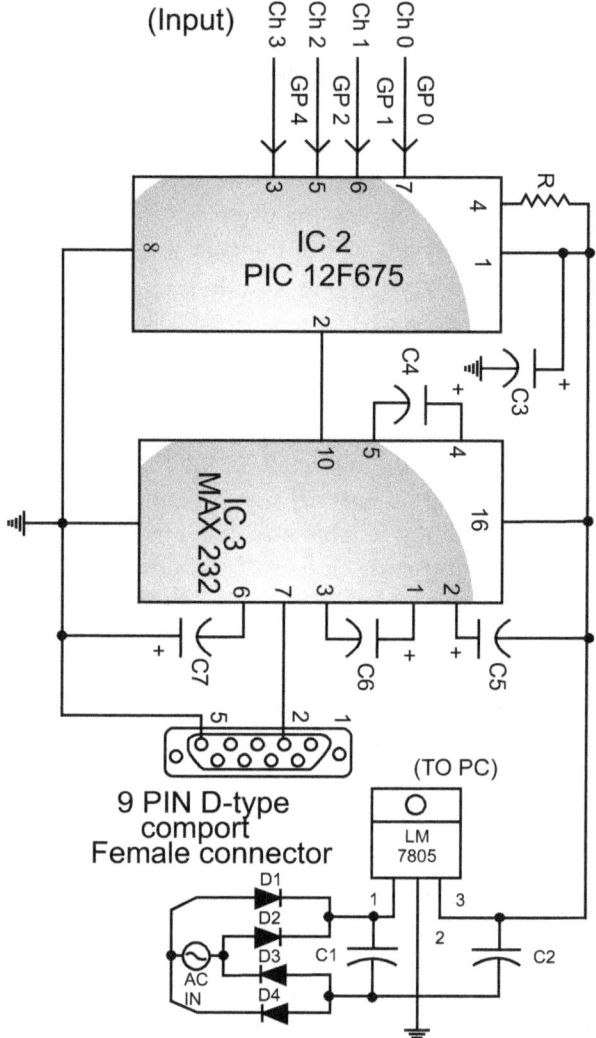

**Fig. 6.1 : The circuit diagram of DAS**

### Signal Source:

A **GW Instek** Function Generator (Model No. SFG-1013) was used as a signal source and applied to the designed DAS in TTL, or after converting it to a uni polar signal (if it is in analog mode). Because, the DAS accepts voltage level between 0 to 5 volt for all the four analog inputs of the PIC microcontroller. Software section

For the proper functioning of the data acquisition system, a firmware was developed and writes to the microcontroller and an application program is also developed in Visual Basic 6. Firmware A BASIC like program was written in Oshonsoft PIC Simulator IDE for proper ADC conversion at a fixed sampling rate and sending the digitized data serially. The program was compiled to make a hex file. The hex file so generated was written to the PIC12F675 microcontroller using PICkit2 programmer. The flowchart of the program so developed is given in Fig. 6.2.

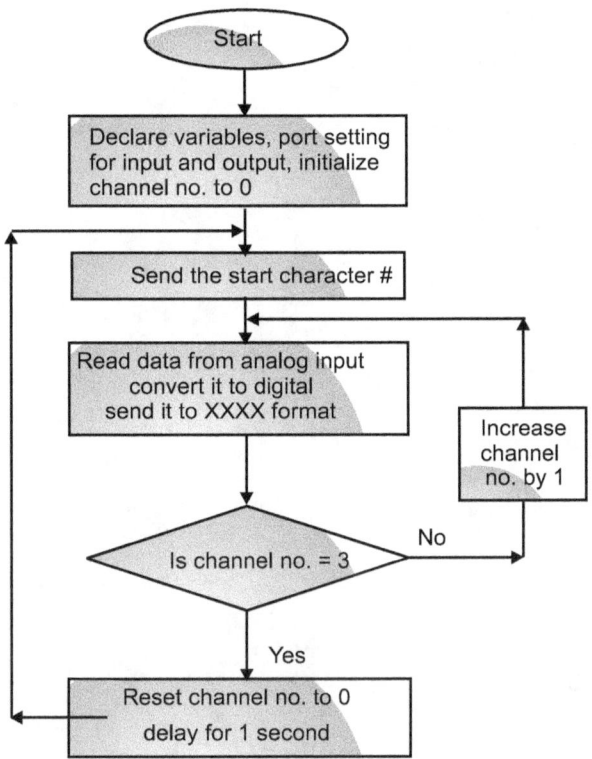

**Fig. 6.2 : Flow chart of the firmware**

DAS collects one sample per second. For studying the DAS, very low frequency signals are applied from the Function Generator. The acquired signals has been displayed numerically, graphically and the data is also stored into the hard disc of the computer in .csv (Comma Separated Value) format, which can be opened directly by MS Excel. The wave form can be reconstructed from the data of the stored file using MS Excel.

**Program :**

```c
#include <P18f4520.h>
#pragma config OSC=HS
#pragma config PWRT=OFF
#pragma config WDT=OFF
#pragma config DEBUG=OFF, LVP=OFF
#define ldata PORTD
#define rs PORTEbits.RE0
#define rw PORTEbits.RE1
#define en PORTEbits.RE2
void DELAY(unsigned int value);
void lcd_init(void);
void lcdcmd (unsigned char value);
void lcddata (unsigned char value);
void val_display(unsigned int);
void main(void)
{
unsigned int temp1;
unsigned char val;
TRISD=0;
PORTD=0;
TRISB=0;
PORTB=0;
TRISC=0;
TRISE=0;
PORTC=0;
TRISAbits.TRISA0=0;
ADCON0 = 0X81;
ADCON1 = 0XCE;
//ADFM=1;
lcd_init();
while(1)
{
DELAY(1);
ADCON0bits.GO = 1;
```

```c
while(ADCON0bits.DONE ==1);
//PORTD=ADRESL;
//PORTC=ADRESH;
temp1=(ADRESH<<8)|ADRESL;
val_display(temp1);
DELAY(10);
 }
}
 void lcdcmd (unsigned char value)
{
ldata=value;
rs=0;
rw=0;
en=1;

DELAY(1);
en=0;
}
 void lcddata (unsigned char value)
{
ldata=value;
rs=1;
rw=0;
en=1;
DELAY(1);
en=0;
}
void lcd_init(void)
{
lcdcmd(0x38);        //4bit mode
lcdcmd(0x0E);
lcdcmd(0x01);
lcdcmd(0x06);
lcdcmd(0x81);
}
```

```
void DELAY(unsigned int value)
{
int i,j;
for(i=0;i<=value;i++)
for(j=0;j<=135;j++);
}
void val_display(unsigned int avg)
{
unsigned int a;
a=avg/1000;
a=a+0x30;
lcdcmd(0xc0);
lcddata(a);
a=avg%1000;
a=a/100;
a=a+0x30;
lcdcmd(0xc1);
lcddata(a);
a=avg%100;
a=a/10;
a=a+0x30;
lcdcmd(0xc2);
lcddata(a);
a=avg%10;
a=a+0x30;
lcdcmd(0xc3);
lcddata(a);
}
```

## 6.2 FREQUENCY COUNTER

**Introduction:**

A frequency counter is an electronic instrument, or component of one, that is used for measuring frequency. Frequency is defined as the number of events of a particular sort occurring in a set period of time. Frequency counters usually measure the number of oscillations or pulses per second in a repetitive electronic signal.

**The Schematic Diagram:**

Most frequency counters work by using a counter which accumulates the number of events occurring within a specific period of time (In this project, I used the counter of Timer1) . After a preset period (1 second, for example), the value in the counter is transferred to a display and the counter is reset to zero.

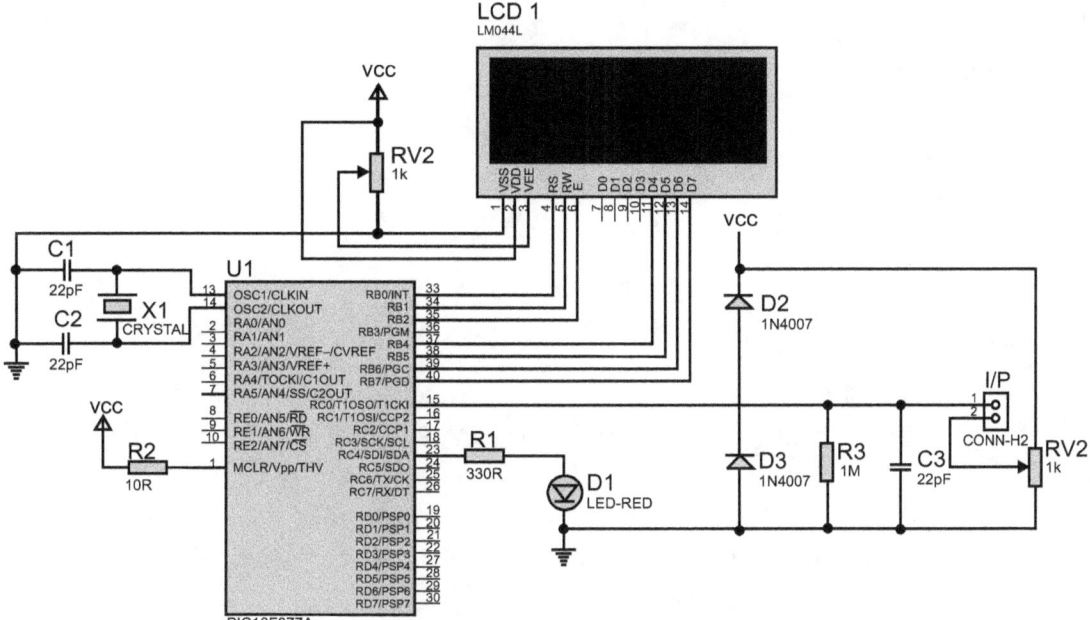

**Fig. 6.3 : Freq. Count. Circuit Diagram**

If the event being measured repeats itself with sufficient stability and the frequency is considerably lower than that of the clock oscillator being used, the resolution of the measurement can be greatly improved by measuring the time required for an entire number of cycles, rather than counting the number of entire cycles observed for a pre-set duration (you can use CCP1/Capture to do that).

**Source Code:**

```
/* Frequency Counter    */
#include <16f877a.h>
#use delay(clock=20M)
#include <lcd420.c>
#include <LCD_D.h>
```

```c
#fuses hs,nowdt,nocpd,nolvp,noprotect
#byte portc=0x07
#bit  led=portc.4

void LCD_D( );
unsigned int16 value;
void main( )
{
    set_tris_c(0x00);
    led=1;
    delay_ms(500);
    LCD_D();
    delay_ms(50);

    while(1)
    {
        set_timer1(0);
        setup_timer_1(t1_external | T1_DIV_BY_1);

        delay_ms(1000);                    // in protues, should be 1000/3
        setup_timer_1(T1_DISABLED);
        value=get_timer1();
        lcd_gotoxy(11,4);
        printf(lcd_putc,"%LU HZ   ",value);
        led=!led;
    }
}
```

## 6.3 DIGITAL MULTIMETER

A multimeter is an electronic measuring instrument that combines several measurement functions in one unit. A typical multimeter may include features such as the ability to measure voltage, current and resistance. There are two categories of multimeters, analog multimeters and digital multimeters.

In our case we designed a digital multimeter with analog inputs, setting one input to each channel, also we added another function to the multimeter, and this was temperature.

To make the measure of temperature we had to use a sensor that consists in a precision integrated circuit whose output voltage is linearly proportional to the Celsius (Centigrade) temperature, with this output voltage, we search for a linear relation in order to establish the real temperature, and then we put this relation in our program.

To measure AC voltage, DC voltage, AC current and DC current we applied our knowledge's of circuits and electronics, using voltage rectifiers, voltage divide, potentiometers and other instruments to complete the measures, that is when we used what we have learned in class of microprocessors and adjust the program to calculate and show the measures in the LCD.

A multimeter or a multitester, also known as a volt/ohm meter or VOM, is an electronic measuring instrument that combines several measurement functions in one unit. A typical multimeter may include features such as the ability to measure voltage, current and resistance.

Modern multimeters are often digital due to their accuracy, durability and extra features. In a Digital Multimeter the signal under test is converted to a voltage and an amplifier with an electronically controlled gain preconditions the signal. A Digital Multimeter displays the quantity measured as a number, which prevents parallax errors. The inclusion of solid state electronics, from a control circuit to small embedded computers, has provided a wealth of convenience features in modern digital meters.

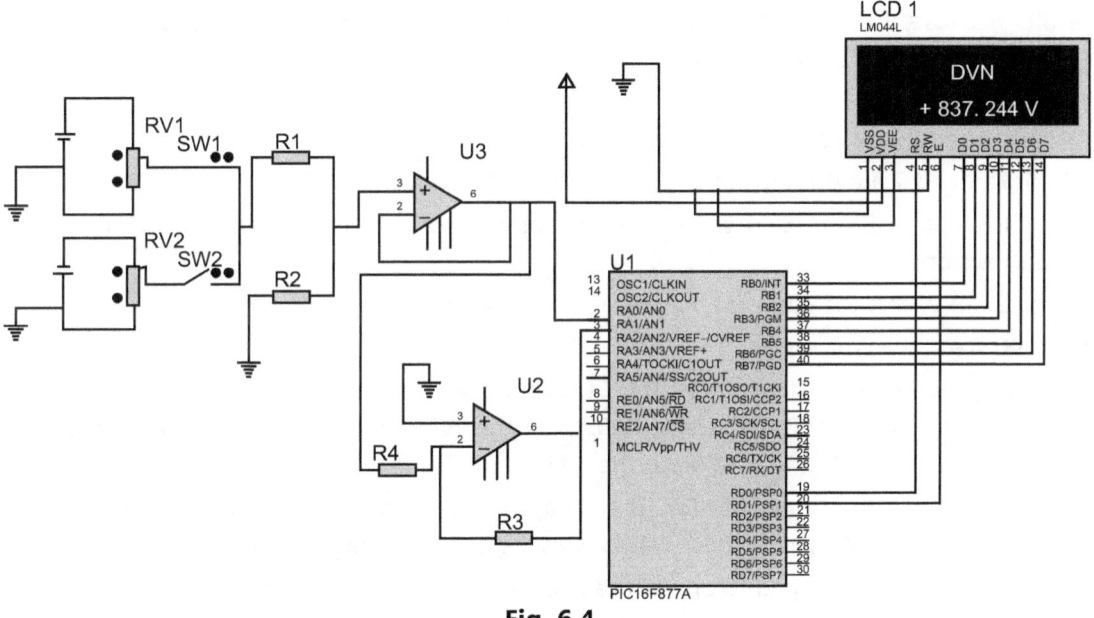

**Fig. 6.4**

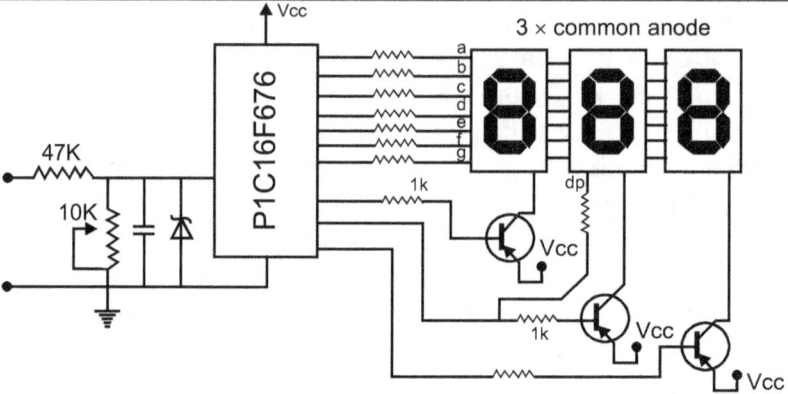

**Fig. 6.5**

This is a simple voltmeter which measures 0-5V at a precision of 4.8 mV. This is a simple design using inbuilt ADC of PIC 16F877A. PIC 16F877A have 8 channel 10bit ADC. Measured voltage is displayed on 16x2 LCD display.

Using one of the most popular 8 bit PIC 16f877A, for instance, reading the datasheet, we'll find that the ADC modules (10 bit) are controlled by four different registers. The first two, **ADCON0** and **ADCON1**, are used to set and start the ADC module. When high level language is used, the programmer doesn't need to care a lot of the register connected to the results because they are normally stored in a variable by a routine of the language itself (*adc_read*, for instance, using mikroc).

### The ADCON0

As we can see this registers are 8 bit registers where.

- bit6 and bit 7 are used to set the frequency of the conversions.
- bits 3, 4 and 5 are used to select the pins of the microcontroller enabled to theadc conversions.
- bit 2 represents the status of the conversion procedure.
- bit 0 starts the conversion.

Regarding the second register, **ADCON1**, it must be set for two reasons: to select the format of the result value (bit 7), to select (bit0…bit3) the reference voltage and to set the port configuration control bits according to the following table

This circuit uses AN0 channel of ADC. The voltage conversion is employed in a logic, 16F877A have 10 bit ADC. That is, it can have 1024 levels. Reference voltage is fixed at

0 – 5 V Analog I/P is mapped to one of the 1024 levels (0-1023 Digital Count)

Resolution = 5/(1024)   (as it is 10 bit ADC)

= 5/1024

= 4.8828 mV  It means that for a change in 4.8828mV, the binary output changes by 1. ADC module of PIC Microcontroller converts the Signals on its analog pin to 10 bit binary data and it has software selectable high and low voltage reference input to some combination of VDD, VSS, RA2 and RA3. The analog input to PIC is limited to 0 to 5. The converted value is in mV. It is then converted to volts and displayed on LCD.

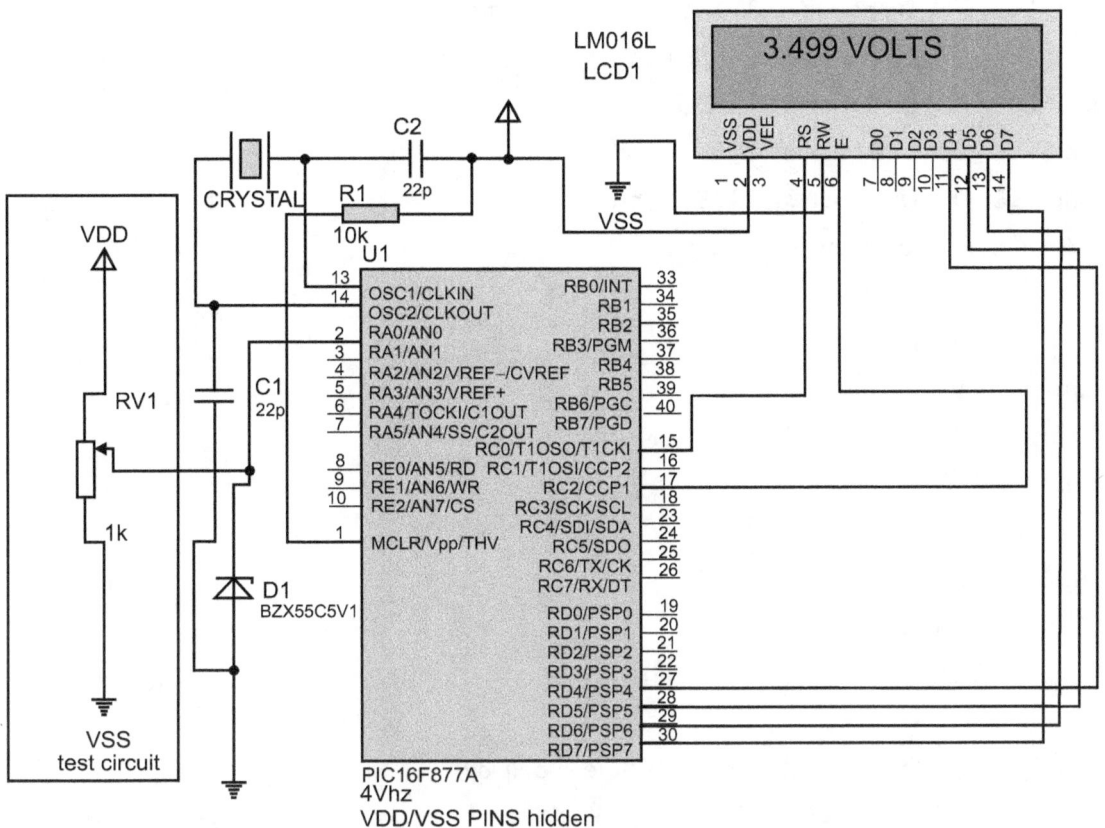

**Fig. 6.6 : Digital Voltmeter using PIC Microcontroller**

**Program :**
```
// LCD module connections
sbit LCD_RS at RC0_bit;
sbit LCD_EN at RC2_bit;
sbit LCD_D4 at RD4_bit;
```

```c
sbit LCD_D5 at RD5_bit;
sbit LCD_D6 at RD6_bit;
sbit LCD_D7 at RD7_bit;

sbit LCD_RS_Direction at TRISC0_bit;
sbit LCD_EN_Direction at TRISC2_bit;
sbit LCD_D4_Direction at TRISD4_bit;
sbit LCD_D5_Direction at TRISD5_bit;
sbit LCD_D6_Direction at TRISD6_bit;
sbit LCD_D7_Direction at TRISD7_bit;
// End LCD module connections

unsigned long temp;
unsigned int i;
char digit[]="0.000 VOLTS";
void main() {
TRISA=0xFF;
ADCON0=0x01;
ADCON1=0x0E;
   Lcd_Init();                 // Initialize LCD

  Lcd_Cmd(_LCD_CLEAR);         // Clear display
  Lcd_Cmd(_LCD_CURSOR_OFF);    // Cursor off
  LCD_Out(1,1,"EMBEDDED");
  LCD_Out(2,1,"PROJECTS BLOG");
  Delay_ms(1000);

  do {
   temp = ADC_Read(0);   // Get 10-bit results of AD conversion
```

```c
    temp=temp*5000/1023;   //Convert ADC value to mV
    digit[0]=(temp/1000)+48;
    digit[2]=((temp%1000)/100)+48;
    digit[3]=(((temp%1000)%100)/10)+48;
    digit[4]=(((temp%1000)%100)%10)+48;

    LCD_Cmd(_LCD_CLEAR);
    LCD_Out(1,1,digit);

      //Carriage Return
    Delay_ms(500);
  } while(1);
}
```

## 6.4 DC MOTOR CONTROL

Motion control plays a vital role in industrial atomization. Different types of motors AC, DC, SERVO or stepper are used depending upon the application; of these DC motors are widely used because of easier controlling. Among the different control methods for DC motor armature voltage control method using pulse width modulation (PWM) is best one. We can realize the PWM using H-bridge built with IGBT switches or transistors. To generate PWM signals we use PIC16F72 microcontroller.

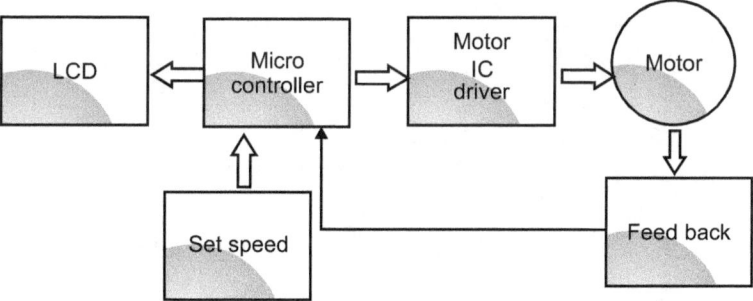

**Fig. 6.7 : Block diagram of DC Motor Control**

I already posted about Interfacing DC Motor with PIC Microcontroller. In our robotics applications we may have to control the speed of the DC Motor. In this tutorial we will see how to control the speedof a DC Motor using Pulse Width Modulation (PWM). By using PWM we can easily control the average power delivered to a load and by thus we can easily control the speed of the DC Motor. You may think that a variable resistor in series with a DC Motor can control its speed. There are three reasons for "Resistor is not a good choice for controlling the speed of a DC Motor". The main problem is that the motor is a varying electrical load so a resistor can't do this task. It needs more power during start up than in running state. It draws more current also when a mechanical load is applied to motor shaft.

The resistor drops excess energy as heat. Thus it is not good for a battery powered device.

We all know that motor requires more current, so resistors with higher power rating are required to drop excess energy.

PWM can be easily generated using the inbuilt CCP module of a PIC Microcontroller. CCP stands for Capture/Compare/PWM. CCP modules are available with a number of PIC Microcontrollers. Most of them have more than one CCP module. MikroC Pro for PIC Microcontroller provides built in library routines for PWM which makes our task very simple. Please refer the following articles.

- Generating PWM with PIC Microcontroller
- Interfacing DC Motor with PIC Microcontroller

In this example project DC Motor is interfaced with PIC Microcontroller using L293D Motor Driver. Two Push Button switches are provided to control the speed of the motor. Here we are using 12V DC Motor and average DC value delivered to motor can be varied by varying the duty ratio of the PWM. The average DC Voltage of 0% duty cycle is 0V, 25% duty cycle is 3V, 50% duty cycle is 6V, 75% duty cycle is 9V and for 100% duty cycle 12V.

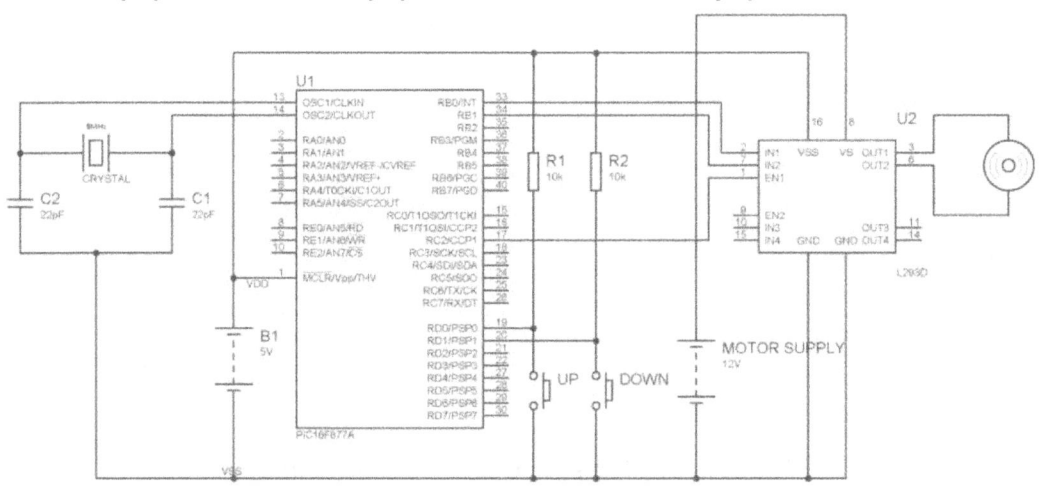

**Fig. 6.8 : Circuit diagram of DC Motor Control**

Note: VDD and VSS of the pic microcontroller is not shown in the circuit diagram. VDD should be connected to +5V and VSS to GND.

Two push button switches are connected to 1st and 2nd pins of PORTD which is used to control the duty ratio of the generated PWM. Pressing the UP switch increases the duty cycle, which increases the motor speed while pressing the DOWN switch decreases the duty cycle, which decreases the motor speed. Here we use CCP1 module of PIC 16F877A to generate PWM and it is given to the enable pin of L293D. The direction of rotation of motor can be control using the 1st and 2nd pins of PORTB.

**Program :**

```
{
 short duty = 0; //initial value for duty
 TRISD = 0xFF; //PORTD as input
 TRISC = 0x00; //PORTC as output
 TRISB = 0x00; //PORTB as output
 PORTB = 0x02; //Run motor in anticlock wise
 PWM1_Init(1000);  //Initialize PWM1
 PWM1_Start();  //start PWM1
 PWM1_Set_Duty(duty); //Set current duty for PWM1
 while (1)    // endless loop
 {
   if (!RD0_bit && duty<250) //if button on RD0 pressed
   {
     Delay_ms(40);
     duty = duty + 10;  //increment current_duty
     PWM1_Set_Duty(duty);  //Change the duty cycle
   }
   if (!RD1_bit && duty >0) //button on RD1 pressed
   {
     Delay_ms(40);
     duty = duty - 10;  //decrement duty
     PWM1_Set_Duty(duty);
   }
   Delay_ms(10);    // slow down change pace a little
 }
void main()
}
```

# QUESTIONS

1. Describe how DAS system is designed with the help of c-program.
2. Describe how frequency counter is interfaced with PIC 18f microcontroller. Output should be displayed on LCD.
3. Design Digital Multi-meter with diagram, flow chart and c-program.
4. Design DC motor control using PWM with diagram, flow chart and c-program.